readers with a comprehensive topics.

Chapter 2, Data Management and Support for Generative AI, covers key topics such as data governance models, data quality management, and security while addressing the challenges and opportunities presented by AI technologies. Readers will gain insights into developing a modern data strategy and implementing effective data stewardship practices to support generative AI initiatives.

Chapter 3, Data Governance in action using AWS Services, covers essential aspects of data governance using AWS services, including data cataloging, quality management, profiling, classification, compliance, security, lineage, and master data management. Readers will learn about key AWS tools like Glue, DataZone, Macie, and Lake Formation, as well as how to implement data governance best practices. The chapter provides practical insights through use cases and case studies, helping readers understand real-world applications of these concepts.

Chapter 4, Democratizing Generative AI: Governing the unstructured data frontier, explores the responsible development and governance of generative AI, focusing on unstructured data. It covers essential aspects such as implementing guardrails, governing the RAG pipeline, ensuring data quality, addressing privacy concerns, and considering ethical implications. Readers will gain insights into monitoring and improving generative AI applications, with an emphasis on speed, cost, and output quality.

Chapter 5, Data Mesh on AWS, explores Data Mesh via the lens of AWS cloud, covering its organizational principles, core concepts, and how it differs from traditional data architectures. Readers will gain insights into decentralized data domains, enterprise data products, federated governance, and self-service sharing, as well as understand the key components of a Data Mesh implementation. This lays the foundation for the data mesh terminology required for the rest of the book.

Chapter 6, Approach to building a Data Mesh on AWS, provides a comprehensive understanding of the building blocks for data mesh on AWS, covering essential services like Amazon S3, AWS Glue, and AWS Lake Formation. It presents architecture reference patterns, introduces AWS Lake Formation for data mesh implementation, and explores data sharing capabilities using Amazon Redshift, offering readers practical insights and best practices for creating a robust data mesh infrastructure.

Chapter 7, Services to power your data mesh: Capabilities to build, manage, and share data products, explores essential AWS services for building, managing, and sharing data products in a data mesh architecture. Readers will learn how to leverage AWS Glue, Amazon EMR, and AWS Clean Rooms to create and expose data products, with a focus on data quality, cataloging, and generative AI capabilities. The chapter provides practical insights into implementing these services for effective data mesh implementation.

Chapter 8, Build a Data Product on a Big Data Platform, explores the creation of data products using AWS big data services. Readers will learn how to load data into S3, create and crawl databases with AWS Glue, transform data using Glue Studio and Amazon EMR Serverless, and query data with Amazon Athena. The chapter provides practical guidance on leveraging these tools to build robust data products on AWS's big data platform.

Chapter 9, Build a Data Product on a Data Warehouse, guides readers through the process of building a data product using Amazon Redshift. It covers loading data into Amazon S3, creating a Redshift Serverless workgroup, and connecting to Redshift. The chapter also explores data transformation techniques and demonstrates how to query data effectively within the Amazon Redshift environment using SQL.

Chapter 10, Self-served data mesh: Democratizing analytics and AI/ML with data products, covers the self-served data mesh framework, focusing on democratizing analytics through data products. It delves into the critical roles of data stewards, analysts, and scientists, providing practical execution steps for each. Readers will learn how to leverage Amazon DataZone to manage data products, enhance SQL analysis, and empower large-scale machine learning and generative AI initiatives.

1. Decoding Data Mesh and Data Governance in the Era of Generative AI

Data has become a critical asset for organizations in the digital age. Managing and governing enterprise data to ensure quality, security, privacy, and maximize value are key priorities. Two emerging concepts aim to address enterprise data challenges - data mesh and data governance. This chapter introduces these concepts through the following questions:

- What is data mesh?
- What is data governance?
- How are data mesh and data governance related?
- When Data mesh is not for you?
- Why AWS for implementing your Data mesh and Data governance?
- What is the role of data in generative AI?

What is Data Mesh?

Data mesh is a methodology, a data architecture, and a set of best practices and principles that introduce a new paradigm by aligning data ownership with organizational domains. Data owners within each domain are responsible for building, operating, serving, and resolving any issues arising from the use of their data.

The data mesh approach is based on 4 key principles:

- Domain Ownership: decentralization and accountability to those who are closest to the data are at the heart of the data mesh. How can the ownership of the various parts of the data ecosystem be broken down and decentralized?
- Data as a product: the goal of the data as a product principle is to solve the long-standing issues with data silos and data quality. Domain data must be treated as a business product rather than as a siloed product with various ownership and use cases for various stakeholders.
- Self-serve data platform: to operate and monitor the services, the data platform can be seen as an extension of the delivery platform. It must give users access to high-level infrastructure abstractions that take the complexity and hassle out of setting up and managing the lifecycle of data products. To achieve it, a self-serve data infrastructure is required as a result.
- Federated computational governance: a distributed system of independent data products is called a data mesh. The governance structure of data mesh supports decentralization and domain self-sovereignty. Additionally, it supports interoperability via global standardization, a dynamic topology, and, most importantly, automated platform decision-making.

These principles empower each business domain to manage and take care of its own data. The decentralized architecture aligns data ownership with the business domain, and by default, it makes data security and compliance the responsibility of each data owner.

The two principles, "Data Ownership" and "Data as a Product," highlight that data mesh and data governance are closely related.

Data owners are identified, and they acquire the role of data producers. They are responsible for all data generated within their domain and for ensuring that meaning and context are correctly communicated to their data customers/consumers. With this approach, organizations can benefit from greater data agility and accuracy because ownership is moved from a central team (which could potentially become a bottleneck) to autonomous domain-aligned teams that can move independently.

Data products refer to a unit of data that's been curated, processed, and made available for consumption by users or other parts of the organization. Each data product encapsulates data, processing logic, and metadata. They are designed to be self-contained and independently deployable, allowing for easier maintenance, scaling, and agility in a complex data ecosystem. The data product concept promotes better data quality, discoverability, and governance by emphasizing the importance of treating data as a product with clear owners, responsibilities, and defined interfaces for consumption.

What is Data Governance?

Data governance establishes who has the authority to make decisions about data and analytics, as well as outlining responsibilities to guide proper practices for assessing, producing, using, and managing data. Having a well-defined strategy and framework for governing data across the organization is pivotal in bringing organizational success with data. Robust data policies, procedures, roles, and responsibilities are the key foundational elements that constitute a comprehensive data governance framework. The core building blocks for these foundation elements, in no specific order of importance, include data stewardship, data quality management, metadata management, master data management, data security, data auditing, data lifecycle management, issue escalation and accountability, and training & communication.

Data governance is the overall management of an organization's data assets. It includes the development and implementation of policies and procedures to ensure the effective use and protection of data. Data governance is typically handled by a data governance committee or data governance board, which is responsible for setting data policies and guidelines, as well as monitoring and enforcing compliance with those policies.

Data governance is important for several reasons. First, it helps to ensure that data is accurate, complete, and consistent. This is essential for making informed decisions and for maintaining trust in the data. Second, data governance helps to protect data from unauthorized access and use. This is important for maintaining the confidentiality and security of sensitive information. Third, data governance helps to ensure that data is properly managed and maintained. This is important for ensuring that data is accurate and up-to-date and that it is accessible to those who need it. It is an important part of any organization's data management strategy. It helps to ensure that data is findable, accurate, high quality, secure, and accessible and that it is properly managed and maintained. It is also important to ensure that data is used effectively and efficiently and that it is aligned with the organization's goals and objectives. Data governance gives businesses the ability to manage their data resources. It involves putting in place the proper personnel, workflows, and technical systems to ensure data quality and suitability for business needs. Data governance teams compromise a core data governance body, data stewards, and central IT teams.

Data governance teams can be setup both centrally and decentralized depending on the teams, use case, and size of the organization:

- **Centralized data governance** team is a model where data is ingested, transformed, and stored in a central data lake. Data consumers discover and get access to the data at a central location to build analytics. The centralized model has several advantages, such as the ability to manage data, but there are several challenges. It can be more difficult to make changes to the data, and the data is managed by a team that may not understand the data really well. The process of making changes to the data is expensive as it involves running data pipelines and data quality jobs.
- **Decentralized data governance** empowers decentralized data product teams to own the data product build, which includes ingestion, transforming, and building data products. Data product teams own and make decisions regarding the data itself and work with data engineers and data experts to build data products. In this model, a central governance team works with decentralized data product teams to set up infrastructure, set rules for data quality, list data in a marketplace, and adhere to compliance policies. The decentralized model has several advantages, such as the ability to share data and access workflow across the organization.

Data governance establishes responsibilities and authority for managing data. It provides policies, procedures, roles, and responsibilities for assessing, producing, using, and governing data. Key elements of a data governance framework include data stewardship, data quality, metadata management, master data management, data security, auditing, lifecycle management, issue escalation/accountability, and communication. Let's see what is the link between data mesh and data governance.

How are data mesh and data governance related?

In a modern data governance and data mesh paradigm, it's important to have a federated and decentralized governance model that includes working across multirole teams and processes. **Decentralized Ownership** provides autonomy to each domain or line of business. Each domain or business unit has ownership of its data. This requires clear communication, collaboration, and alignment among teams responsible for different data sets.

Data as a product mindset brings new roles within the governance, consumers, and data product teams. Data product teams are cross-functional teams that are responsible for the entire lifecycle of a specific data product. They include data engineers, data experts, data scientists, domain experts, and others needed to create, maintain, and evolve the data product. One of the key roles in a data product team is data steward or domain data product owner, who is responsible for the maturity and lifecycle of a data product. Data stewards are also responsible for approving a data product to be listed in a catalog by assessing the key metrics like quality, lineage, classification, and conformation to standards approved by the organization. Data stewards also receive requests for new features in an existing data product or a new data product for their domain. Data products evolve over time, and it is critical to have a change management process that includes the people across governance, data products, and consumers because changing schemas and maintaining backward compatibility are important to avoid disruptions in downstream applications.

The data mesh approach highlights that data governance and underlying data platforms should be aligned to the operation structures of the organization (i.e., Conway's Law). An organization with centralized governance and operations would naturally look towards a centralized data platform to achieve organizational efficiencies: operational, governance, and compliance concerns are being centralized with dedicated teams who have the required specialisms. A highly federated organization may not be as operationally "efficient," but it will be significantly more agile, as each business unit can move at its own pace. Such organizations might perhaps prefer a domain-aligned approach to governance and data platforms, enabling each autonomous business unit to maintain operational control over a self-service data platform and the creation, discovery, and subscription of data products.

Data governance, along with a decentralized data product model defined by the data mesh concept, sets guidelines for the following:

- **Data Policies:** rules and regulations that govern the use and management of data. These policies are typically set by the data governance board and data product teams.
- **Data Guidelines:** best practices and recommendations for how to manage and use data. These guidelines are typically set by the data governance board and data product teams.
- **Data Compliance:** helps the data product team build data products that adhere to the rules and regulations set by the data governance board that align with the industry-specific compliance needs.
- **Data Confidentiality:** the practice of keeping data secure and private so that it is not accessible or shared with unauthorized individuals. This is important for maintaining trust in the data and for protecting sensitive information.
- **Data Security:** the practice of protecting data from unauthorized access and use and of ensuring that data is not compromised or stolen. This includes implementing a self-

service workflow for consumers to request access to the data that can be routed to the right person responsible for approving or denying the requests.

- **Data Lineage:** the practice of tracking the flow of data, which helps in understanding the data and its transformation. Data lineage helps understand and track the data.

- **Data Marketplace:** The data marketplace is setup by the governance teams and enriched by various process and data products experts. This marketplace helps consumers locate and request access to the data.

Data governance and data mesh are linked through decentralized and federated governance models. Does it mean that data mesh is a must or a pre-requisite for implementing data governance?

When data mesh is not for you?

While there are no doubts about the benefits of a data mesh, it should also be noted that a true data mesh implementation is a non-trivial effort and requires significant time, effort, and capital investments. For most organizations, the investments will span beyond technology. A successful data mesh implementation is not only about technology—it is equal parts about your organizational culture, your people, and your processes. Data mesh principles like domain ownership and data as a product are relatively new to the scene and require leadership support and commitment to drive the necessary mindset across the organization to empower employees to own beyond their current responsibilities. For example, domain ownership demands that people not only just own the function but also the value of the outcome that the function produces, while the data as a product principle requires them to ensure the value is as desired by the business.

A data mesh design promotes higher agility and greater autonomy, democratizes data management, and streamlines governance. However, it would be remiss on the part of the organization not to first undertake a careful assessment of their current situation and analyze the risks versus the benefits. Pragmatically speaking, a data mesh will not make sense for all types of organizations.

There are a few thumb-rules that organizations can leverage to do a quick and dirty "back of a napkin" assessment:

- Size, scale, diversity, and complexity of your current ecosystem.
- Maturity levels of your data platforms.
- Degrees of cross-functional collaboration.
- Appetite for experimentation and failure.
- Frequency of issues, escalations, breakdowns, and time-to-recover.
- Available expertise and resources.
- Funding capacity.

The data mesh principles are not mutually inclusive. You may also benefit from a piece-meal approach. For example, you can start by introducing domain ownership and defining data products that are curated by domain owners who understand the data, the business operations for it, and the permissible requirements for it. Regardless of whether you are looking at implementing a full data mesh or parts of it, it is imperative to assess the value proposition realities of a data mesh for your organization.

Implementing a data mesh involves changing organizational culture, people, and processes. Leadership commitment is needed to drive new mindsets around domain ownership and treating data as a product. The organizations should carefully assess their readiness to evolve in regard to the data mesh goals.

Data Mesh Goals

The ultimate goal of a data mesh is to drive business value through better data utilization by making data more accessible and usable. While organization-specific goals may vary from one organization to another, there are a few key ubiquitous outcomes that a data mesh design provides:

- **Scalability:** a scalable architecture that can handle the growing volume, variety, and velocity of data in modern organizations. By decentralizing data ownership and management, it helps distribute the workload and prevents bottlenecks.

- **Data governance:** promotes domain-specific ownership of data, which can lead to improved data quality and better governance.

- Agility enables organizations to quickly adapt to changing data needs and business requirements by allowing domain teams to iterate and evolve their data products independently.

- **Data democratization:** makes data more accessible to different teams and individuals within an organization. By providing self-serve data access and data discovery, it empowers a broader range of stakeholders to leverage data for decision-making.

- **Cross-functional collaboration:** fosters collaboration between different functional groups, including data engineering, data science, domain experts, and business analysts.

- **Reduced data silos:** breaks down data silos by treating data as a product and encouraging the creation of data products that can be reused across the organization.
- **Improved data discovery:** promotes data discovery by providing metadata catalogs, data lineage, and similar features that help users find and understand the available data assets.

A data mesh aims to improve business value by making data more usable and accessible. Key outcomes include scalability to handle growing data volumes, better governance through domain-owned data, agility to adapt to changing needs, and democratization of data access for the business stakeholders. In the next section, let's see why AWS is an accelerator for building a data mesh architecture.

Why AWS for implementing your Data mesh and Data governance?

AWS provides a set of services that enable you to support a wide range of architectural patterns for building your data mesh and data governance foundations. It allows different teams to leverage the technical stack that they prefer by having their own dedicated AWS accounts that they can customize based on their preference.

The flexibility provided by AWS brings a lot of value for the organizations:

- Reducing the time and effort to build your data mesh architecture (if it's compatible with the company's strategy) allows different units to continue to operate with the stack they know how to use.
- Because of the previous point, this might mean lower resistance to change (at least from technical teams) when different areas of the business have to be integrated.

- Overall, facilitates the integration of new areas of the business, as they don't need to adapt to an existing stack.
- Freedom of evolution of different units is no longer tied to having to conform to a single stack.
- With the data mesh's technological freedom, teams have the opportunity to choose for themselves the right tool for their use case.

The AWS services such as **AWS Lake Formation**, **Amazon DataZone**, and **AWS Glue Data Catalog** are the blocks for building your data mesh and data governance.

AWS Lake Formation provides the ability to enforce data governance within each data domain and across domains to ensure data is easily discoverable and secure.

Amazon DataZone is a data management service that makes it faster and easier for customers to catalog, discover, share, and govern data stored across AWS, on-premises, and third-party sources. With Amazon DataZone, administrators and data stewards who oversee an organization's data assets can manage and govern access to data using fine-grained controls. These controls are designed to ensure access with the right level of privileges and context.

AWS Glue Data Catalog stores metadata about various data sources, transformations, and targets used in your data integration and analytics workflows. AWS Glue Data Catalog acts as a centralized metadata store, capturing metadata (e.g., tables, schemas, columns) about your data sources, making it easier to manage and query data. It automatically discovers and infers the schema of your data from various sources, reducing the need for manual schema definition.

The use of these AWS services will generate a direct impact by reducing the time-to-market for new business initiatives:

- Rather than having to ask different parts of the organization, "Do we have this data?" the team can directly investigate a well-curated catalog of enterprise data.
- Once the right data source(s) has been identified, there is no need to set up a complex integration: with a simple, centralized, and granular access control, the team can be assigned access to the data source.
- As the team starts to use data, it is likely going to be well-documented and high quality as it's been prepared by subject matter experts - this saves a lot of time in getting a basic understanding of data and figuring out how to clean it up according to business rules.
- The team can then process data using the preferred technical stack - no time spent learning and adapting to a different stack that it's not familiar with.

Role of Data in Generative AI

The bedrock of generative AI's prowess lies in its voracious appetite for data, the lifeblood that courses through its silicon veins. These sophisticated digital alchemists transmute vast oceans of information into golden insights, learning to mimic the intricate tapestry of human expression across myriad domains. By gorging on billions of examples, these artificial savants decode the cryptic language of human creativity, unraveling the threads that weave our collective knowledge.

The potency of an AI's digital sorcery is inextricably linked to the quality of its cerebral nourishment. A well-balanced diet of diverse, representative data ensures the AI can conjure outputs that are not only coherent but also imbued with the subtle flavors of context and style. This carefully curated cognitive feast shapes the AI's ability to comprehend and respond to the incantations we call prompts, fueling its capacity for both whimsical and purposeful creation. However, one must tread carefully in this realm of digital sustenance, for the biases and limitations lurking within the data can manifest as unwelcome specters in the AI's creations, potentially amplifying society's existing prejudices.

The hunger for data persists beyond the AI's formative years, with many implementations constantly imbibing fresh streams of information to tailor their outputs. This perpetual feast allows for the generation of content that resonates with the zeitgeist and caters to individual tastes. Furthermore, the AI's palate is refined through a continuous feedback loop, sampling the reactions of its human interlocutors to hone its skills and adapt to the ever-shifting landscape of user expectations.

As we navigate this brave new world of artificial cognition, responsible stewardship of data becomes paramount. We must don the mantle of digital custodians, implement robust governance practices, adhere to regulatory guidelines, and maintain transparency in our use of this precious resource. As generative AI continues to weave itself into the fabric of our industries and lives, data remains the loom upon which we can craft a future that balances technological potential with ethical imperatives and societal well-being.

Summary

The key takeaways of this chapter:

- Data mesh is a decentralized data architecture approach that is based on domain ownership of data, treating data as products, self-serve platforms, and federated governance. It aims to improve data access, usage, and value for organizations.

- Data governance establishes rules, roles, and processes for managing enterprise data assets to ensure quality, security, and compliance. It involves setting policies, standards, and guidelines.
- Data mesh and governance are related through decentralized models that assign domain ownership of data and see data stewards as product owners responsible for associated data products.
- The goals of a data mesh include scalability, improved governance, and making data more accessible and usable for business users through democratization.

The fundamentals have been presented; now, let's dive deep into data governance.

2. Data Management and Support for Generative AI

In this chapter, you will learn about the foundation of a good data landscape that makes it easy to ingest, process, discover, and consume data at scale. We are going to cover the following main topics.

- **People and Process Problem**

  Skills learned: Understand the role of people and process dimensions in data management and data governance

- **Data Governance models (Centralized vs Decentralized)**

  Skills learned: Learn the differences between a centralized data governance model and a decentralized model. Understand how the organization can influence using generative AI on data management and data governance for both structured and unstructured data.

- **Modern data strategy and Generative AI**

  Skills learned: Learn why you need a modern data architecture and how it differs from traditional strategy. Also, learn the objectives of a data-driven organization and how you should think of integrating your data strategy with generative AI.

- **Data Governance Fundamentals**

  Skills learned: Understand the core concepts and main activities involved in building robust data governance for your organization.

How you organize your data and the 4 V's of traditional data management, which include volume, velocity, variety, volume, and veracity, play a pivotal role in your success with generative AI. Foundation models are built to take a variety of data inputs and produce an output for a given task without complex machine-learning techniques such as labeling and training. However, these models cannot work with all volumes of data. Following are some considerations with respect to the 4 V's.

Volume: Most models today can only support between 4K tokens and 16K token input tokens, and each token represents roughly 4 characters. So, based on the match, you cannot use any volume as input for the foundation model. There are methods to chunk large volumes of data before feeding it into a foundation model, and specific data management techniques are required to achieve that.

Volocity: Performance varies when running inferences with foundation models depending on the total number of input and output tokens requested. These models are not designed to provide sub-second or low latencies, which you may be familiar with some tradition machine learning model inferences that can achieve millisecond response times. So, you need to keep in mind what velocity of data can provide acceptable SLAs for your business applications and work with that.

Variety: Not all foundation models can support all varieties of data since not all models are trained on all types of data. When using certain models that require prompts or user input in specific formats, for example, Anthropic Claude v2 is seen to perform best when providing XML prompts; you want to perform data management techniques to convert your data to support those formats.

Veracity: Garbage in, garbage out. This is not only true for traditional machine learning models but is also applicable to foundation models.

The highest quality of data that accurately represents data for a specific business problem will provide more accurate results from the foundation models. You need to use traditional data management techniques to ensure data is trustworthy and ready for insights before using generative AI foundation models.

People and Process Problem

In a modern data governance and data mesh paradigm, it's important to have a federated and decentralized governance model that includes working across multirole teams and processes. **Decentralized Ownership** provides autonomy to each domain or line of business. Each domain or business unit has ownership of its data. This requires clear communication, collaboration, and alignment among teams responsible for different data sets.

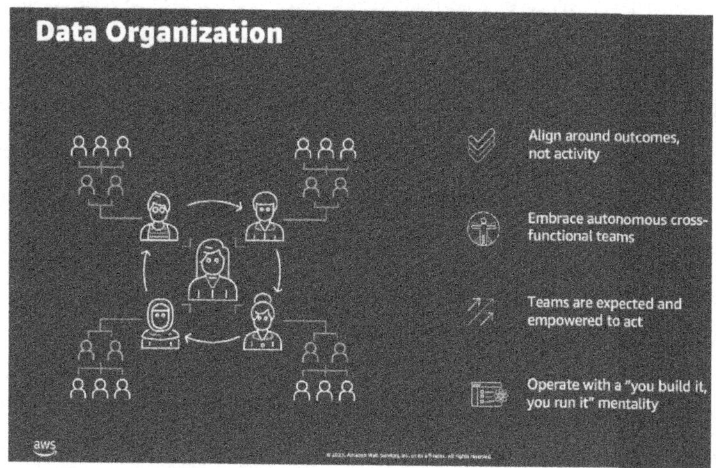

Figure 2.1: Organizing Data

Data as a product mindset brings new roles within the governance, consumers, and data product teams. Data product teams are cross-functional and are responsible for the entire lifecycle of a specific data product. They include data engineers, data experts, data scientists, domain experts, and others needed to create, maintain, and evolve the data product. One of the key roles in a data product team is data steward or domain data product owners, as they are responsible for the maturity and lifecycle of a data product. Data stewards are also responsible for approving a data product to be listed in a catalog by assessing the key metrics like quality, lineage, classification, and conformation to standards approved by the organization. Data stewards also receive requests for new features in an existing data product or a new data product for their domain.

The data governance team or central IT is responsible for infrastructure, automation, and building the core components of a central catalog and authorization workflow. Data lake admins in the Central IT team are responsible for setting up a catalog for data products and also responsible for building automation to create an environment for data products, automation for policy management, and a platform to build data products. Centralized data catalogs help discover and understand available data products, making it easier for teams to find and use data across the organization. Data products evolve over time, and it is critical to have a change management process that includes the people across governance, data products, and consumers because changing schemas and maintaining backward compatibility are important to avoid disruptions in downstream applications.

Interactions between teams are crucial. Teams collaborate on defining data contract quality standards and sharing data in a standardized way, often using APIs or data platforms. Processes and guidelines are established for data quality, security, compliance, and privacy. These ensure that data products meet organizational standards. Different teams might use various tools and technologies for analysis and processing. The ecosystem should be flexible enough to support this diversity.

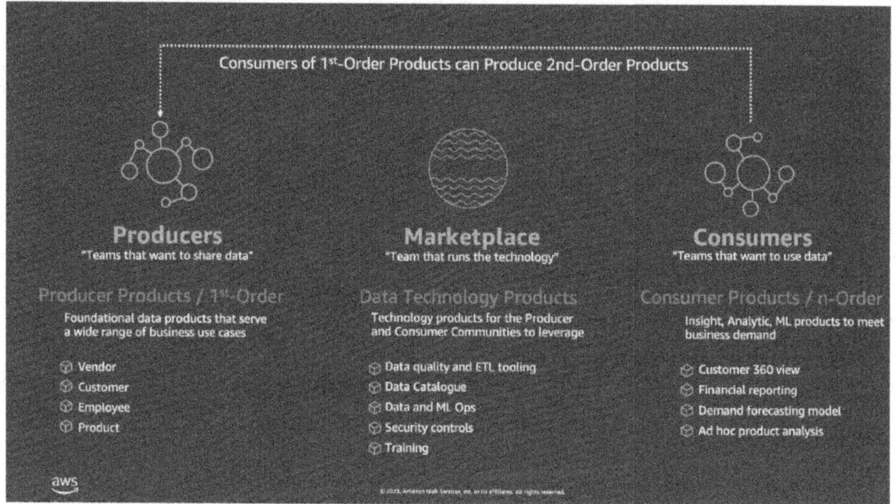

Figure 2.2: Data Producers and Consumers

Measurement and Feedback: Metrics are used to assess the impact and effectiveness of data products. Teams learn from usage patterns and continuously improve their products.

Education and Training: Training programs and resources help teams understand their roles and responsibilities. Periodic retraining ensures the organizational changes are well informed from time to time between both producers and consumer teams.

Overall, the "People and Process" aspect of Data Mesh focuses on fostering a culture of collaboration, autonomy, and accountability among cross-functional teams to effectively manage and utilize data across the organization.

In this section, you have seen the role of people and processes come together in establishing a data mesh and how decentralized ownership between producers and consumers forms the basis of a data mesh. In the next section, you will see various data governance models and understand how generative AI can influence data management and data governance.

Data Governance Models (Centralized versus Decentralized)

Data governance is the overall management of an organization's data assets. It includes the development and implementation of policies and procedures to ensure the effective use and protection of data. Data governance is typically handled by a data governance committee or data governance board, which is responsible for setting data policies and guidelines, as well as monitoring and enforcing compliance with those policies.

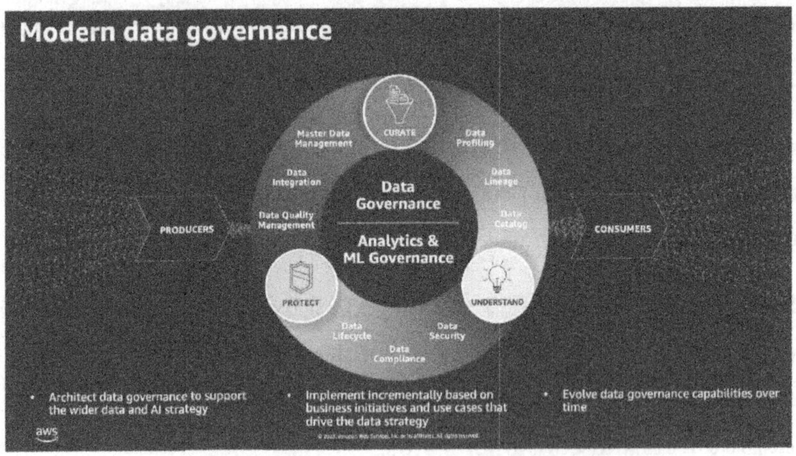

Figure 2.3: Data Governance Concepts

Data governance is important for a number of reasons. First, it helps to ensure that data is accurate, complete, and consistent. This is essential for making informed decisions and for maintaining trust in the data. Second, data governance helps to protect data from unauthorized access and use. This is important for maintaining the confidentiality and security of sensitive information. Third, data governance helps to ensure that data is properly managed and maintained. This is important for ensuring that data is accurate and up-to-date and that it is accessible to those who need it.

Overall, data governance is an important part of any organization's data management strategy. It helps to ensure that data is findable, accurate, high quality, secure, and accessible and that it is properly managed and maintained. It is also important to ensure that data is used effectively and efficiently and that it is aligned with the organization's goals and objectives.

Data governance needs to align with ML and FMOPS governance to build an end-to-end platform for building insights to drive business outcomes. Data governance core pillars are spread across data producers, data governance teams, and data consumers. For example, data governance has three main categories: security, understand, and unify. These categories need a good data quality framework, self-service access workflow, single pane of data access policies management, decentralized data product ownership, building a business catalog, data sharing, and data lineage, just to mention a few.

Data governance provides businesses the ability to manage their data assets. It involves establishing the policies, procedures, roles, and technologies to ensure data quality and fitness for business purposes. A typical data mesh governance consists of a central data governance body, data stewards embedded in business units, and IT teams. Together, they define and enforce rules for how data is accessed, protected, improved, and used across the organization. The goal is to maximize the value of data while minimizing risk.

A data governance body is a group of individuals who are responsible for setting data policies and guidelines, building a data discovery platform, and monitoring and enforcing compliance with those policies. The data governance board works with data stewards from data product domains to make sure that data products are built as per the organization's standards and meet compliance needs. The data governance board is typically made up of senior leaders from across the organization, as well as experts in data management and governance.

Data governance, along with a decentralized data product team, sets guidelines for the following:

- **Data Policies:** rules and regulations that govern the use and management of data. These policies are typically set by the data governance board and data product teams.
- **Data Guidelines:** best practices and recommendations for how to manage and use data. These guidelines are typically set by the data governance board and data product teams.
- **Data Compliance:** helps the data product team build data products that adhere to the rules and regulations set by the data governance board that align with the industry-specific compliance needs.
- **Data Confidentiality:** the practice of keeping data secure and private so that it is not accessible or shared with unauthorized individuals. This is important for maintaining trust in the data and for protecting sensitive information.
- **Data Security:** the practice of safeguarding and protecting data from unauthorized access and use and of ensuring that data is not compromised or stolen. This includes implementing a self-service workflow for consumers to request access to the data that can be routed to the person responsible for approving or denying the request.
- **Data Lineage:** the practice of tracking the flow of data, which helps in understanding the data and its transformation. Data lineage helps understand and track the data.

- **Data Marketplace:** The data marketplace is setup by the governance teams and enriched by various process and data products experts. This marketplace helps consumers locate and request access to the data.

Data governance teams can be setup both centrally and decentralized depending on the teams, use case, and size of the organization.

A centralized data governance team is a model where data is ingested, transformed, and stored in a central data lake solution. Data consumers discover and get access to the data at a central location to build analytics. The centralized model has several advantages, like the ability to manage data, but there are several challenges in this model; it can be more difficult to make changes to the data, and the data is managed by a team who may not understand the data really well. The process of making changes to the data is expensive.

The decentralized data governance approach empowers decentralized data product teams to own the data product generation, which includes ingestion, transforming, and building data products. Data product teams own and make decisions regarding the data itself and work with data engineers and data experts to build a matured data product. In this model, a central governance team works with decentralized data product teams to set up infrastructure, set rules for data quality, list data in a marketplace, and adhere to compliance policies. This is a more recent model and is becoming more popular as organizations become more agile. The decentralized model has several advantages, such as the ability to more easily adapt to changing needs and the ability to share data with other parties.

Influence of Gen AI on Data Management and Data Governance

In order to get high-quality responses from a generative AI foundation model, you need to have good-quality data fed into the foundation model. You require a strong data foundation using AWS's purpose-built data analytics services to ensure you are delivering the right quality data at desired SLAs and with desired performance at the lowest cost. Enterprises today are building their data and analytical platform using FAIR data principles to support a self-serve analytics architecture that helps in building business insights faster. Data mesh and federated data governance are leveraged across many organizations to reduce time spent building high-performing and cost-effective analytics that feed data into the foundation models.

This means building an end-to-end strategy that leverages Generative AI models to build consolidated and linked metadata, enhance search experience using semantic search and custom embeddings, and build analytics using Generative AI models. This can also include generating queries and codes, text generation, summarization of results, and integration with chatbots and coding assistants.

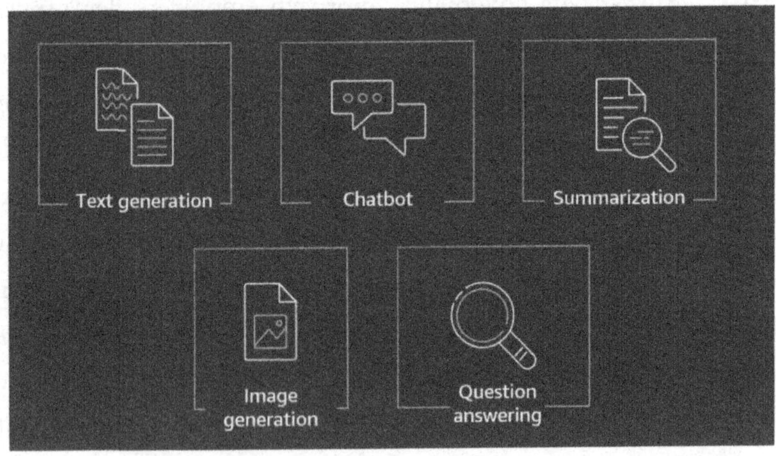

Figure 2.4: Generative AI Use Cases

Industry-specific metadata can be generated using Generative AI models. As an example, in Healthcare and Life sciences, business metadata and glossaries can be generated using existing metadata like electronic lab notebooks and industry-specific clinical ontologies and data concepts, including notebooks, databases, technical catalogs, and unstructured data. The auto-generated descriptions provide additional context and insights into the data assets. Generative AI models can be leveraged to build a contextual and semantic data-findable solution.

Modern Data Strategy and Generative AI

Speaking to several leaders across organizations, the following five trends are driving a change in thinking about data strategies.

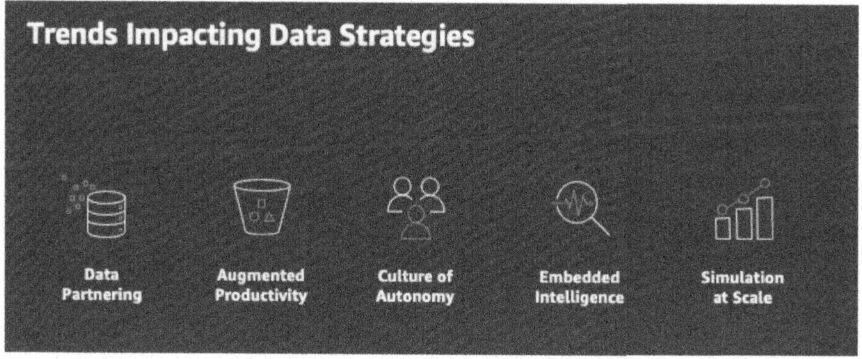

Figure 2.5: Data Strategy Trends

Organizations are increasingly partnering across industries and value chains to connect internal and external data to broaden the context of their decision-making and differentiate themselves.

The trend of using **AIML** to augment productivity is growing fast. It's being used to supplement gaps in specialist talent and augment tasks in creative, research, and administrative areas. It's freeing up team members to focus on activities that create more value.

Many organizations are removing the traditional bottlenecks created by managing data centrally. More companies recognize the need to use small, lean, empowered teams that adopt a "data as a product" mentality to be more autonomous.

Companies are using near-real-time intelligence to provide insights "at the moment that matters." This is driving hyper-personalization that improves customer experiences.

Last but not least, cloud services that support infinite scaling and the instrumentation of the real-world using **IoT** are enabling organizations to develop models that simulate complex "what if" scenarios.

Many companies are struggling to leverage these trends to create value using data.

According to a study in 2023 by New Vantage Partners, 99% of leading companies are investing in using data in new ways, but only 24% report seeing the results they aspire to. The main causes cited for this gap are not related to technology. In fact, the key challenges are related to culture, people, and processes. The organizations that get it right are the ones that are able to bring mindset, people, process, and tech together to create a modern data strategy. They form the pillars of a strategic modern data strategy, as depicted below. Our view on how to develop a modern data strategy is informed by our work with several customers and our own experience at Amazon.com.

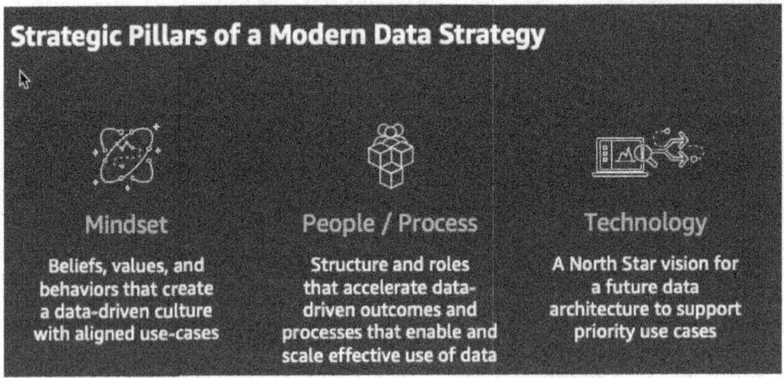

Figure 2.6: Strategic Pillars of Modern Data Strategy

For Mindset, one key difference is adopting a product-oriented mindset vs. a platform-oriented mindset. A modern mindset doesn't start with implementing a technology platform that you then go looking for ways to use to show value. It's about working backward from the "customer" to define the product and experience.

For People/Process, it's establishing joint ownership of the strategy by business and technology leaders that reflects the importance of data in the modern world. Moving away from monolithic "data teams" to smaller, domain-oriented, "data product" teams with more autonomy. And creating governance models and tooling that enable teams versus control teams.

Finally, for Technology, a modern data strategy is built upon an extendible, cloud-based architecture where you utilize the best fit-for-purpose services based on the business needs at hand.

Now that we've defined our view of a modern data strategy, let's explore HOW data and machine learning come together to strengthen your modern data strategy.

Data and ML Strategy – Better Together!

Traditionally, in many organizations, people are still responsible for high effort but less creative work, which includes tasks such as documentation operations work like monitoring and identifying issues, to name a few. In recent times, organizations have placed more emphasis on their workforce to generate new value via investments through automation and machine learning, as illustrated in the figure below.

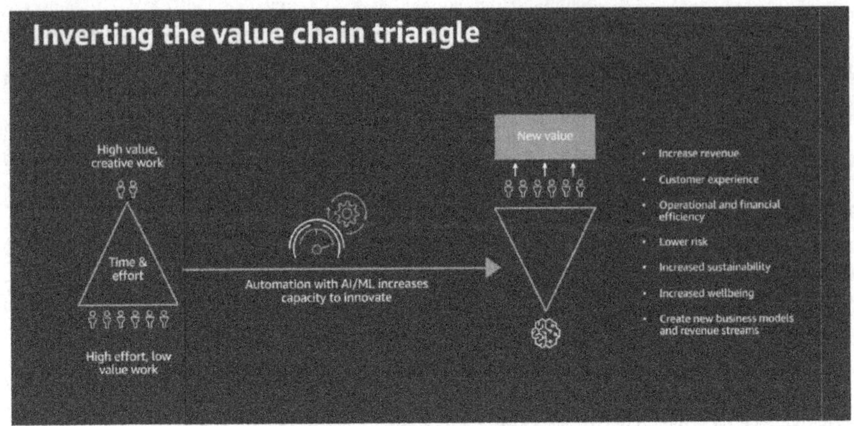

Figure 2.7: AI/ML Value Chain

The resulting effect is an inversion of where people can now spend their time. As high-effort, low-value work is automated, people have the capacity to focus on generating new value, innovating, and creating better customer experiences. Future roles will comprise high-value, creative work. All industries and business models will be disrupted as all components of the value chain are automated. This, in turn, continues to feed the machine with new data feedback loops, continually raising the bar on the quality of ML inference.

ML is assisting us in so many activities across the value chain, including sensing, automating, optimizing, predicting, and assisting.

- In sales, we see customers delivering increasing personalization and automated sales assistance.
- In fraud, we see financial companies proactively detecting fraud patterns without impeding customer service.
- In legal, we see companies automating how they search for case law and getting faster time to answers all possible due to the use of machine learning with data.

Now, generative AI is added to the mix, and organizations want their applications to be not only data-driven but also able to integrate seamlessly into their GenAI vision. The following depicts a call center agent chatbot application as an example of how data-driven organizations quickly gain value by integrating their data to gain differentiating insights from the foundation AI models.

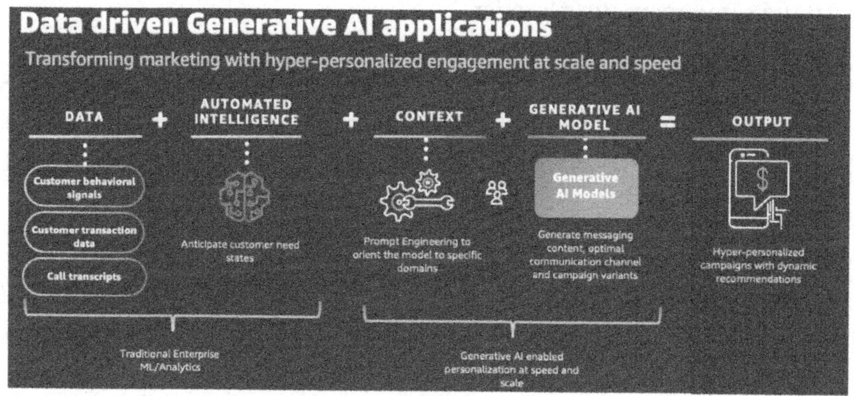

Figure 2.8: Data-driven Generative AI Application

A typical marketing campaign flow starts with some kind of a portfolio of ML models that take in customer data – e.g., behavior signals like online activity patterns, transaction data, and interactions like call transcript data to develop predictions. For example, ML models would generate a Customer LifeTime Value prediction propensity to churn. These would then be used to bucket the customers into segments, and for each segment, the marketing teams would design and deploy campaigns. Each of these campaigns gets executed for each customer segment and, where possible, with multiple variants that are instrumented and evaluated on an ongoing basis. This process is capacity-constrained for marketing teams to design campaigns and monitor/tweak them on an ongoing basis. Can we solve this problem with GenAI?

In the above example scenario, an AI-powered foundation model generates ad/campaign messaging content for each recommended communication channel, which can then be tweaked by the marketing teams. This can provide a significant productivity boost to the marketing teams – a study by McKinsey in 2023 estimated that GenAI can improve the productivity of marketing teams by 5-15% in terms of throughput with the same marketing budgets.

There are many such use cases that are possible across entire value chains within Enterprises and across almost all business functions. We are getting started! We should expect to see many, many such use-cases deployed in the next few years.

Another common use case is the use of data-powered virtual agents to resolve customer queries in an automated way, either using chatbots or Q&A interfaces. This is depicted in more detail below.

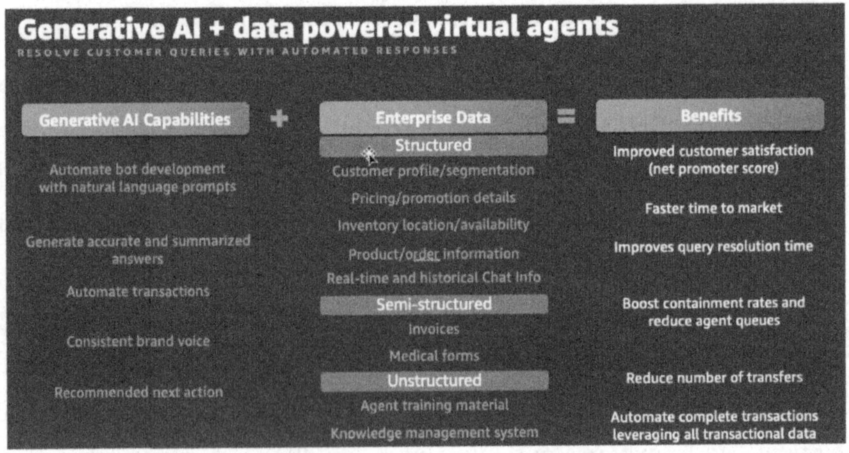

Figure 2.9: Gen AI-Powered Virtual Agents

These virtual agents use enterprise data in any format, structured, semi-structured, or unstructured, to be fed into a generative AI model to gain an improved customer experience. In some cases, the data needs to be enriched, as in traditional machine learning use cases.

You have seen how these generative AI use cases influence data management in the modern data strategy. Now, let's look at some of the fundamentals of data governance.

Data Governance Fundamentals

Data explosion is creating a balancing act between access and control. Organizations like to become data-driven and need a centralized, consistent data protection and governance strategy to protect their businesses and democratize data to take competitive advantage.

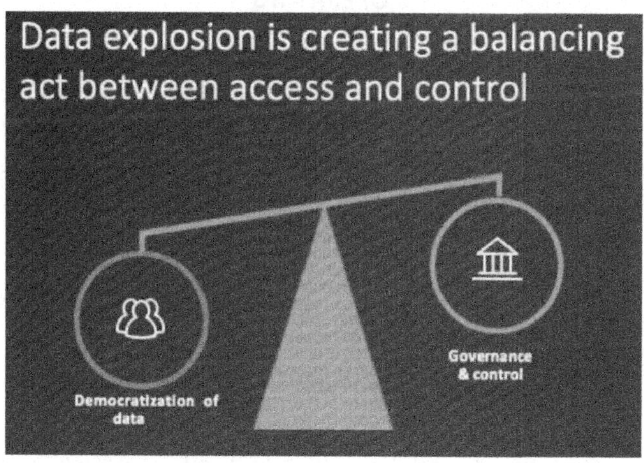

Figure 2.10: The Balancing Act of Data Management

Having a well-defined strategy and framework for governing data across the organization is pivotal in bringing organizational success with data. Robust data policies, procedures, roles, and responsibilities are the key foundational elements that constitute a comprehensive data governance framework. The core building blocks for these foundation elements, in no specific order of importance, include Data stewardship, Data quality management, metadata management, master data management, data security, data auditing, data lifecycle management, issue escalation and accountability, and training & communication.

The following diagram depicts a successful approach to data governance. Notice that the operating model is centered around people, process, and technology, which is a lynchpin to data governance success, as outlined in the section on the people and process problem.

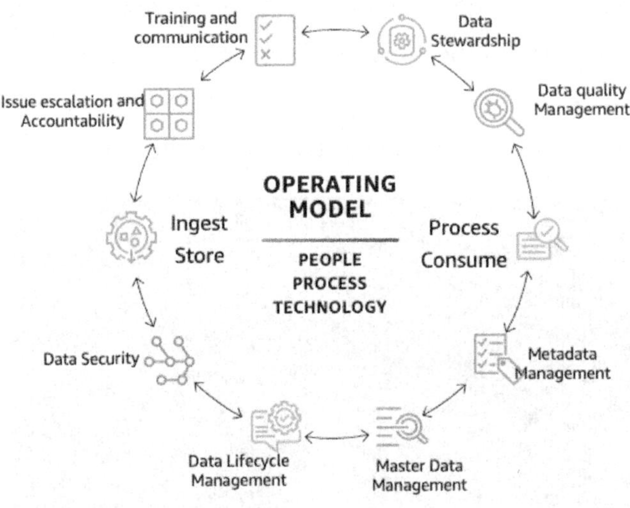

Figure 2.11: Data Governance Operating Model

The data governance operating model is explained in more detail below.

Data Stewardship

Data stewardship is about appointing data stewards who are responsible for managing and governing specific data domains or datasets. Stewards serve as key points of contact and accountability. When assigning data stewards, identify key personnel to take responsibility for managing and governing specific data domains. Stewards have an in-depth understanding of the data and serve as an advocate and caretaker. Stewards can come from any part of the organizational structure but are more commonly seen between the business teams or an IT liaison who has a strong understanding of both the business usage terminology and can translate them to technical teams.

Defining stewardship roles and responsibilities requires clearly outlining the duties of data stewards, such as maintaining standards, policies, issue resolution, quality control, metadata management, and user access controls. Data stewards should also play a role in defining benchmarks and metrics for data quality, accuracy, completeness, consistency, etc. This includes developing data quality rules and procedures and working closely with IT teams if the organization structure requires IT teams to manage data quality rules.

When managing data policies and procedures, stewards assist in formulating and enforcing data policies, guidelines, and processes for activities like data acquisition, storage, integration, access, archiving, etc. Data stewards are also responsible for ongoing data quality monitoring, auditing, issue tracking, and working with IT teams to resolve any quality problems. Educating stakeholders on proper data usage, lineage, definitions, and meaning is a key stewardship duty. This improves overall data reliability and helps promote data literacy.

When maintaining metadata, stewards should maintain descriptive metadata, including definitions, sources, lineage, etc. Complete and accurate metadata is crucial for governance. Data stewards grant appropriate data access privileges to users and set data security protocols aligned to policies and legal/regulatory mandates. They need to work with IT to build a people and process workflow that allows them to intake data access requests and get notified on requests with most details required to make a decision to either approve or deny the requests.

Data Quality Management

The information you derive is only as valuable as the data's quality. You should thus make sure that the data you are feeding into building the insights is of the highest quality. Establishing processes to monitor, measure, and improve data quality on an ongoing basis is paramount to producing high-quality data at all times. This includes data profiling, data cleansing, data monitoring, issue tracking, root cause analysis, reference data management, training, issue escalation, remediation, and continuous improvement.

Data profiling: Analyzing data to understand its structure, content, relationships, etc., is referred to as data profiling. This helps identify data quality issues and areas for improvement. Maintaining a data profiling dashboard by application not only allows you to quickly identify anomalies and data issues but also helps downstream consumers to quickly glean patterns within the data and accelerates time to insights.

Data cleansing: Data cleansing is all about detecting and correcting corrupt, inaccurate, incomplete, duplicate, or irrelevant data. This may involve standardization, deduplication, pattern matching, etc.

Data Monitoring: Establishing processes and checks to monitor data quality over time and prevent new issues from arising. This includes metrics, dashboards, data validation, etc.

Issue tracking: Having a system to log, prioritize, and track the resolution of identified data quality issues. This provides visibility into the types of problems and progress.

Root cause analysis: Diving deep into the source of where the data quality issue originated is important. This is not always easy to accomplish due to the complexities involved between data silos, lack of proper lineage during and after ETL processing, and lack of consensus in documenting the right quality of data. That said, having a sound understanding of where the symptom lies vs. the actual source that caused this symptom in the data pipelines is critical in fixing data quality issues.

Reference data management: Centralizing management of master data used across systems like product catalogs, customer info, geographic data, etc. This eliminates inconsistencies.

Data quality rules: Defining business rules, validation checks, thresholds, etc., to enforce data quality standards, accuracy, integrity, and validity.

Training: Educating data stewards, business users, and IT staff on maintaining data quality and their roles. Improves accountability.

Issue escalation: Clearly defining thresholds and processes for escalating unresolved critical data quality issues to senior management. Enforces priority.

Continuous improvement: Regular assessment of data quality KPIs, audits, and feedback loops to refine policies, processes, and controls to improve data quality over time.

All of the above collectively provide a robust way to establish, monitor, and improve data quality.

Metadata Management

Maintaining detailed metadata about data assets to understand lineage, meaning, usage, etc., provides an effective way to understand what data exists within the organization and validates the fidelity of the data. This provides context for effective governance. Considerations for robust metadata management include the following.

- Establish metadata standards with consistent schemas, taxonomies, and dictionaries, thereby building consistency across organizational assets no matter where they reside in the organization. That includes standards for metadata creation, storage, and integration across files, databases, and associated objects, streaming topics, ML models and endpoints, APIs, etc.

- Maintaining centralized, searchable repositories of metadata to provide a "single source of truth" for data meaning, context, lineage, etc. This could include business glossaries, data catalogs, and ML model cards.
- Metadata access controls are required to maintain integrity, which can be achieved by setting user access permissions and security protocols for creating, updating, and viewing metadata based on roles and responsibilities.
- Using automated tools for technical metadata collection from data sources vs manual processes improves the completeness and freshness of data. This further allows data democratization at scale.
- Track all changes made to metadata over time for auditing. Build a notification mechanism to notify source and destination data teams of schema drift. Establish a human review/approve process for changes to sensitive metadata before committing to repositories.
- Develop automated flows across systems to propagate metadata changes bidirectionally. It is pivotal to leverage lineage and keep technical, business, and operational metadata in sync when drift occurs.
- Setup dashboards, reports, and alerts to monitor metadata health - completeness, accuracy, freshness, etc. Flag issues for resolution and track impacted data objects, applications, and owners to notify them of progress.
- After establishing a business glossary, enable business users to

update definitions of business terms to the technical catalog. Establish a governed process that aligns metadata with changing business needs.

- Capturing end-to-end data flows and transformations from source to destination allows for comprehensive data lineage tracking. This is critical for regulatory compliance and preventing broken data chains.

- Defining KPIs for metadata completeness, conformity to standards, and rate of schema drifts allows for measuring and improving metadata quality over time.

- Metadata audits periodically involve conducting audits to identify metadata gaps, inconsistencies, and quality issues. The audit process should be followed by recommending corrective actions.

These considerations collectively provide robust metadata management capabilities.

Master Data Management

Master data refers to the critical, core business entities that are essential for an organization's operations and analytics. It includes data on customers, products, suppliers, employees, assets, locations, etc. Master data is typically scattered across multiple systems and silos within an organization. These silos risk the accuracy of insights, lead to data duplication, and introduce operational challenges in maintaining a single source of truth. Master data is the essential "oil" that keeps the organization running smoothly. **Master data Management (MDM)** removes the "grit" from this oil by managing master data at an enterprise level. It is a strategic investment that pays both tactical and long-term dividends.

Organizations should build MDM systems for the following benefits:

- MDM consolidates master data from different sources into one consistent version. This provides one single source of truth across the organization.
- MDM eliminates duplicates and inconsistencies in master data coming from different systems. This greatly improves data reliability and quality.
- MDM establishes clear accountability, policies, and stewardship over master data domains. This ensures master data is trustworthy and secure.
- With clean, uniform master data, organizations can derive better insights from analytics and reporting. MDM is a key enabler for advanced analytics.
- With reliable master data, organizations can respond faster to changing business needs and innovate more quickly.
- MDM provides the trusted data foundation for new digital business models and initiatives like self-service customer portals.

The following figure illustrates the high-level activities you need to perform in no specific order to build a robust MDM system.

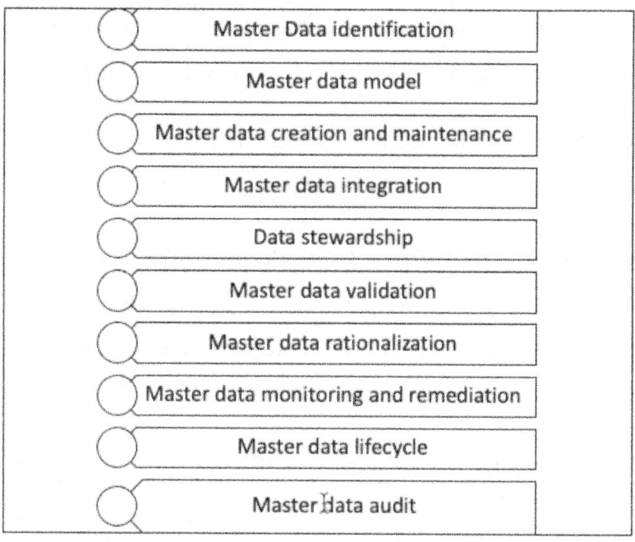

Figure 2.12: Master Data Management Activities

Master data identification: Determining which business entities, like customers, products, suppliers, etc., will be considered master data and managed centrally.

Master data model: Defining a consistent data model to provide a uniform view for master data entities with attributes, relationships, taxonomy, metadata, etc.

Master data creation/maintenance: Establishing unified processes for creating, updating, and retiring master data. It may require business user workflows and approval chains.

Master data integration: Linking master data across source systems consistently through ETL processes to prevent siloed, contradictory master data.

Master data security: Setting up access controls, editing privileges, and reading permissions for master data based on use and application roles. This prevents unauthorized changes that would otherwise compromise exposing and altering master data.

Data stewardship: Appointing data stewards accountable for the quality and governance of master data within their business domain.

Master data validation: Defining business rules for master data quality checks. Preventing bad data from entering systems.

Master data rationalization: Resolving conflicts between master data records through merging, purging, etc., to maintain a single version of truth. This is a step that should be automated within the ETL data integration framework.

Master data monitoring and remediation: Ongoing data profiling, analytics, and dashboards to monitor master data quality for completeness, accuracy, and compliance. Formal issue/exception workflow for master data errors or changes creates a way for rapid resolution of issues.

Master data lifecycle: Establish a master data life cycle that includes a combination of people and processes that clearly defines how master data will be discovered, integrated, unified, published, and retired.

Master data audits: Regular master data health checks through audit assessments to identify issues and drive improvements.

These activities bolster the maturity of your master data, allowing data applications to better trust and use it as a single source of truth for master data.

Data Security

Securing data is ***job zero***, as it protects sensitive information from unauthorized access and misuse. As individuals, we rely on data security to safeguard our personal and financial information from threats like hackers, fraudsters, and cybercriminals. Businesses need data security to protect intellectual property, trade secrets, strategies, and proprietary information that gives them a competitive edge. Proper data security allows companies to avoid costly compliance violations and penalties associated with regulations like HIPAA (Health Information Portability and Accountability Act) and PCI-DSS (Payment Card Industry Data Security Standard). It also reduces business disruption from breaches and cyberattacks while building customer trust through a demonstrated commitment to data protection and privacy. Overall, investing in robust data security measures reduces risk, prevents identity theft and fraud, maintains privacy, secures sensitive assets, avoids noncompliance, minimizes business disruption, builds reputation, and saves money in the long run.

The activities that help you build robust data security in your organization include:

Data classification: This involves categorizing data based on sensitivity and criticality to a business function that, in turn, helps determine appropriate security levels, access controls, and protection policies.

Access controls: Understand all the stakeholders for given data and their role within the organization. Leveraging role-based access controls, least privilege access, authentication, and authorization to grant access to data on a need-to-know basis.

Encryption: Applying encryption for data at rest and in transit to ensure confidentiality and protect against unauthorized access.

Data masking: Masking sensitive data for non-production use cases like development, testing, and analytics. Ensures security while enabling business use.

Data loss prevention: Data loss prevention ensures the authorized users of data do not misuse handling data. Implementing controls to prevent unauthorized sharing, leakage, or exfiltration of sensitive data like PII, IP, financial data, etc.

Data auditing: With a data map in place, organizations can then develop policies, procedures, and technical controls for monitoring access and changes to important data. This includes implementing logging to create audit trails of user activity, configuring alerts for suspicious access, and utilizing data loss prevention tools. Periodic audits should be conducted to review logs, verify controls are functioning, and identify potential vulnerabilities, issues, or incidents.

Data erasure: Ensuring sensitive data is completely erased and unrecoverable when no longer required as per data retention policies.

Data anonymization: Removing personally identifiable information from data sets to enable broader analytics while adhering to privacy regulations.

Data sovereignty: Maintaining data within geographic boundaries based on regulatory obligations and data residency laws. **General Data Protection Regulation** (**GDPR**) is a good example of data sovereignty, which safeguards how organizations can transfer data across borders.

Incident response: outlines the key steps an organization should take when a breach or cyberattack involving sensitive data occurs. The first priority is to quickly identify and contain the incident to limit damage and prevent further unauthorized access. This is followed by an in-depth investigation to determine the root cause, affected systems, and exact data compromised. Notification should go out to impacted individuals and authorities as required by law. Short-term response often involves resetting passwords, applying patches, taking affected systems offline, and blocking suspicious IP addresses. Longer-term recovery focuses on eliminating vulnerabilities that led to the incident and improving defenses to prevent recurrence. Formal documentation, monitoring, and analysis are critical throughout the response process. Having clear roles and responsibilities assigned to incident response team members ensures coordination and accountability. Proper planning to develop, test, and refine incident response procedures makes execution smooth when an actual breach occurs. With the increasing frequency of attacks, having robust incident response capabilities is crucial for minimizing harm from data security threats.

Training: Educating data users on security practices and their responsibilities in protecting data as per the governance policies.

All these activities, in no specific order, bring a robust data security posture to your organization.

Data Lifecycle Management

Data lifecycle management (**DLM**) refers to the policies and procedures for managing data throughout its useful lifespan within an organization. DLM considers the entire data journey from creation and acquisition through its useful life until it is no longer needed and can be deleted. Key stages are depicted in the following diagram.

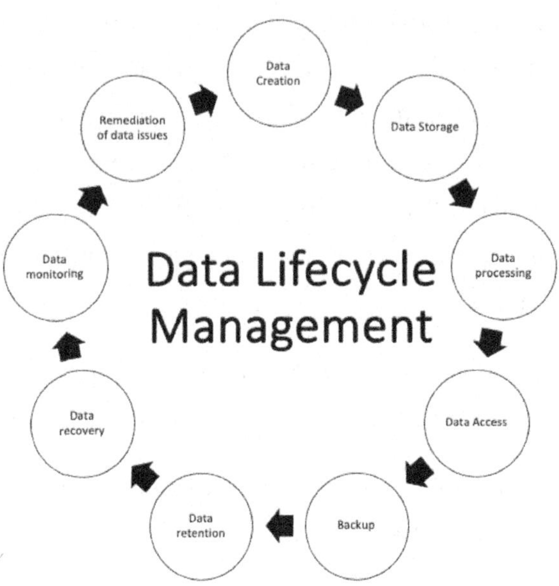

Figure 2.13: Data Management Life Cycle

- **Data Creation:** Define standards for how data gets created and captured in systems. Ensures proper input validation and error handling.
- **Data Storage:** Determine the appropriate storage system required for business applications to store different types of data, between structured, semi-structured, and unstructured data. Optimizing storage for cost, availability, performance, and security. This includes less frequently used data stored on a low-cost and lower-performance storage system if that meets business requirements.
- **Data Processing:** Establish data processing controls, workflows, and standards to maintain integrity during transformations, integrations, cleansing, etc.
- **Data Access:** Manage data access through role-based controls

and security policies that allow the right stakeholders access to data. For instance, audit teams require access to entire historical data, but reporting teams only require access to the last 1 or 2 years of data for business intelligence reporting purposes.

- **Backup:** Define backup schedules, retention periods, and storage for different business data types to enable restore from any point in time.
- **Data Retention:** Implement data deletion and retention schedules in compliance with regulatory obligations for how long certain data should persist and define how to delete all data objects associated with the object that is required to be deleted. Building archive policies to move inactive/older data to cheaper storage tiers while retaining accessibility. Following proper destruction techniques such as the **National Institute of Standards and Technology** (**NIST**) standards, ***erasing data objects in the cloud*** allows you a safe harbor approach when destroying data.
- **Data Recovery:** Establish recovery protocols in case of failures, outages, disasters, etc., to resume operations with minimal data loss.
- **Data Monitoring:** Track data and its usage across the lifecycle to ensure controls are working as intended. Understanding data heuristics to find the most used data objects establishes data availability SLAs for consumers along with performance SLAs, allowing you to provide an agile and effective way to democratize data.
- **Remediation of Data Issues:** Assess issues found during monitoring to enhance data lifecycle management controls. This

includes a customer-centric value chain perspective that allows customers to be agile and provides a system that helps with faster time to market.

These stages of the data management lifecycle, in no specific order, allow organizations to keep their business data secure and relevant to business needs.

Issue Escalation and Accountability

Having clear procedures to escalate data issues and ensuring accountability for remediation is pivotal in achieving organizational success with data management. The lack of this enforcement undermines data governance. The following are the activities for data leaders to stay on top.

- **Issue Documentation:** Have a standard process to document data issues/problems as they arise. This includes details like issue description, data affected, owner, and upstream and downstream applications impacted. Create transparent communication with data stakeholders as soon as the impact is identified.

- **Issue Prioritization:** Classify and prioritize data issues based on severity, impact, urgency, etc., to determine escalation timelines and resources needed.

- **Escalation Thresholds:** Define quantitative and qualitative thresholds for escalating data issues to higher levels, such as the number of records affected, type of data, SLA breaches, etc.

- **Escalation Hierarchy:** Maintain a clear escalation hierarchy with defined roles and responsibilities for data issue resolution. Starts from data stewards to IT, business leaders, and executive sponsors.

- **Resolution Tracking:** Monitor data issue resolution progress via standard metrics and KPIs. Ensure issues don't remain open indefinitely.

- **Post-Resolution Review:** Conduct root cause analysis on resolved significant issues to address underlying factors and prevent recurrence.

- **Accountability Framework:** Designate data stewards accountable for data quality in their domain. Include SLAs for issue resolution.

- **Ownership Transparency:** Publicize data stewardship responsibilities across the organization for transparency into data accountability.

- **Consequence Management:** Institute consequences for recurring data quality failures like missed SLAs through warnings, additional training, loss of access or role, etc.

- **Compliance Reporting:** Regularly report to senior management on metrics related to data quality, issue resolution, accountability, etc., for continued sponsorship.

- **Continuous Improvement:** Analyze data issue metrics to identify systemic gaps and enhance policies to improve issue resolution.

These activities, in no specific order, allow organizations to stay proactive and avoid large-scale disruptions due to data issues.

Training and Communication

When speaking to leaders in several organizations, there is a consensus on the lack of proper emphasis on training and communication. The role of people in data governance operations is paramount, and leaders across organizations agree that it is often overlooked. People training, when performed, leaders mentioned that it is a one-time set and one deal and never looked back. The problem is exacerbated when people switch roles, new members are hired across data teams, and there is a lack of proper training to level set their role in data governance. The following guidance helps you to stay on top of required training and communication for effectively operating your data governance at scale.

- **Awareness Training:** Conduct training for all data stakeholders on the basics of data governance, including policies, procedures, principles, roles, and responsibilities. This creates organizational alignment.
- **Targeted Training:** Provide in-depth training on data management to key roles like data stewards, data owners, and IT teams. Provide adequate training to improve their proficiency in implementing governance.
- **Ongoing Education:** Create ongoing learning opportunities through certifications, seminars, and workshops to sustain and refresh data governance skills.
- **Training Measurement:** Assess training effectiveness through surveys, exams, and audits of employee data governance knowledge. Identify gaps and remediate them.
- **Training Material:** Maintaining up-to-date training documents, videos, and use cases that provide practical examples tailored to the organization by personas with desired responsibilities.
- **Communication Workflow:** Establish a cadence for regular communication on data governance updates, metrics, issues, and successes with all stakeholders.

- **Multi-channel Communication:** Leverage emails, newsletters, town halls, intranet portals, etc., to communicate through preferred mediums of different audiences.
- **Executive Sponsorship:** Having executive leaders endorse and advocate for the data governance program across the organization is when the rubber meets the road. This improves buy-in and instigates stakeholders to perform their desired role effectively. Leaders in several organizations have mentioned that this lack of proper executive sponsorship across the company was a huge hindrance in effectively enforcing data governance.
- **Continuous Improvement:** Create centralized channels like forums and email inboxes for stakeholders to provide input, ask questions, and get support on data governance. The use of generative AI chatbots can accelerate awareness, improve support posture, simplify enforcement, and allow feedback via a single pane of glass.
- **Success Broadcast:** Publicize data governance wins and deliver value to demonstrate real-world impact. This builds further commitment and brings more stakeholders to the platform who would like to repeat similar success.

Keeping your teams and stakeholders well informed of data tools, technologies, processes, and changes ensures long-term success with data.

Summary

The chapter provided an overview of various aspects of data management and governance that are important for organizations to democratize data for enterprise use cases, including AI technologies like generative AI. The role of people, processes, and technologies together in managing data as a strategic asset is a cornerstone for a successful data organization. Key concepts covered include data quality, data security, data lifecycle management, metadata, master data, and operational readiness with data.

These learnings help you understand how to build a robust data foundation to enable advanced analytics and AI initiatives. Well-governed, high-quality data is crucial for generating accurate and reliable insights. The chapter outlined best practices that allow organizations to improve the findability, reliability, and accessibility of data at scale. By implementing these data governance fundamentals, readers can empower their teams to innovate with data while minimizing risk. Overall, these learnings can help organizations accelerate their modern data strategies to unlock more value.

3. Data Governance in Action using AWS Services

The previous chapters have introduced data governance and presented several challenges in managing data at scale. A core challenge of data governance is coordinating data management across large, complex organizations with many teams and stakeholders. This requires aligning data standards, policies, and procedures. Data mesh faces additional difficulties in distributing data ownership to domain teams. While this can empower teams, it also risks creating data silos and inconsistencies without proper coordination. Both approaches must balance centralized oversight and guidance with distributed data control. Key tasks include developing frameworks for metadata, data quality, security, and access that work across the organization. Overall, successful data governance and data mesh require cultural change, stakeholder alignment, and adaptive processes to manage distributed yet interconnected data at the enterprise scale.

This chapter will explain how Amazon Web Services (AWS) can support organizations in implementing effective data governance. AWS provides various services that can assist with key data governance activities like establishing policies and procedures, classifying data, improving data quality, securing sensitive data, enabling collaboration and stewardship, providing metadata management, and monitoring data usage.

Data Catalog & Discovery

From customer preferences and market trends to operational metrics and financial insights, the abundance of data holds immense potential for driving informed decision-making and fueling innovation. However, with this deluge of data comes the challenge of managing, organizing, and extracting meaningful insights from it effectively.

Data catalogs have emerged as a crucial component in addressing these challenges by providing a centralized repository of metadata, which acts as a comprehensive index for all available data assets within an organization. Among the myriad of data catalog solutions available, AWS Glue Data Catalog stands out as a powerful tool offered by Amazon Web Services (AWS), designed to streamline data management and enable efficient data discovery, understanding, and governance.

This section aims to delve into the realm of data cataloging, with a particular focus on AWS Glue Data Catalog and Amazon DataZone. We will explore the fundamentals of data catalogs, the key features and capabilities of AWS Glue Data Catalog, and delve into practical aspects such as setting up and managing metadata, data discovery, governance, integration with other AWS services, optimization strategies, and real-world use cases. By understanding and harnessing the capabilities of AWS Glue Data Catalog, organizations can unlock the full potential of their data assets, fostering a data-driven culture and gaining a competitive edge in today's dynamic business landscape. Let's embark on this journey to explore the transformative power of data catalogs in modern data management practices.

Definition and Purpose

In the ever-expanding landscape of data management, data catalogs serve as indispensable tools for organizing and navigating the vast seas of data within organizations. At their core, data catalogs are centralized repositories that store metadata or data about data, providing a comprehensive index of all available data assets.

Data catalogs are designed to capture, store, and manage metadata related to an organization's data assets. This metadata encompasses a wide range of information, including data source, format, schema, quality, ownership, and usage statistics. By consolidating this metadata in one centralized location, data catalogs enable users to easily search, discover, understand, and utilize data assets across the organization. Implementing a data catalog improves the findability and accessibility of data sources, provides transparency into how data is used and facilitates trust in data for analytics and decision-making. Overall, a data catalog is a critical tool for organizations to inventory data assets, enforce data management best practices, and enable users to get the most value from their data. By cataloging and standardizing how it is, data catalogs give users a single source of truth about available data. This improves the findability and accessibility of data, allowing users to leverage data more effectively.

Data catalogs typically consist of several key components, each playing a crucial role in facilitating efficient data management:

- **Metadata Repository:** The core component of a data catalog, the metadata repository, stores all metadata associated with data assets, providing a unified view of the organization's data landscape.

- **Data Discovery Interface:** A user-friendly interface that allows users to search, browse, and explore data assets within the catalog based on various criteria, such as keywords, tags, data types, and attributes.

- **Integration and Interoperability:** Mechanisms for integrating with other data management tools, platforms, and services to facilitate seamless data exchange and interoperability.

Data catalogs can be classified into different types based on their scope, deployment model, and functionality. Some common types of data catalogs include:

- **Enterprise Data Catalogs:** catalogs that span across the entire organization, capturing business metadata from various data sources.
- **Technical Data Catalogs:** catalogs designed to capture the technical metadata from across disparate systems to standardize how the data is defined and described.

Understanding these fundamental aspects of data catalogs lays the groundwork for exploring the capabilities and applications of AWS Glue Data Catalog in the subsequent sections of this chapter.

Introduction to AWS Glue

AWS Glue is a serverless data integration service that makes it easy to discover, prepare, and combine data for analytics, machine learning, and application development. It consists of three main components - AWS Glue ETL for extracting, transforming, and loading data, AWS Glue Data Catalog as a central metadata repository, and AWS Glue DataBrew for visual data preparation without coding.

AWS Glue is a fully managed extract, transform, and load (ETL) service that simplifies the process of preparing and loading data for analytics. It supports extracting data from various sources, transforming it to meet business needs, and loading it into destinations. It uses the Apache Spark engine to distribute big data workloads across worker nodes for faster transformations with in-memory processing. At the heart of AWS Glue lies its data catalog, which serves as a central metadata repository for all data assets within the AWS environment. By automating the discovery, cataloging, and organization of data, AWS Glue empowers organizations to derive insights from their data more efficiently.

The key Features and Capabilities of AWS Glue Data Catalog are:

- **Centralized Metadata Repository:** AWS Glue Data Catalog provides a unified view of metadata from various data sources and formats, including databases, data lakes, and streaming data. This centralized metadata repository facilitates data discovery, understanding, and lineage tracking.

- **Schema Discovery and Inference:** AWS Glue Data Catalog automatically discovers and infers schemas from data sources, eliminating the need for manual schema definition. This feature accelerates the data preparation process and ensures data consistency and accuracy.

- **Integration with AWS Services:** AWS Glue Data Catalog seamlessly integrates with other AWS services such as Amazon S3, Amazon Redshift, Amazon Athena, and Amazon EMR, enabling smooth data exchange and interoperability across different data platforms.

- **Data Governance and Security:** AWS Glue Data Catalog supports data governance initiatives by providing features such as data classification, access controls, and encryption. This ensures compliance with regulatory requirements and enhances data security.

- **Scalability and Performance:** Being a fully managed service, AWS Glue Data Catalog scales automatically to handle large volumes of data and concurrent users. It offers high availability and reliability, ensuring consistent performance even under heavy workloads.

- **Cost-Effectiveness:** AWS Glue Data Catalog follows a pay-as-you-go pricing model, where users only pay for the resources they consume. This cost-effective pricing structure, coupled with serverless architecture, helps organizations optimize their data management costs.

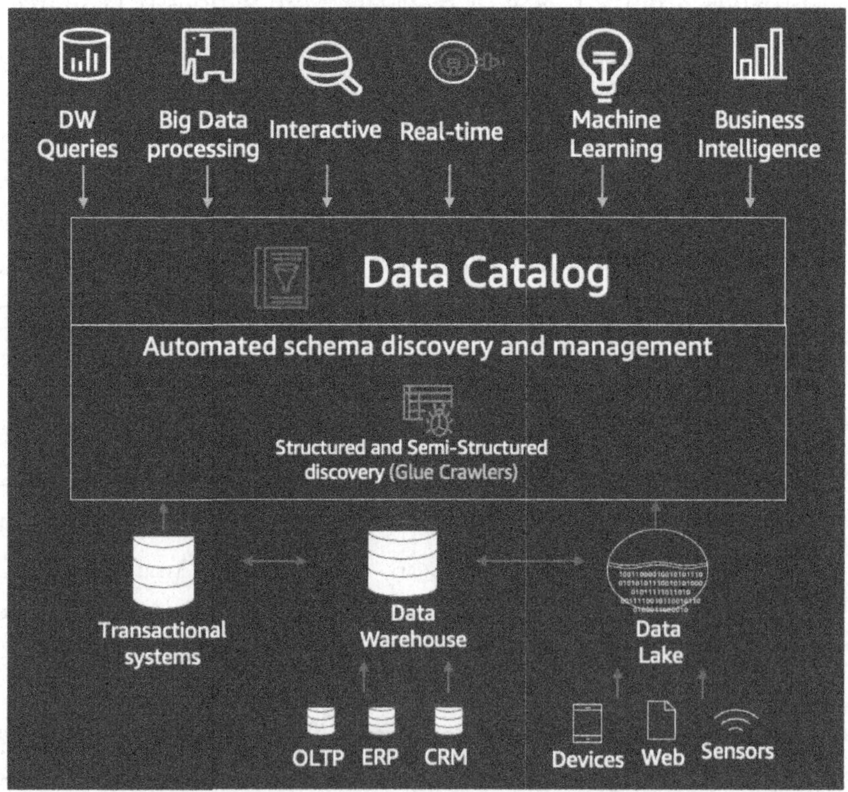

Figure 3.1: Glue Data Catalog

Figure 3.1 illustrates how the glue data catalog integrates with other data stores. The advantages of using AWS Glue Data Catalog:

- **Simplified Data Management:** AWS Glue Data Catalog automates the tedious tasks associated with data management, such as metadata discovery, schema inference, and data preparation, allowing organizations to focus on deriving insights from their data.

- **Improved Data Accessibility:** By providing a centralized metadata repository and intuitive data discovery interface, AWS Glue Data Catalog enhances data accessibility and enables self-service analytics for business users and data analysts.
- **Accelerated Time-to-Insights:** With its schema discovery and inference capabilities, the AWS Glue Data Catalog expedites the data preparation process, reducing the time-to-insights and enabling faster decision-making.
- **Enhanced Data Governance:** AWS Glue Data Catalog facilitates data governance by enforcing policies for data classification, access control, and encryption, ensuring compliance with regulatory requirements and enhancing data security.

This overview sets the stage for exploring the practical aspects of setting up, managing, and leveraging the AWS Glue Data Catalog.

Managing Metadata in AWS Glue Data Catalog

Effective metadata management lies at the core of the AWS Glue Data Catalog, enabling organizations to gain insights into their data assets, maintain data quality, and ensure compliance with regulatory requirements. This section delves into the various aspects of managing metadata within the AWS Glue Data Catalog, including extraction, import, update, and maintenance.

AWS Glue Data Catalog captures a wide range of metadata types, including schema information, partition, and data source details.

The approaches to extract and import Metadata:

- **Automated Metadata Extraction:** AWS Glue Data Catalog employs automated metadata extraction techniques, "the AWS Glue Crawler," that enables the discovery of and infer schemas from various data sources, including relational databases, data lakes, and streaming data. This eliminates the need for manual schema definition, accelerating the metadata extraction process.

- **Metadata Import:** In addition to automated extraction, AWS Glue Data Catalog supports manual metadata import, allowing users to import metadata from external sources such as Apache Hive metastores, Apache Atlas, and other data catalog systems. This enables seamless integration with existing metadata repositories and ensures data consistency.

By effectively managing metadata in the AWS Glue Data Catalog, organizations can unlock the full potential of their data assets, drive data-driven decision-making, and ensure compliance with regulatory requirements.

Introduction to Amazon DataZone for business Metadata

Amazon DataZone provides a central place to discover, understand, and manage data across an organization. This allows companies to track where sensitive data resides, establish access controls, and get insights into how data is used. DataZone also enables data democratization by making it easy for employees to find relevant datasets. Overall, the introduction of DataZone reflects how modern data platforms need robust data governance and catalog capabilities to manage data at scale, ensure security and compliance, and maximize the business value of data assets.

Amazon DataZone simplifies business metadata management:

- DataZone provides a central catalog to store, manage, and access business metadata. This eliminates siloed metadata spread across various systems and tools.

- It has an intuitive interface that allows business users to easily search, browse, and manage metadata without needing technical skills. Users can manage glossaries, data models, metrics, etc.
- DataZone automatically harvests metadata from data sources like databases, data warehouses, BI tools, etc. This saves time compared to manually capturing metadata.
- It enables collaboration by allowing different users to access, edit, review, and approve metadata changes. This ensures consistency and accuracy of metadata.
- DataZone integrates with data governance tools to apply policies and controls for metadata. This ensures metadata security and compliance with regulations.
- The catalog can be accessed via API, allowing metadata to be consumed across various applications. This avoids duplication of metadata efforts.
- It enables metadata-driven automation of data pipelines, quality checks, etc. Reducing manual processes.
- DataZone provides pre-built connectors to many data sources and BI tools that accelerate metadata indexing and governance.

In summary, DataZone provides a centralized and collaborative metadata management platform to unlock the value of metadata across the organization. Its automated harvesting and intuitive interfaces simplify metadata capture and consumption.

Data Discovery and Exploration

Data discovery and exploration are essential aspects of data management, enabling users to efficiently locate, understand, and utilize data assets within an organization. This section focuses on leveraging the AWS Glue Data Catalog for effective data discovery and exploration, encompassing features, capabilities, and best practices.

Leveraging AWS Glue Data Catalog for Data Discovery:

- **Intuitive Search Interface:** AWS Glue Data Catalog offers an intuitive search interface that allows users to discover data assets based on different criteria, such as keywords, tags, data types, and attributes.
- **Customizable Filters:** Users can apply customizable filters to refine search results and narrow down their exploration based on specific requirements, facilitating targeted data discovery.
- **Search Capabilities and Filters:**
    - **Keyword Search:** Users can perform keyword searches within the AWS Glue Data Catalog to find relevant data assets based on specific terms or phrases associated with metadata attributes such as table names, column names, or descriptions.
    - **Tag-based Search:** AWS Glue Data Catalog supports the tagging of data assets, enabling users to categorize and search for data based on predefined tags, facilitating easier organization and discovery of related data assets.
    - **Attribute-based Search:** Users can leverage attribute-based search to discover data assets based on specific attributes such as data type, format, size, or ownership, allowing for

more precise exploration.

By harnessing the data discovery and exploration capabilities of AWS Glue Data Catalog and adopting best practices, organizations can empower users to efficiently locate, understand, and leverage data assets to drive informed decision-making and unlock business value.

Leveraging Amazon DataZone for Data Discovery:

- Amazon DataZone is a data catalog service that makes it easy to find, understand, and manage data in AWS. It helps discover data across data lakes, data warehouses, databases, and other data stores.
- With DataZone, users can quickly search for and discover data assets. It maintains metadata like data schema, lineage, glossary, and statistics to provide context around the discovered data.
- DataZone automatically crawls data sources like Amazon S3 buckets, Amazon Athena, and Amazon Redshift to infer schema and populate the catalog. Users can leverage this automated schema inference and cataloging to accelerate data discovery.
- The data catalog provides a central place to find data and understand what it contains without having to access the underlying data sources. This makes it faster and easier to locate relevant data for analytics and applications.
- By leveraging DataZone's data catalog and discovery capabilities, organizations can break down data silos, reduce time spent searching for data, and deliver data to users for faster analytics and insights.
- Key features like search, automated profiling, fine-grained access control, and integration with data processing engines enable self-

service data discovery and governance.

Use Cases and Case Studies

Data catalogs, particularly AWS Glue Data Catalog, have found widespread adoption across various industries and use cases, empowering organizations to harness the value of their data assets. This section explores real-world use cases and case studies that highlight the diverse applications and benefits of data catalogs in driving business outcomes.

The use cases for AWS Glue Data Catalog

Use Case 1: Data Lakes and Analytics

Challenge: Managing and cataloging vast amounts of data within a data lake for analytics purposes.

Solution: AWS Glue Data Catalog provides a centralized metadata repository, making it easier to organize and discover data assets within the data lake. Users can seamlessly integrate with analytics services like Amazon Athena, allowing for ad-hoc querying and analysis.

Use Case 2: Data Warehousing

Challenge: Efficiently managing metadata in a data warehouse environment with numerous tables and schemas.

Solution: AWS Glue Data Catalog automates the discovery and inference of data schemas, reducing the manual effort required for metadata management. It integrates seamlessly with Amazon Redshift, facilitating metadata synchronization and ensuring consistent data definitions.

Use Case 3: Data Governance and Compliance

Challenge: Ensuring data governance and compliance with regulatory requirements.

Solution: AWS Glue Data Catalog supports data classification, access controls, and encryption, helping organizations enforce data governance policies. It provides audit trails and metadata lineage, aiding in compliance monitoring and reporting.

Use Case 4: Cross-Platform Data Integration

Challenge: Integrating data from various sources, including on-premises databases, cloud-based storage, and third-party applications.

Solution: AWS Glue Data Catalog offers seamless integration with different AWS services and supports interoperability with third-party tools. This enables organizations to achieve cross-platform data integration while maintaining a unified metadata view.

The case studies leveraging the AWS Glue Data Catalog

Case Study 1: E-commerce Platform Optimization

Challenge: A global e-commerce platform faced challenges in efficiently managing and utilizing the vast amount of customer behavior data for personalized recommendations.

Solution: Implementing the AWS Glue Data Catalog enabled the organization to centralize metadata, improve data discovery, and enable faster analytics. This resulted in more accurate product recommendations, enhancing the overall customer experience.

Case Study 2: Financial Services Data Governance

Challenge: A financial services firm needed to enhance data governance and comply with strict regulatory requirements.

Solution: AWS Glue Data Catalog was deployed to enforce data governance policies, including data classification, access controls, and encryption. The organization achieved regulatory compliance and improved the security and integrity of sensitive financial data.

Case Study 3: Healthcare Analytics and Reporting

Challenge: A healthcare provider struggled with disparate data sources and the need for timely analytics to improve patient outcomes.

Solution: AWS Glue Data Catalog streamlined metadata management, allowing the organization to integrate diverse healthcare data sources. This facilitated faster analysis and reporting, leading to improved decision-making and patient care.

These use cases and case studies underscore the diverse applications of AWS Glue Data Catalog across industries. By leveraging its capabilities, organizations can overcome data management challenges, enhance analytics, and drive innovation in their respective domains.

In the ever-evolving landscape of data management, the AWS Glue Data Catalog stands out as a powerful tool for organizations seeking to harness the full potential of their data assets. Throughout this section, we have explored the fundamental aspects, key features, and practical applications of the AWS Glue Data Catalog, highlighting its role in streamlining data management, enabling efficient data discovery, and ensuring robust data governance. AWS Glue Data Catalog plays a crucial role in enabling data governance and compliance with regulatory requirements. Its support for data classification, access controls, and encryption helps organizations enforce data governance policies and safeguard sensitive data.

Looking ahead, the introduction of Amazon DataZone promises to further enhance the capabilities of AWS Glue Data Catalog. Amazon

DataZone is a new data management service designed to simplify data governance. By extending the capabilities of AWS Glue Data Catalog, Amazon DataZone will enable organizations to seamlessly manage metadata and data assets across diverse environments, unlocking new possibilities for data-driven innovation. So, AWS Glue Data Catalog, along with the upcoming Amazon DataZone, represents a paradigm shift in data management, empowering organizations to extract maximum value from their data assets. By embracing these technologies and adopting best practices for metadata management, organizations can drive innovation, improve decision-making, and achieve competitive advantage in today's data-driven world. Let's dive deep into how AWS can enable and simplify Data Quality management.

Data Quality

In the fast-paced landscape of data-driven decision-making, the quality of data serves as the bedrock upon which organizations build their insights, strategies, and actions. High-quality data ensures the accuracy, reliability, and relevance of analyses, enabling businesses to make informed decisions that drive growth and innovation. Conversely, poor data quality can introduce errors, biases, and uncertainties, leading to flawed conclusions and misguided actions. Recognizing the critical role of data quality, organizations are increasingly investing in tools and technologies to assess, monitor, and improve the quality of their data assets. Within the Amazon Web Services (AWS) ecosystem, AWS Glue Data Quality emerges as a comprehensive solution designed to address the multifaceted aspects of data quality management.

This chapter delves into data quality, exploring its definition, significance, and dimensions. We then turn our attention to AWS Glue Data Quality, offering an in-depth overview of its features, capabilities, and integration with AWS services and data catalog. From assessing data quality through profiling and analysis to implementing data quality best practices and monitoring data quality in real-time, AWS Glue Data Quality equips organizations with the tools and insights needed to achieve data quality excellence.

Definition and Purpose

Data quality is the cornerstone of any successful data-driven initiative. In today's interconnected digital landscape, where organizations generate and consume vast amounts of data at an unprecedented rate, ensuring the accuracy, reliability, and relevance of data has become paramount. The ability to make informed decisions, drive innovation, and maintain a competitive edge hinges upon the quality of the underlying data.

Data quality encompasses various dimensions that collectively determine the fitness for use of data in a given context. These dimensions include but are not limited to accuracy, completeness, consistency, timeliness, validity, and relevance. Achieving high-quality data involves ensuring that data meets predefined standards and requirements, aligning with the specific needs and objectives of the organization.

Data quality is a multidimensional concept that encompasses various attributes and characteristics of data. The following dimensions collectively determine the overall quality and fitness for use of data in different contexts:

- **Accuracy:** refers to the correctness and precision of data in relation to the real-world phenomenon it represents. Accurate data is free from inconsistencies and inaccuracies, providing a reliable representation of reality. Achieving accuracy involves ensuring that data values are recorded correctly, validated against known standards or reference data, and updated as needed to reflect changes in the underlying reality.

- **Completeness:** refers to the extent to which all required data elements are present and accounted for in a dataset. Complete data contains all relevant attributes, fields, or records necessary for the intended analysis, decision-making, or operational use. Incomplete data may result from missing values, null entries, or omitted records, which can lead to gaps in information and biased or incomplete analyses.

- **Consistency:** refers to the uniformity and coherence of data across different sources, systems, or time periods. Consistent data maintains the same meaning, format, and structure across various contexts, ensuring interoperability and comparability. Inconsistent data may arise from discrepancies in data formats, naming conventions, or data definitions, leading to confusion, ambiguity, and potential errors in analysis and interpretation.

- **Timeliness:** refers to the currency and relevance of data in relation to the time at which it is needed for decision-making or analysis. Timely data is available when required, reflecting the most up-to-date information relevant to the specific context or use case. Timeliness considerations may vary depending on the nature of the data and its intended use, with some data requiring real-time updates while others may be suitable for periodic or batch processing.

- **Relevance:** refers to the degree to which data aligns with the specific needs, objectives, and requirements of users or stakeholders. Relevant data is tailored to the intended audience and purpose, providing meaningful insights and actionable information. Assessing relevance involves understanding the context in which data will be used and ensuring that it addresses the pertinent questions or concerns of the intended audience.

- **Validity:** refers to the extent to which data conforms to predefined rules, constraints, or standards established for a particular domain or purpose. Valid data is accurate, reliable, and fit for its intended use, adhering to specified criteria or quality thresholds. Validity checks may involve verifying data against predefined business rules, regulatory requirements, or logical constraints to ensure its integrity and trustworthiness.
- **Accessibility:** refers to the ease of accessing and retrieving data when needed for analysis, reporting, or decision-making purposes. Accessible data is readily available to authorized users or systems, enabling efficient data discovery, retrieval, and utilization. Accessibility considerations encompass factors such as data storage locations, data formats, security permissions, and integration with data management systems.
- **Precision:** refers to the level of detail or granularity present in data, reflecting the accuracy and specificity of measurements or values. Precise data is characterized by fine-grained distinctions and minimal variability, providing a high level of resolution and accuracy in representing underlying phenomena. Precision considerations may vary depending on the nature of the data and the requirements of the intended analysis or application.

In summary, data quality encompasses a range of dimensions that collectively define the integrity, reliability, and usability of data. By understanding and managing these dimensions effectively, organizations can ensure that their data meets the highest standards of quality and reliability, supporting informed decision-making, driving innovation, and achieving strategic objectives.

Introduction to AWS Glue Data Quality

AWS Glue provides a comprehensive suite of features and tools to assess and improve data quality within data pipelines and workflows. Leveraging AWS Glue's capabilities, organizations can implement robust data quality checks, profiling, and monitoring to ensure the integrity and reliability of their data assets. In this section, we will explore the key features of AWS Glue Data Quality:

- **Data Quality Assessment:** AWS Glue enables users to perform data quality assessments as part of the data preparation and ETL (Extract, Transform, Load) processes. It automatically computes statistics, recommends quality rules, monitors, and alerts you when it detects issues. Glue Data Quality uses ML algorithms to recommend Data Quality checks.
- **Pre-built Data Quality Rules:** AWS Glue provides pre-built data quality 25+ out-of-the-box DQ rules that users can leverage to assess various aspects of data quality, including completeness, accuracy, consistency, and timeliness. These pre-built rules can be easily integrated into data pipelines and workflows using AWS Glue jobs. Users can define custom data quality rules and thresholds based on their specific requirements and use cases.
- **Integration with Other AWS Services for Data Quality:** AWS Glue seamlessly integrates with other AWS services to enhance data quality management capabilities. By integrating AWS Glue with other AWS services, organizations can implement end-to-end data quality solutions that span data ingestion, transformation, storage, and analysis.

In summary, AWS Glue provides a comprehensive set of features and tools for assessing and improving data quality within AWS environments. By leveraging AWS Glue Data Quality features, organizations can ensure the integrity, reliability, and usability of their data assets, enabling informed decision-making, driving innovation, and achieving business objectives.

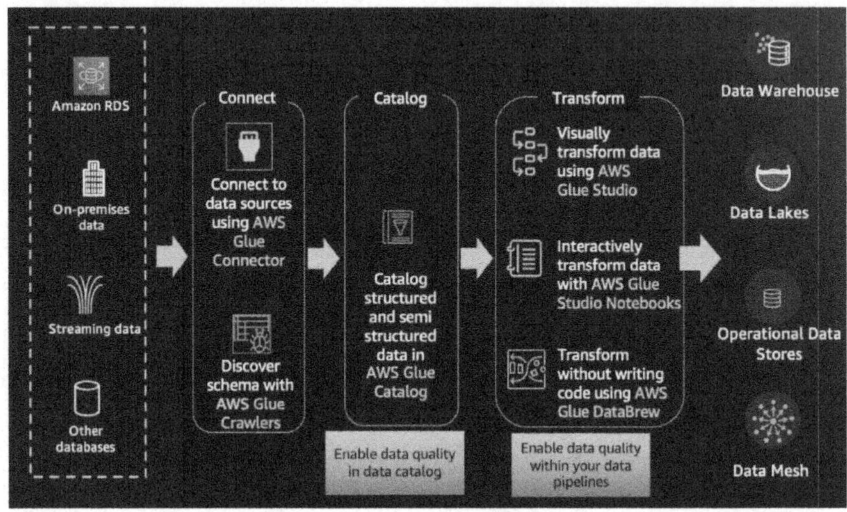

Figure 3.2: AWS Glue Ecosystem

Figure 3.2 illustrates the AWS Glue ecosystem that showcases the breadth and depth of capabilities from data connectors to ingest data, catalog for discoverability, rich transformations that span between complex data transformations, and data quality.

Implementing Data Quality Checks in AWS Glue

AWS Glue provides powerful capabilities for implementing data quality checks within data pipelines and workflows. By leveraging AWS Glue's features and tools, organizations can automate the detection and remediation of data quality issues, ensuring the integrity and reliability of their data assets. In this section, we will explore how to implement data quality checks in AWS Glue:

- **Defining Data Quality Rules:** Before implementing data quality checks in AWS Glue, it is essential to define data quality rules that align with the specific needs and objectives of the organization. Data quality rules define the criteria for assessing the quality of data based on predefined standards, thresholds, and constraints. These rules may encompass various dimensions of data quality, including accuracy, completeness, consistency, and validity.

- **Configuring Data Quality in AWS Glue:** AWS Glue Data Quality automatically computes statistics for your datasets. It uses these statistics to recommend a set of quality rules that checks for freshness, accuracy, integrity, and even hard-to-find issues. You can adjust recommended rules, discard rules, or add new rules as needed. If it detects quality issues, AWS Glue Data Quality also alerts you so that you can act on them.

- **Monitoring Data Quality Checks:** Users can leverage AWS CloudWatch metrics and logs to monitor the status, performance, and execution history of data quality jobs in AWS Glue.

- **Implementing Remediation Actions:** In the event of data quality issues detected during data quality checks, data quality managers can implement remediation actions to address and resolve the issues automatically. Remediation actions may include data cleansing, enrichment, or transformation tasks to correct errors, fill in missing values, or reconcile inconsistencies in the data. By implementing automated remediation actions, organizations can maintain data integrity and reliability while minimizing manual intervention.

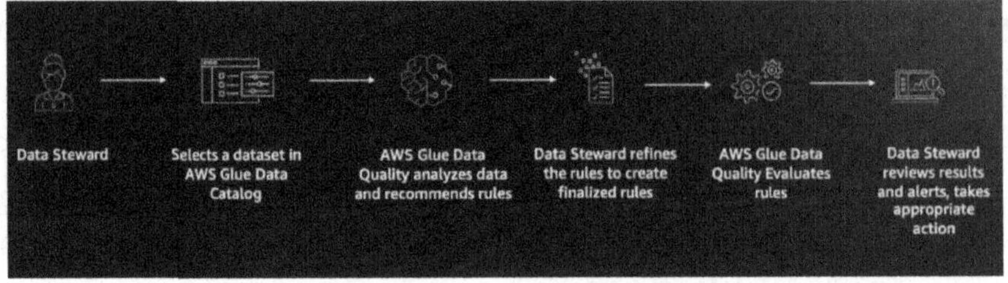

Figure 3.3: Role of Data Steward

Figure 3.3 illustrates the role of the data steward in the context of data AWS Glue and its data quality. You will also see a more detailed view of this role in Chapter 10 of this book, which focuses more on business glossary and data security.

In summary, AWS Glue Data Quality provides robust capabilities for implementing data quality checks within data pipelines and workflows. By defining data quality rules, configuring data quality jobs, monitoring data quality checks, and implementing remediation actions, organizations can ensure the integrity and reliability of their data assets in AWS environments.

Case Studies: Data Quality Stories with AWS Glue Data Quality

In this section, we will explore real-world case studies highlighting successful implementations of AWS Glue Data Quality features to address data quality challenges and achieve business objectives.

Case Study 1: Improving Data Quality in Retail Analytics

Challenge: A retail organization was struggling with data quality issues in its analytics platform, leading to inaccurate sales forecasts and inventory management.

Solution: The organization implemented AWS Glue Data Quality features to profile and assess the quality of its sales and inventory data. Using AWS Glue Data Quality, data analysts were able to identify inconsistencies and missing values in the dataset. They used pre-built data quality metrics to measure completeness, accuracy, and consistency and implemented data quality rules to enforce data standards.

Case Study 2: Ensuring Data Quality in Healthcare Analytics

Challenge: A healthcare organization faced challenges with data quality in its analytics platform, impacting the accuracy and reliability of patient outcomes analysis.

Solution: The organization deployed AWS Glue Data Quality features to assess the quality of its healthcare data, including patient records, medical diagnoses, and treatment outcomes. AWS Glue DataBrew was used to profile and cleanse the data, identifying errors and inconsistencies in patient demographics, diagnosis codes, and treatment procedures.

Case Study 3: Data Quality Assurance in Financial Services

Challenge: A financial services firm faced data quality challenges in its risk management and regulatory reporting processes, leading to compliance issues and operational inefficiencies.

Solution: The firm implemented AWS Glue Data Quality features to assess and improve the quality of its financial data, including transaction records, customer accounts, and regulatory reporting data. AWS Glue DataBrew was used to profile and cleanse the data, identifying anomalies and discrepancies in transaction amounts, customer identifiers, and regulatory reporting fields.

In summary, these case studies demonstrate the value of AWS Glue Data Quality features in addressing data quality challenges and achieving business objectives across various industries. By leveraging AWS Glue's capabilities, organizations can ensure the integrity, reliability, and usability of their data assets, enabling informed decision-making, driving innovation, and achieving strategic goals.

Data quality is a fundamental aspect of modern data management and analytics, playing a critical role in enabling informed decision-making, driving business insights, and ensuring regulatory compliance. In this chapter, we have explored various aspects of data quality, including its definition, dimensions, factors influencing it, methods for assessment, strategies for improvement, and future trends.

We have learned that data quality is a multidimensional concept encompassing attributes such as accuracy, completeness, consistency, timeliness, relevance, validity, accessibility, and precision. Achieving and maintaining high-quality data requires organizations to address a myriad of factors, including data collection methods, data entry processes, data storage and retrieval systems, data cleaning and preprocessing techniques, human error, technological limitations, and cultural and organizational factors. Furthermore, we have explored the role of AWS Glue Data Quality features in addressing data quality challenges within AWS environments. AWS Glue provides a comprehensive suite of features and tools for implementing data quality checks, profiling, monitoring, and remediation, enabling organizations to ensure the integrity and reliability of their data assets in data pipelines and workflows.

In conclusion, ensuring high-quality data is essential for organizations to derive maximum value from their data assets, drive innovation, and achieve strategic objectives. By understanding the complexities of data quality management and implementing effective strategies and tools for assessing and improving data quality, organizations can unlock the full potential of their data and gain a competitive edge in today's data-driven world.

Data Profiling and Classification

Data classification is the process of classifying data according to risk and sensitivity assessments, whereas data profiling is the analysis of data to determine its suitability for use downstream. Let's examine each of these characteristics in more detail, considering both their advantages and implementation difficulties.

Data Profiling

Examining, purifying, converting, and evaluating data in order to identify its relationships, structure, substance, and shortcomings is the process known as data profiling. Finding quality problems, anomalies, patterns, and other valuable insights entails creating metadata and metrics about the data using automated technologies and statistical analysis. By revealing any quality issues that, if left unattended, could affect analysis findings and system performance, data profiling makes it possible to evaluate the preparedness of data for business intelligence and reporting. In order to improve quality and dependability, strong data management processes and data remediation can be designed with the use of actionable information from effective data profiling.

It drives data management and preventive quality control procedures for mission-critical systems. It provides useful insights to enhance current data assets and direct the approach to obtaining trustworthy, high-quality data. When data concerns and needs are identified early on in the process, it lowers risk, effort, and expense compared to reactive corrections made later on in analytics or operational procedures. Organizations gain from data profiling in a variety of ways, including:

- **Enhances Data Quality:** By identifying data inaccuracies, inconsistencies, duplicate entries, and integrity problems that may affect reporting and analytics later on, profiling helps improve the quality of data.

- **Facilitates Data Governance:** Programs for data lifecycle management, storage, security, and compliance are informed by insights gleaned by profiling.

- **Promotes Integration Projects:** Profiling assists in determining readiness and identifying transformation requirements when transferring or combining data from other systems.

- **Tracks Data Drift:** Regularly profiling production databases allows for the tracking of important metrics and the sending of alerts regarding any unforeseen shifts, anomalies, or problems with quality.

While the benefits of data profiling are tangibly significant, successful implementation requires overcoming technical and procedural challenges:

- Complex data - It might be computationally costly to profile large data from several sources with sparse patterns or linkages.

- Data that is updated frequently - Production databases receive regular changes. Periodic re-profiling is necessary to maintain consistency in profiling metadata.

- Tooling limitations: Blindspots are caused by profiling tools' inability to detect some data irregularities, uniqueness, functional dependencies, etc.

- Legacy systems – Particularly in older systems, connecting profiling tools may be restricted by incompatible or proprietary storage formats.

- Lack of clear business context: Technical statistical insights obtained just from profiling may fail to completely qualify the data due to a lack of business data definitions, norms, and policies.

- Process integration: Over time, the impact of profiling is diminished when it is not included in continuous data integration, quality, and governance programs.

Strong, scalable data discovery tools, better integration with data management stacks, and frameworks to capture important metadata for business users are all necessary to overcome obstacles.

Introduction to AWS Glue DataBrew

With AWS Glue DataBrew, users can prepare data visually and code-free while cleaning and normalizing data. The time it takes to prepare data for analytics and machine learning can be decreased by using DataBrew. To automate data preparation operations like screening anomalies, transforming data to standard formats, and fixing erroneous values, you can select from more than 250 pre-made transformations.

AWS Glue DataBrew has a job subsystem that serves two purposes:

1. Applying a data transformation recipe to a DataBrew dataset.

2. Analyzing a dataset to create a comprehensive profile of the data.

A dataset is subjected to a series of evaluations by profile jobs, which output the results to Amazon S3. You may better understand your dataset and choose the type of data preparation procedures to use in your recipe jobs with the help of the information gathered by data profiling. The profile task can be set up at the column or dataset level. To view the degree of relationship between the values in several columns, you may also enable a correlations matrix at the dataset level.

To find out more about building and managing AWS Glue DataBrew profile jobs, visit the developer guide.

Data Classification

The process of classifying data involves arranging information according to various degrees of sensitivity and business significance. The intention is to assist businesses in implementing use policies, governance techniques, security measures, and access controls that are appropriate for the various classification levels. Personal data, intellectual property, legal compliance, data kind, value to the organization, ease of access or dissemination, and the repercussions of unauthorized disclosure or breach are among the considerations that go into data classification. Policies such as authorization for access, necessary encryption, limitations on remote storage, guidelines for retention, and permissible usage can be outlined for each category after they have been classified. Maintaining track of categorization levels between systems makes it easier to conduct compliance audits for laws governing personal data, such as GDPR and HIPAA. It also lessens the likelihood of being exposed to theft or loss.

In order to properly manage information assets throughout their lifecycle in line with business objectives, proactive classification-driven data governance is becoming more and more necessary due to the emergence of a data-driven philosophy and growing sensitivity around consumer data. Organizations can benefit from data classification in a number of ways.

- Promotes data security and privacy - By classifying data, appropriate security measures, such as sensitivity-based masking, encryption, and access limits, can be implemented. This aids in preventing breaches involving intellectual property or sensitive personal data and illegal access.

- Aids in regulatory compliance: laws such as GDPR and HIPAA demand additional security measures and audits for the use of personal data. A framework for identifying, monitoring, and ensuring controls on sensitive data is provided by data classification, supporting compliance.

- Lower company risk: In the event of an incident like data theft or unintentional disclosure of private information, classification helps to reduce the chance of regulatory penalties, harm to one's reputation, and loss of customer trust. Data protection is matched to risk levels by it.

- Encourages data governance: Classification-derived insights inform data retention, storage, sharing, and lifecycle management rules that are tailored to the needs of the business and the level of risk tolerance. This keeps data from being misused and allows for its reuse.

- Enhances data quality – Knowing when and how to handle sensitivity and criticality enables data quality best practices to be concentrated on high-priority data that has a bigger influence on operations, analytics, and decisions.

An architectural plan for methodically managing data based on its business context is provided by data classification. It serves as a crucial link between data-driven business goals and requirements for data governance, security, privacy, and quality. When implementing a data classification program, firms must overcome challenges like:

- **Manual Classification:** It takes a lot of time, money, and error to classify massive amounts of data manually. An automated tool's absence may impede adoption.

- **Changing Data:** Data is created dynamically and changes over time. It is challenging to monitor and update classifications on a regular basis.

- **Absence of Standards:** Businesses frequently classify data inconsistently or non-standardly, which results in data that is incorrectly labeled and control gaps.
- **Preserving Context:** Content-only classification ignores the context-driven use of data that determines its level of sensitivity.
- **Embedded/Unstructured Data:** Unless tools are used to assess embedded contextual content, pertinent data found in unstructured files such as papers, source code, and logs cannot be classified.
- **Legacy Systems:** Enforcing regulations can be challenging due to incompatible legacy systems that lack embedded controls for new classifications.

The AWS Well-Architected Framework

The AWS Well-Architected Framework helps you understand trade-offs for decisions you make while building workloads on AWS. You will gain knowledge of the most recent architectural best practices for creating and managing dependable, secure, productive, economical, and sustainable cloud workloads by utilizing the Framework. It gives you a mechanism to regularly compare your workload to industry best practices and pinpoint areas in which you may improve.

The framework is based on six pillars:

- Operational Excellence
- Security
- Reliability

- Performance Efficiency
- Cost Optimization
- Sustainability

The Security pillar of the AWS Well-Architected Framework lists the best practices for categorizing organizational data based on criticality and sensitivity. AWS has also published a comprehensive whitepaper on data classification to help organizations plan their approach to determining the appropriate level of controls for the confidentiality, integrity, and availability of their data based on risk to the organization.

Introduction to Amazon Macie

Amazon Macie is a data security solution that uses machine learning and pattern matching to find sensitive data, gives you insight into data security threats, and lets you set up automated defenses against those threats. Macie continuously assesses your S3 buckets for security and access controls and generates findings to alert you to issues like unencrypted buckets, publicly accessible buckets, and buckets shared with AWS accounts outside of your organization. This helps you manage the data security posture of your Amazon S3 environment. After that, Macie creates an interactive data map showing the locations of your sensitive data across accounts in S3, automatically samples and examines objects in your S3 buckets to check for sensitive data, such as personally identifiable information (PII), and assigns a sensitivity score to each bucket. The interactive data map can help you decide whether to undertake targeted, sensitive data discovery jobs with Macie to conduct more in-depth analyses of particular S3 buckets. You can comply with laws like the General Data Privacy Regulation (GDPR) and the Health Insurance Portability and Accountability Act (HIPAA) by conducting targeted sensitive data discovery jobs. In order to start automated remediation, such as preventing public access to your S3 storage, all Macie discoveries are submitted to Amazon EventBridge and can also be published to AWS Security Hub.

Data Compliance and Privacy

The processes and procedures that businesses implement to guarantee that the gathering, storing, using, and sharing of data conforms with legal requirements, organizational policies, and other guidelines are referred to as data compliance. Data compliance is becoming more and more crucial across sectors as data becomes a more valuable asset and privacy concerns increase. Organizations create data compliance programs to understand how laws and regulations relate to their data practices. Finding every system and procedure that interacts with covered data categories is usually the task of a cross-functional data compliance team. After that, they carry out risk assessments to identify any possible gaps in compliance and set up policies, procedures, and regular audits to help reduce such risks. Technical precautions include data loss prevention measures, encryption, and access controls for securing sensitive data flows and preventing unauthorized access.

In order to assist you in meeting security and compliance standards for the banking, retail, healthcare, government, and other industries, AWS routinely obtains third-party validation for hundreds of global compliance requirements that it continuously monitors. Customers may better grasp the strict controls that AWS has put in place to ensure cloud security and compliance by participating in the AWS Compliance Program. AWS Compliance Enablers expand on conventional programs by connecting governance-focused, audit-friendly service features with relevant compliance or audit standards. This assists clients in setting up and managing an AWS security control environment. You may also read the AWS Risk and Compliance whitepaper, which describes the risk management strategies that AWS has put in place for its portion of the Shared Responsibility Model, as well as the resources that customers can use to make sure these strategies are being followed in the letter.

Data Privacy

Organizations are gathering, storing, and sharing an exponential amount of sensitive customer, employee, and company data as digital technologies progress and more parts of life shift online. Because of this, creating strong data privacy protocols is now essential for all companies. The laws, rules, and practices put in place to guard against illegal access, use, or disclosure of personal data are collectively referred to as data privacy.

From the standpoint of compliance, a lot of laws and rules already require minimum standards and procedures for data privacy. Federal legislation in the US that is industry-specific, such as GLBA and HIPAA, provides controls for financial and personal health data. State-level laws requiring openness, such as the Virginia Consumer Data Protection Act and the California Consumer Privacy Act, also grant citizens new rights around data access, correction, and deletion. The General Data Protection Regulation (GDPR) of the European Union gives people of the EU additional protections wherever their data is processed. Customers must receive explicit privacy notices at the time of data collection so they are fully aware of how their data will be used. When appropriate, they should also be provided options regarding data sharing, such as the ability to opt-in for optional processing operations and go beyond what is needed to fulfill a service request. Within businesses, role-based permissions and a need-to-know approach should be used to give access to covered data sets only when required for specific job functions.

Our top goal at AWS is protecting our customers' data, and we do this by putting strict contractual, technological, and organizational safeguards in place to ensure its availability, confidentiality, and integrity regardless of the AWS Region a customer has chosen.

AWS adheres to ISO 27018, a set of guidelines for safeguarding private information in the cloud. The regulation requirements for the protection of personally identifiable information (PII) or personal data in the context of public cloud computing are covered by this extension of ISO Information Security Standard 27001. It also provides implementation guidance based on ISO 27002 controls that are relevant to PII processed by public cloud service providers. Visit the AWS ISO 27018 Compliance portal for further details or to view the AWS ISO 27018 Certification.

The American Institute of CPAs (AICPA) developed the SOC 2 Privacy Trust Criteria, which establishes criteria for evaluating controls related to how personal data is collected, used, retained, disclosed, and disposed of in order to meet the entity's objectives. Based on these criteria, AWS also publishes a SOC 2 Type II Privacy report. According to our Privacy Notice, the AWS SOC 2 Privacy Type II report offers third-party certification of our systems and the appropriateness of the privacy controls' design. The privacy report's scope covers the services and locations covered by the most recent AWS SOC reports, as well as our approach to handling and protecting any content you upload to AWS. You can get the SOC 2 Type II Privacy report via the AWS Management Console by using AWS Artifact.

Introduction to AWS Artifact

The self-service audit artifact retrieval portal AWS Artifact, accessible through the console, gives users on-demand access to AWS and Independent Software Vendor (ISV) compliance documents as well as AWS agreements. Downloads of AWS security and compliance documentation, including Payment Card Industry (PCI), System and Organization Control (SOC) reports, and AWS ISO certifications, are available from AWS Artifact Reports. If the terms and circumstances pertaining to the particular AWS compliance report allow you to do so, you may immediately share the reports with your customers.

Data Access Security

Policies, practices, and technological advancements aimed at limiting access to an organization's data to just authorized people and applications are collectively referred to as data access security. Businesses are increasingly using data to inform critical decisions and operations; therefore, securing access to that data is essential for competitive advantage, trust, and compliance.

Introduction to AWS Lake Formation

It is simpler to centrally manage, secure, and exchange data internationally for analytics and machine learning (ML) using AWS Lake Formation. Using the AWS Glue Data Catalog, you can centralize data security and governance with Lake Formation, managing metadata and data rights in a single location with features akin to those found in a database. In addition, it offers fine-grained data access control, allowing you to guarantee that users have the proper data accessible right down to the row and column levels. After that, you can distribute permissions among your users. Additionally, by facilitating data sharing within your company, between Regions, and outside through AWS Data Exchange, Lake Formation enables you to meet other data-sharing requirements without requiring the relocation of data. This allows you to establish a data mesh. Additionally, Lake Formation offers thorough data access auditing to assist in guaranteeing that the appropriate data was accessed by the appropriate users at the appropriate time since it logs data interactions by role and user.

You can link to your AWS data sources using services like Amazon Athena or Amazon Redshift and third-party business apps like Tableau and Looker. You can be guaranteed that access to your data is restricted and governed no matter which application you use because access is handled by both Lake Formation and the underlying AWS Glue Data Catalog. Similarly, Ahana, Dremio, Privacera, Collibra, and Starburst are a few of the third-party tools that interface with Lake Formation.

Permissions can be managed at the column, row, and cell levels with Lake Formation fine-grained access control (FGAC). FGAC simplifies the process of adhering to stricter corporate rules, implementing enhanced data governance, and skillfully safeguarding and handling sensitive customer data. You can manage rights for your data and metadata in one location by centralizing permission management for all of your resources—including databases and tables—in the AWS Glue Data Catalog. Using well-known database-like grants, you can design and control access for users and apps by role in the Data Catalog, giving your data lake the ease of use of data warehouses and databases.

- **Scaling permissions with AWS Lake Formation:** Data attributes are used by Lake Formation tag-based access control (LF-TBAC) to assist in maintaining current permissions when data changes. Administrators can use LF-TBAC to tag their data appropriately, and then the rules already in place will enforce the desired access to newly created data resources. This saves time and effort on management by helping to scale rights management over a large number of AWS Glue Data Catalog resources.
- **Data sharing with AWS Lake Formation:** By making cross-account data sharing easier, Lake Formation enables you to meet other data-sharing requirements or build a data mesh with less data transportation. Its cross-account capabilities ensure

appropriate data governance so that data owners control who has access to their data and enable users to confidently exchange distributed data across multiple AWS accounts, AWS Organizations, AWS Regions, or directly with IAM principals in another account. Additionally, it works with AWS Data Exchange, allowing you to share data with outside companies without having to move or duplicate it.

- **Monitoring and auditing with AWS Lake Formation:** With AWS CloudTrail, Lake Formation offers thorough audit logs that are useful for tracking access and proving adherence to centrally specified policies. With Lake Formation, you can audit the history of data access for analytics and machine learning services that access the data in your data lake. This enables you to view which roles or users have tried to access what information, when, and through which services.

Data Lineage

In the realm of data management, understanding the journey of data from its origin to its current state is crucial for ensuring data integrity, compliance, and informed decision-making. This understanding is encapsulated in the concept of data lineage. Data lineage provides a comprehensive view of the lifecycle of data, tracing its path through various stages of acquisition, transformation, and consumption within an organization's data ecosystem.

Definition and Purpose

Data lineage can be defined as the detailed documentation and visualization of the flow of data from its source to its destination, including all intermediate steps and transformations. It encompasses the identification of data sources, the mapping of data transformations and dependencies, and the tracking of data usage across different systems, processes, and applications.

Data lineage plays a pivotal role in ensuring data quality, governance, and compliance within organizations. By providing visibility into the origins and transformations of data, data lineage enables organizations to:

- **Ensure Data Quality:** Understanding the lineage of data helps organizations identify and address issues related to data accuracy, consistency, and completeness, thus improving overall data quality.
- **Facilitate Regulatory Compliance:** Data lineage aids in demonstrating compliance with regulatory requirements such as GDPR, CCPA, HIPAA, and others by documenting how data is collected, processed, and used.
- **Support Impact Analysis:** Data lineage enables organizations to conduct impact analysis by tracing the effects of changes in data sources, structures, or processes on downstream systems and stakeholders.
- **Enhance Data Governance:** By documenting data flows and dependencies, data lineage contributes to the establishment of robust data governance frameworks, ensuring data security, privacy, and accessibility.
- **Enable Effective Decision-Making:** Access to accurate and reliable data lineage information empowers stakeholders to make informed decisions based on a clear understanding of data origins, transformations, and usage patterns.

The primary objectives of data lineage include:

- **Visibility:** Providing visibility into the flow of data across systems and processes, enabling stakeholders to understand the origins and transformations of data.
- **Traceability:** Enabling traceability of data from its source to its destination, including all intermediate steps and transformations, to support data governance and compliance efforts.
- **Quality Assurance:** Facilitating the identification and resolution of data quality issues by tracing data lineage and identifying potential sources of inaccuracies or inconsistencies.
- **Impact Analysis:** Supporting impact analysis by tracing the effects of changes in data sources, structures, or processes on downstream systems and stakeholders.
- **Compliance:** Facilitating compliance with regulatory requirements by documenting how data is collected, processed, and used and demonstrating adherence to data privacy and security regulations.

In summary, data lineage serves as a foundational concept in modern data management, providing organizations with the visibility, traceability, and insights needed to ensure data quality, governance, and compliance. By understanding the origins and transformations of data through data lineage, organizations can make informed decisions, mitigate risks, and drive strategic initiatives effectively.

Understanding Data Lineage

Data lineage is a fundamental concept in data management that provides organizations with insights into the flow of data across systems, processes, and transformations. Understanding data lineage involves exploring its components, types, and implications for data management. We will delve into the key aspects of understanding data lineage.

Data lineage comprises several components that collectively contribute to its understanding:

- **Data Provenance:** Data provenance refers to the origin or source of data, including information about how and where data was collected or generated. Understanding data provenance is essential for tracing the lineage of data and establishing its credibility and reliability.

- **Data Flow:** Data flow represents the movement of data from its source to its destination through various intermediate stages and transformations. It includes information about data paths, routes, and dependencies within data pipelines or workflows.

- **Data Transformation:** Data transformation refers to the processes and operations applied to data as it moves through the data pipeline. This may include data cleaning, enrichment, aggregation, or other transformations that alter the structure or content of the data.

Data lineage can be categorized into different types based on the directionality and scope of the lineage:

- **Forward Lineage:** Forward lineage traces the flow of data from its source to its destination, following the path of data propagation through various stages of processing. It provides insights into how data is transformed and used in downstream processes or applications.

- **Backward Lineage:** Backward lineage traces the lineage of data from its destination back to its source, identifying the origins and transformations of data leading up to its current state. It helps stakeholders understand the history and evolution of data, enabling effective data governance and compliance efforts.

- **Horizontal Lineage:** Horizontal lineage focuses on the relationships and dependencies between different datasets or data entities within a given system or environment. It provides insights into how data is related or interconnected, facilitating data discovery, integration, and analysis.

In summary, understanding data lineage involves exploring its components, types, and implications for data management. By gaining insights into the flow, transformation, and usage of data through data lineage, organizations can enhance data governance, quality management, regulatory compliance, and impact analysis efforts effectively.

Implementing Data Lineage

Implementing data lineage involves establishing processes, tools, and frameworks to capture, document, and visualize the flow of data across systems, processes, and transformations. We will explore the steps and considerations involved in implementing data lineage effectively.

Discovering and capturing data lineage information can be challenging, especially in environments with limited documentation and metadata. Visualizing data lineage in a meaningful and intuitive way is essential for enabling stakeholders to understand and analyze data flows effectively. Organizations should invest in automated lineage discovery tools and techniques to identify data sources, transformations, and dependencies accurately.

There are various tools available in the market specifically designed for capturing, documenting, and visualizing data lineage. These tools often provide features such as automated lineage discovery, metadata management, impact analysis, and lineage visualization.

Amazon DataZone is a data management service that makes it faster and easier for customers to catalog, discover, share, and govern data stored across AWS, on-premises, and third-party sources. With Amazon DataZone, administrators and data stewards who oversee an organization's data assets can manage and govern access to data using fine-grained controls. Amazon DataZone provides data lineage capabilities [*to be completed in April 2024 for the data lineage release*]:

- Visual representation of the lineage graph viewed with interactions such as filtering, zoom, panning, drag & drop
- Capture lineage for Glue tables/views and for Redshift tables/views in an automated manner.
- Show connection of DataZone objects (Domain, Project, Subscribing Project, Asset)

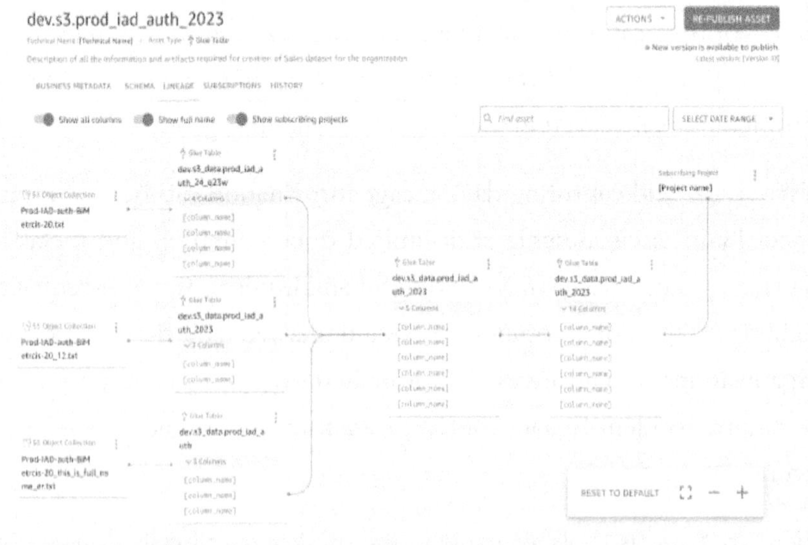

Figure 3.4: Data Lineage in Amazon Datazone

Figure 3.4 illustrates how lineage would appear in Amazon Datazone service, which showcases all the way how the data transitioned from S3 file objects to Glue catalog-backed tables and to a transformed set of tables before ending up in Datazone's project. Other alternatives for data lineage are:

- Data lineage tools such as Collibra Data Lineage or Informatica Enterprise Data Catalog.
- Metadata management platforms play a crucial role in implementing data lineage by capturing and managing metadata about data sources, transformations, and usage. These platforms enable organizations to establish a centralized repository of metadata that can be used to trace the lineage of data across the organization's data ecosystem.
- Data integration platforms such as Apache NiFi, Talend, and Informatica PowerCenter include features for capturing and documenting data lineage as part of data integration and ETL (Extract, Transform, Load) processes. These platforms enable organizations to implement data lineage within data pipelines and workflows, providing visibility into data flows and transformations.

The use of tools is not the only lever for the implementation of data lineage; it also implies the use of frameworks. Establishing data lineage standards and best practices is essential for ensuring consistency and interoperability across data lineage implementations. Organizations should define standardized formats, metadata schemas, and data lineage conventions to facilitate the exchange and integration of data lineage information.

Data lineage governance is another dimension to consider; it involves defining roles, responsibilities, and processes for managing data lineage within the organization. This includes establishing policies, procedures, and controls for capturing, documenting, and validating data lineage information, as well as ensuring compliance with regulatory requirements. Integrating data lineage into existing data management and governance processes is critical for maximizing its value and adoption within the organization. This may involve integrating data lineage with metadata management, data governance, data quality, and data cataloging initiatives to provide a holistic view of data across the organization.

Implementing data lineage at scale can be challenging, particularly in large and complex data environments with heterogeneous data sources and systems. Organizations should adopt scalable architectures and technologies that can handle the volume, velocity, and variety of data lineage information effectively. The use of cloud solutions could be a solution that overcomes such challenges.

In summary, implementing data lineage involves leveraging tools, technologies, and frameworks to capture, document, and visualize the flow of data across systems, processes, and transformations. By establishing data lineage standards, governance, and integration practices, organizations can enhance data management, governance, and decision-making capabilities effectively.

Data lineage is a critical aspect of modern data management, providing organizations with insights into the flow, transformation, and usage of data across systems, processes, and transformations. In this chapter, we explored the foundational concepts, components, and implications of data lineage, as well as the steps and considerations involved in implementing data lineage effectively.

Master Data Management

Master Data Management (MDM) is a comprehensive approach to managing and harmonizing an organization's critical data assets, known as master data, to ensure consistency, accuracy, and reliability across the enterprise. In today's complex data landscape, where organizations collect and utilize vast amounts of data from various sources and systems, mastering and governing core data entities is essential for driving business value and maintaining competitive advantage.

Definition and Purpose

Master Data Management (MDM) can be defined as a set of processes, policies, and technologies designed to create and maintain a single, consistent, and accurate view of an organization's master data entities across disparate systems and data sources. Master data entities typically include critical business entities such as customers, products, employees, suppliers, and other core data elements that are shared across multiple business units and applications.

Master data serves as the foundation for key business processes and decisions within an organization. It provides a centralized and authoritative source of truth for critical business entities, ensuring data consistency and reliability across various business units, applications, and channels. Effective management of master data is essential for:

- **Driving Business Insights:** Master data enables organizations to gain deeper insights into customer behavior, product performance, and other key aspects of their operations, facilitating informed decision-making and strategic planning.
- **Enhancing Operational Efficiency:** By maintaining accurate and consistent master data, organizations can streamline business processes, reduce data duplication and redundancy, and improve

operational efficiency across the enterprise.

- **Enabling Regulatory Compliance:** Master data management helps organizations comply with regulatory requirements such as GDPR, CCPA, HIPAA, and others by ensuring the accuracy, completeness, and security of sensitive data.
- **Supporting Digital Transformation:** In the era of digital transformation, mastering core data entities is essential for enabling seamless integration, interoperability, and innovation across digital channels, platforms, and ecosystems.

The primary objectives of Master Data Management (MDM) include:

- **Data Consistency:** Ensuring that master data entities are consistent, accurate, and up-to-date across all systems and applications within the organization.
- **Data Governance:** Establishing policies, processes, and controls for managing master data throughout its lifecycle, from creation to archival.
- **Data Integration:** Facilitating the integration of master data from disparate systems and sources to create a single, unified view of critical business entities.
- **Data Quality:** Improving the quality and reliability of master data by implementing data quality assessment, cleansing, and enrichment processes.
- **Business Agility:** Enabling organizations to respond quickly to changing business requirements and market conditions by providing a reliable foundation of master data.

In summary, Master Data Management (MDM) is a foundational discipline that enables organizations to effectively manage and govern their critical data assets, ensuring consistency, accuracy, and reliability across the enterprise. By mastering core data entities and implementing robust MDM processes and technologies, organizations can drive business value, enhance operational efficiency, and maintain a competitive edge in today's data-driven world.

Master Data Management Architecture

Master Data Management (MDM) architecture serves as the foundation for implementing MDM processes and technologies within an organization. It encompasses the structure, components, and integration points necessary to manage and govern master data effectively. We will explore the key components and deployment models of MDM architecture.

The components of an MDM Architecture are:

- The **master data repository** is the central repository or database where master data entities are stored, managed, and accessed. It serves as the authoritative source of truth for critical business entities such as customers, products, employees, and suppliers. It can be implemented by a database service such as **Amazon Relational Database Service, Amazon Aurora**, or **Amazon DynamoDB**.

- The **data integration layer** is responsible for integrating master data from disparate systems and sources into the master data repository. It includes tools and technologies for data extraction, transformation, and loading (ETL), as well as data synchronization and replication. An ETL service such as **AWS Glue** can be used as an integration component for the MDM.

- The **data quality tools** are used to ensure the accuracy, completeness, and consistency of master data within the MDM environment. These tools include data profiling, cleansing, deduplication, and enrichment capabilities to improve the quality of master data. As highlighted previously, **AWS Glue Data Quality** can be used as a data quality tool; it can be combined with **AWS Entity Resolution** for deduplication.

- **Metadata management** is essential for capturing and managing metadata about master data entities, including their definitions, relationships, and usage. Metadata management tools provide capabilities for metadata discovery, cataloging, and lineage tracking to facilitate data governance and compliance. **Amazon DataZone** is a service for metadata management.

The Master Data Management can be structured and deployed in one of the following models:

- **Hub-and-spoke model**, a centralized MDM hub serves as the core repository for master data, while individual business units or systems (spokes) interact with the hub to access and update master data. This model provides a centralized governance and control mechanism for managing master data across the enterprise.

- **Centralized model**, a single, centralized MDM system, is deployed to manage master data across the organization. This model offers simplicity and consistency in managing master data but may face scalability challenges in large, complex organizations.

- **Distributed model**, master data management responsibilities are distributed across multiple systems or business units within the organization. Each system or business unit manages its own master data with limited central coordination. This model provides flexibility and autonomy but may result in data inconsistencies and duplication.

- **Registry model**, a centralized registry or index, is used to manage metadata and mappings for master data entities while the actual master data remains distributed across multiple systems. This model enables federated access to master data while maintaining data sovereignty and autonomy within individual systems.

In summary, Master Data Management (MDM) architecture encompasses components such as the master data repository, data integration layer, data quality tools, and metadata management capabilities. Organizations can choose from deployment models such as the hub-and-spoke model, centralized model, distributed model, or registry model based on their specific requirements and business needs. By implementing a robust MDM architecture, organizations can effectively manage and govern master data to drive business value and achieve operational excellence. It involves establishing a data governance framework, assessing and improving data quality, implementing data integration strategies, and addressing data security and privacy considerations. By following these key steps and considerations, organizations can effectively manage and govern master data to drive business value and achieve operational excellence.

In conclusion, Master Data Management (MDM) is a foundational discipline that enables organizations to effectively manage and govern critical data assets, ensuring data consistency, accuracy, and reliability across the enterprise. By implementing robust MDM practices and technologies, organizations can drive business value, enhance operational efficiency, and maintain a competitive edge in today's data-driven world.

Summary

This chapter explores how Amazon Web Services (AWS) can support organizations in implementing effective data governance, from establishing a centralized data catalog and assessing data quality to ensuring data compliance and managing data lineage. It highlights how AWS services like Glue Data Catalog, Glue Data Quality, and DataZone provide comprehensive capabilities to address the challenges of data management at scale. The document also delves into the importance of master data management and how AWS enables organizations to effectively govern their critical data assets. Overall, the AWS ecosystem offers a robust set of tools and services to help enterprises tackle complex data governance initiatives and drive data-driven decision-making.

4. Democratizing Generative AI: Governing the Unstructured Data Frontier

In this chapter, we start with some of the most commonly used cases of generative AI. You will see how unstructured data plays a pivotal role in generative AI use cases. Traditional methods of data governance are not applicable to unstructured data, and novel methodologies are warranted to govern this new data frontier. The chapter covers new methodologies to govern unstructured data while also ensuring Responsible AI practices are in play.

Figure 4.1 illustrates the most commonly seen categories and use cases with generative AI.

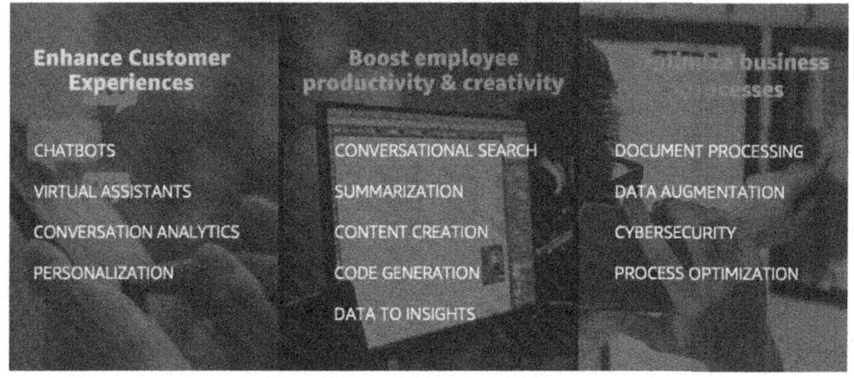

Enhance Customer Experiences
CHATBOTS
VIRTUAL ASSISTANTS
CONVERSATION ANALYTICS
PERSONALIZATION
Boost employee productivity & creativity
CONVERSATIONAL SEARCH
SUMMARIZATION
CONTENT CREATION
CODE GENERATION
DATA TO INSIGHTS
DOCUMENT PROCESSING
DATA AUGMENTATION
CYBERSECURITY
PROCESS OPTIMIZATION

Figure 4.1: Most common use cases with Generative AI

If you have already tried building a gen AI application for any of these use cases in these 3 categories, you will agree that most of the data needed to serve these use cases is in unstructured format such as text, pdf, code, etc.

The advent of generative AI has proliferated the use of unstructured data at a rapid clip, and organizations have put innovation at the forefront. However, since the advent of chatGPT, there have been several incidents related to the use of foundation models that have led to organizational risks and unintended consequences, such as perpetuating biases, generating harmful or misleading content, or infringing on privacy and intellectual property rights.

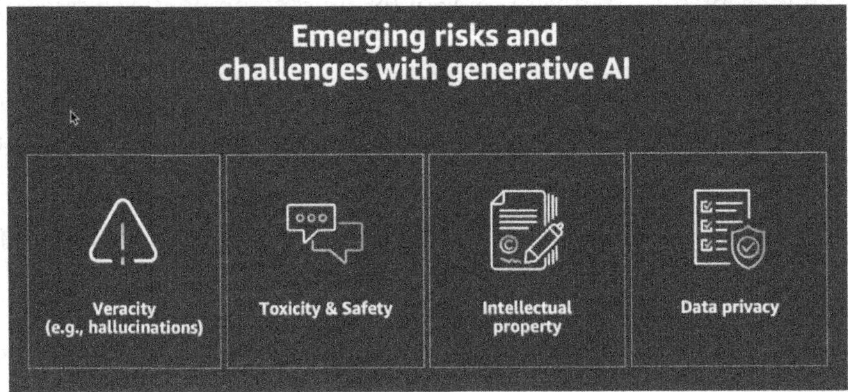

Figure 4.2: Emerging risks with GenAI

The risks, as outlined in Figure 4.2, illustrate what organizations have to deal with when working with generative AI.

Veracity: refers to the truthfulness or accuracy of the information generated or provided by these models.

Toxicity & safety: refers to the potential for these models to generate harmful, offensive, biased, or unsafe content.

Challenges with intellectual property refer to the potential infringement or misuse of copyrighted or proprietary content by these AI systems.

Data privacy: refers to the potential privacy risks and violations that can arise from the data these models are trained on as well as produced. For example, handling sensitive data such as PII.

Building with Responsible AI

It is essential you manage the risks and challenges outlined in the last section upfront when building a generative AI application. Let's look at some ways you can manage these risks.

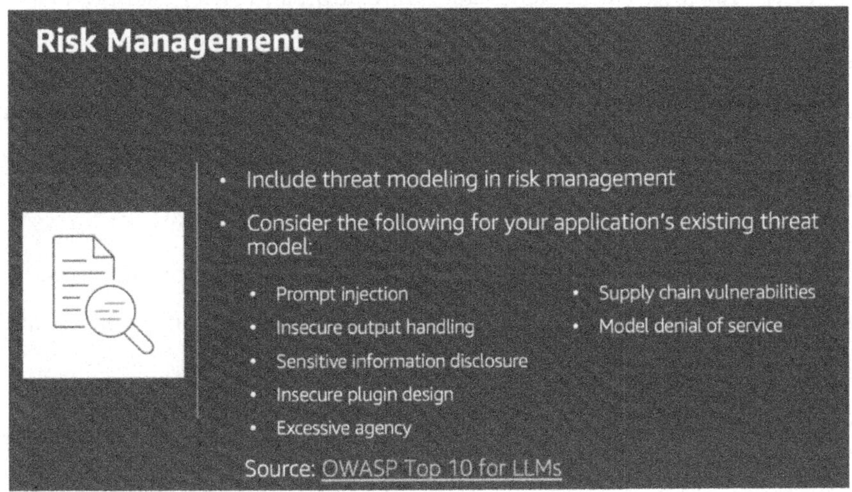

Risk Management
Include threat modeling in risk management
Consider the following for your application's existing threat model:
Prompt injection
Insecure output handling
Sensitive information disclosure
Insecure plugin design
Excessive agency
Supply chain vulnerabilities
Model denial of service
Source: OWASP Top 10 for LLMs

Figure 4.3: Managing Risks with Gen AI

As you delve into generative AI use cases, the core principles of your threat model are likely to remain unchanged. However, you'll need to account for specific risks introduced by these novel applications. In this context, we want to emphasize how your application will handle input and output, interact with third-party APIs, and manage the data flow within its confines.

Figure 4.3 illustrates a few top considerations to mitigate the risks outlined earlier. The OWASP Top 10 for Large Language Models (LLM's) serves as a valuable resource, highlighting additional considerations. Among the key concerns within this top 10 list are:

Prompt Injection: Crafty inputs can manipulate LLM's, causing unintended actions. Direct injections overwrite system prompts, while indirect ones exploit external input sources.

Insecure Output Handling: Accepting LLM outputs without scrutiny can expose backend systems, potentially leading to severe consequences.

Sensitive Data Disclosure: LLM's may inadvertently reveal confidential information, resulting in unauthorized access, privacy violations, and security breaches. Implement data sanitization and strict user policies to mitigate this risk.

Insecure Plugin Design: Insecure inputs and insufficient access control in LLM plugins can enable attackers to exploit vulnerabilities, potentially leading to remote code execution.

Excessive Agency: Granting excessive functionality, permissions, or autonomy to LLM-based systems may lead to unintended and potentially harmful actions.

Training Data Poisoning: Manipulating training data or fine-tuning processes can introduce vulnerabilities, backdoors, or biases, compromising the model's security, effectiveness, or ethical behavior.

Supply Chain Vulnerabilities: Using third-party datasets, pre-trained models, and plugins can introduce vulnerabilities throughout the LLM application lifecycle, enabling security attacks.

Model Denial of Service: Resource-heavy operations on LLM's, exacerbated by the unpredictability of user inputs and the resource-intensive nature of LLM's, can lead to service degradation or high costs.

Model Theft: Unauthorized access, copying, or exfiltration of proprietary LLM models can result in economic losses, compromised competitive advantage, and potential access to sensitive information. Navigating these risks is further complicated by a rapidly evolving compliance landscape surrounding generative AI applications.

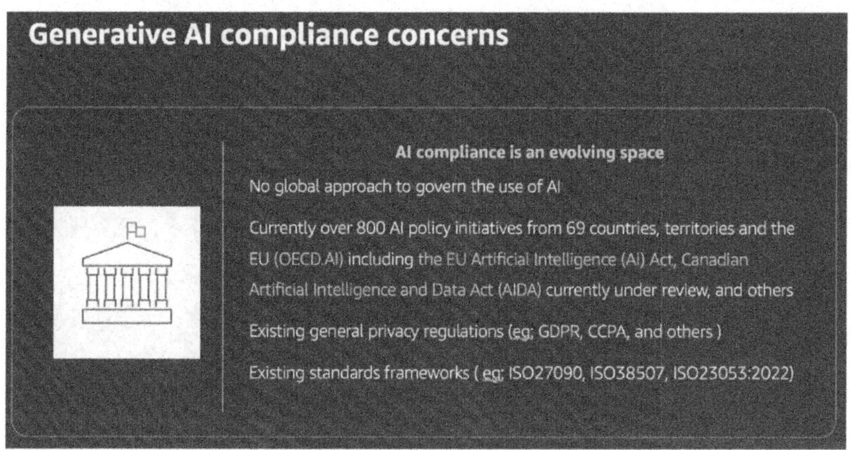

Generative AI compliance concerns
AI compliance is an evolving space
No global approach to govern the use of AI
Currently over 800 AI policy initiatives from 69 countries, territories and the EU (OECD.AI) including the EU Artificial Intelligence (AI) Act, Canadian Artificial Intelligence and Data Act (AIDA) currently under review, and others
Existing general privacy regulations (eg; GDPR, CCPA, and others)
Existing standards frameworks (eg; ISO27090, ISO38507, ISO23053:2022)

Figure 4.4: Gen AI Compliance Concerns

AI compliance is an evolving space, and there is no single standard framework or entity that regulates it. Figure 4.4 illustrates the compliance concerns and the evolving nature of this compliance paradigm in its current state. Model providers like Anthropic, Amazon, and AWS are rapidly adopting constitutional AI principles to make generative AI safe for your use. Today, it's a shared responsibility between the providers and you, the customer, to overcome the risks and challenges highlighted by generative AI.

When building generative AI applications on AWS, the big question that customers ask us is how AWS can help them with building generative AI applications responsibly.

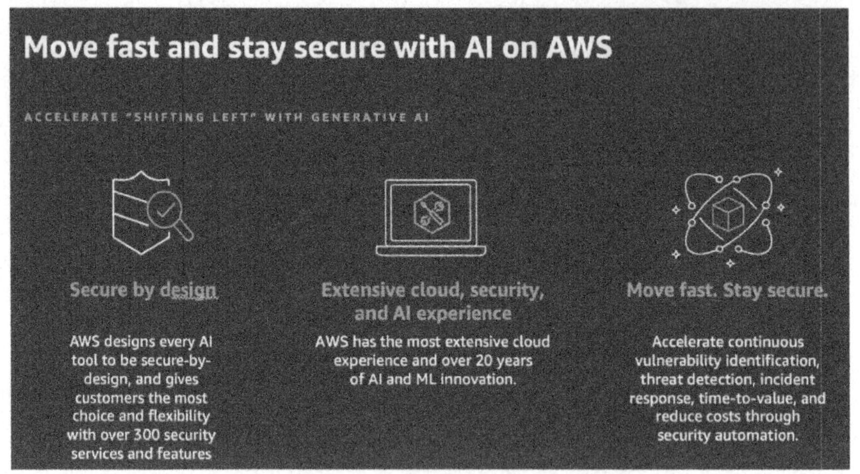

Move fast and stay secure with AI on AWS
ACCELERATE "SHIFTING LEFT" WITH GENERATIVE AI
Secure by design
AWS designs every AI tool to be secure-by-design, and gives customers the most choice and flexibility with over 300 security services and features
Extensive cloud, security, and AI experience
AWS has the most extensive cloud experience and over 20 years of AI and ML innovation.
Move fast. Stay secure.
Accelerate continuous vulnerability identification, threat detection, incident response, time-to-value, and reduce costs through security automation.

Figure 4.5: AWS, your trusted Security Partner

Figure 4.5 shows how AWS is your trusted security partner in managing AI responsibly. AWS is built to be secure by design, and our security services and features are integrated into over 200 AWS services. This allows our customers to innovate more securely from the start, rather than adding security to the end of a process, which slows innovation and makes it more expensive to fix later.

AWS has the most extensive cloud experience and over 20 years of experience with AI/ML innovation. Combined with AWS being engineered to be the most secure cloud infrastructure, this positions AWS as the best place for customers to develop guardrails to innovate quickly and securely with generative AI.

AWS provides the broadest and deepest set of security and governance capabilities to integrate generative AI and security together, as depicted in Figure 4.5.

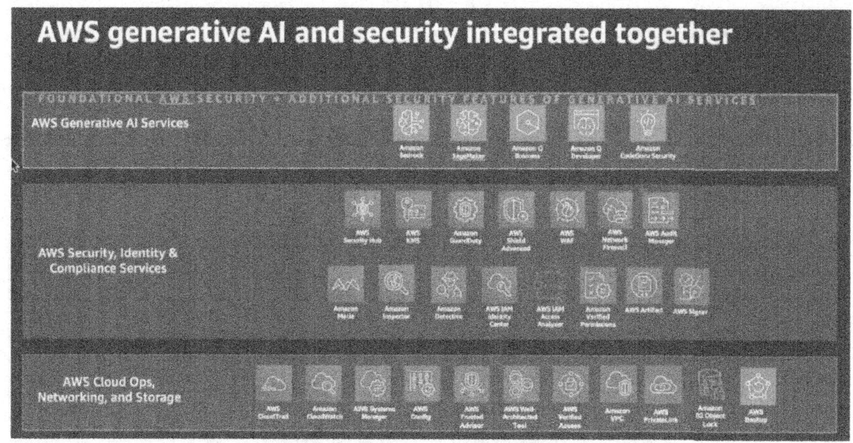

Figure 4.6: Broadest and deepest gen AI Security

Figure 4.5 may appear busy with a lot of AWS services to deal with, but you don't need to use all of these services to build a comprehensive security fabric for generative AI. These services are purpose-built and can seamlessly integrate with your genAI application for any use case to provide robust security. We recommend starting with a few core services like IAM, VPC, and Identity Center that can lay a secure foundation that lets you accelerate and launch generative AI services and products using the topmost layer.

In the AWS shared security model, let's take a look at how AWS integrated security can be leveraged so you can build additional security and governance over what comes out of the box in the generative AI service offerings.

Generative AI service offerings:

- Amazon Bedrock
- Guardrails for Amazon Bedrock
- Amazon Q
- Amazon Titan foundation models

Amazon Bedrock

Amazon Bedrock is a fully managed one, place-stop shop for building GenAI applications with a choice of top-performing models in the world.

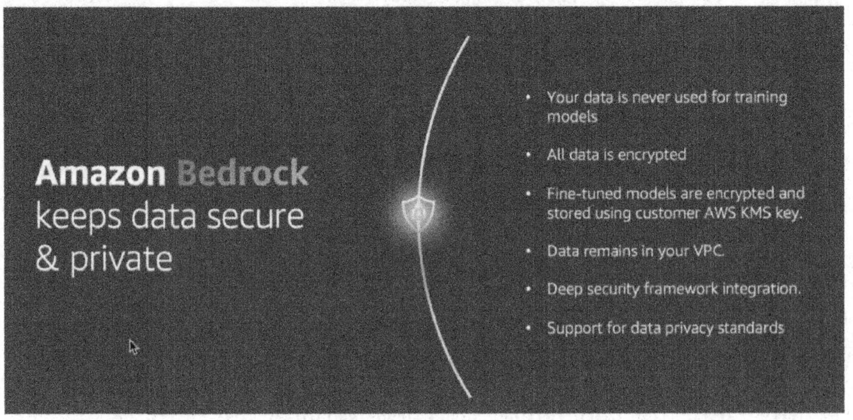

Figure 4.7: Security with Amazon Bedrock

Leveraging Amazon's Bedrock offering, the service was engineered to be inherently resilient and conform to stringent security protocols by default. This is what that it means, as depicted in Figure 4.6:

- None of the client's data is utilized to train the underlying foundational models.
- All information is encrypted at rest using AWS Key Management Service (KMS) and encrypted in transit with Transport Layer Security (TLS) 1.2 (minimum requirement). Additionally, it supports Amazon Managed keys or Customer-Managed Keys (CMKs).
- Fine-tuned models are encrypted and stored utilizing the customer's AWS KMS key. Only you possess access to your customized models.

- Data employed to personalize models remains confined within your Virtual Private Cloud (VPC).
- Incorporates seamless security integration. For instance, Integration with Identity and Access Management (IAM) is used for granular access controls, and GuardDuty is used for threat detection.
- Complies with data privacy standards, including the General Data Protection Regulation (GDPR), Health Insurance Portability and Accountability Act (HIPAA), and Payment Card Industry (PCI) standards.

Bedrock helps you address the OWASP top 10 security recommendations.

Figure 4.8: Amazon Bedrock support to address OWASP Top 10

Figure 4.7 shows the shared security model, where you can see how the top 10 OWASP security recommendations can be addressed based on what comes out of the box from the model provider, Amazon Bedrock, and you, the customer.

Guardrails for Amazon Bedrock

Guardrails for Amazon Bedrock assesses user prompts and generative model responses based on use case-specific guidelines, offering an extra layer of safeguards irrespective of the underlying language model. These protective measures can be implemented across all sizeable language models (LLM's) on Amazon Bedrock, encompassing fine-tuned variants. Clients can craft protective barriers using multiple guardrails, each configured with a distinct combination of controls, and utilize these across diverse applications and use cases. Furthermore, these protective barriers can be integrated with Agents and Knowledge Bases for Amazon Bedrock to construct generative AI applications aligned with your responsible AI policies.

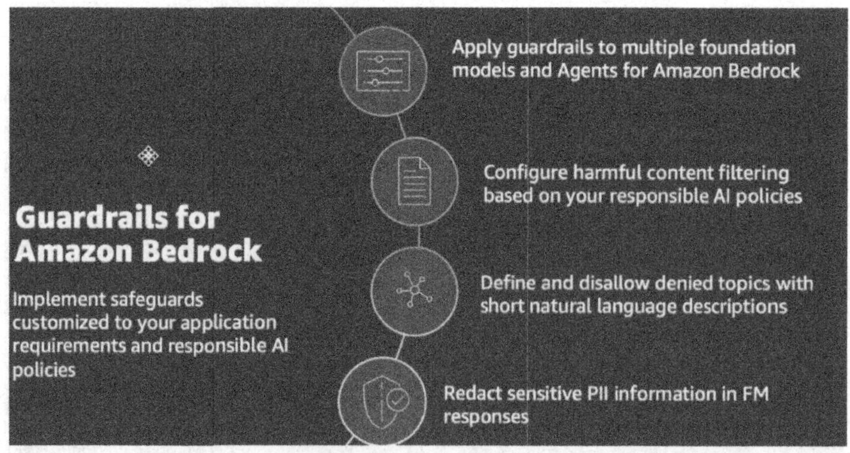

Guardrails for Amazon Bedrock
Implement safeguards customized to your application requirements and responsible AI policies
Apply guardrails to multiple foundation models and Agents for Amazon Bedrock
Configure harmful content filtering based on your responsible AI policies
Define and disallow denied topics with short natural language descriptions
Redact sensitive PII information in FM responses

Figure 4.9: Guardrails for Amazon Bedrock Capabilities

Let's dig a bit deeper into the capabilities highlighted in Figure 4.9. Guardrails can be applied to both the inputs sent to your foundation models and/or the outputs from the FM's, as depicted in Figure 4.10.

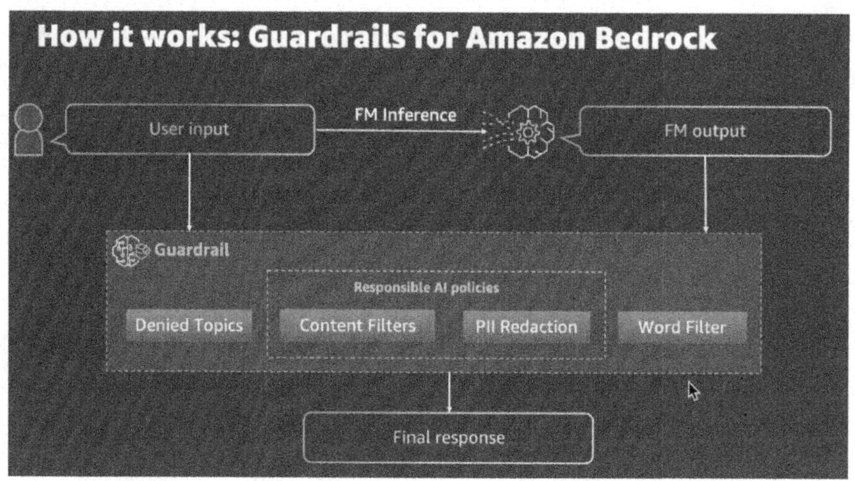

Figure 4.10: How Guardrails Work

You can choose to further apply content filters using specific custom blocked words that you do not want your application to use, apply filters such as a profanity filter, and even respond with a preconfigured custom message when these blocked words are detected.

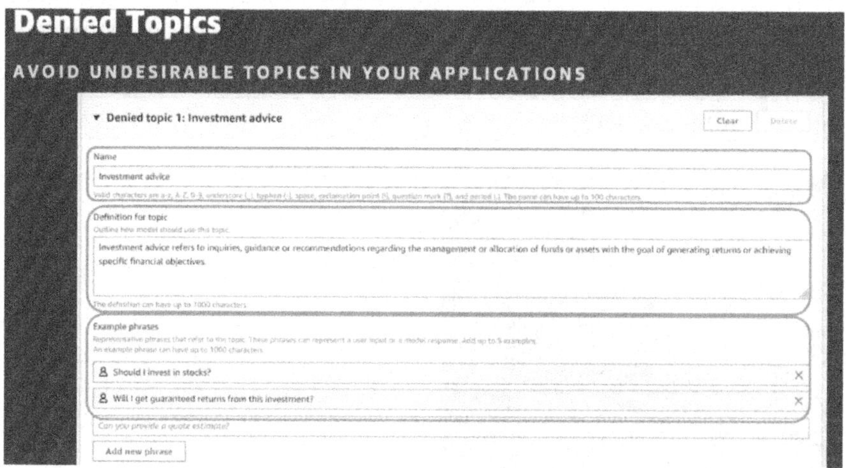

Figure 4.11: Guardrails Denied Topics Configuration

Figure 4.11 depicts how easy it is to configure for denied topics using example phrases that can not only filter specific words but also use the examples to understand the right intent so it can block sentences with that meaning.

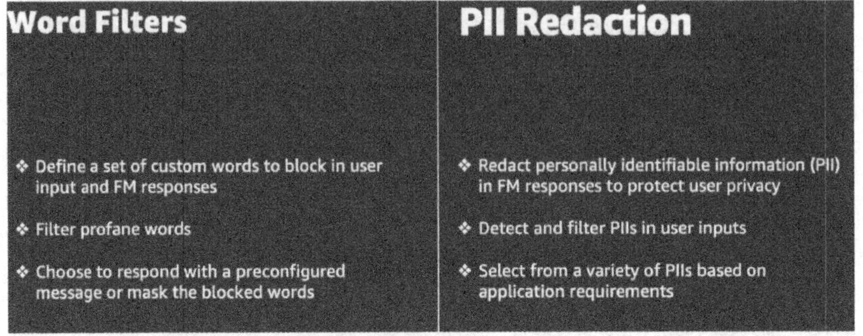

Word Filters
Define a set of custom words to block in user input and FM responses
Filter profane words
Choose to respond with a preconfigured message or mask the blocked words
PII Redaction
Redact personally identifiable information (PII) in FM responses to protect user privacy
Detect and filter PIIs in user inputs
Select from a variety of PIIs based on application requirements

Figure 4.12: Guardrails word Filtering and PII Redaction

When dealing with sensitive data, it is essential to NOT persist sensitive data in your vector stores and use your data pipelines to de-sensitize data before sending the data to your embedding model to persist into the vector store. However, there may be scenarios where PII data can be introduced into the prompt by the end-user or within an augmented prompt. In these scenarios, the guardrail's PII redaction feature can either redact or mask the sensitive fields based on your configuration, as outlined in Figure 4.12.

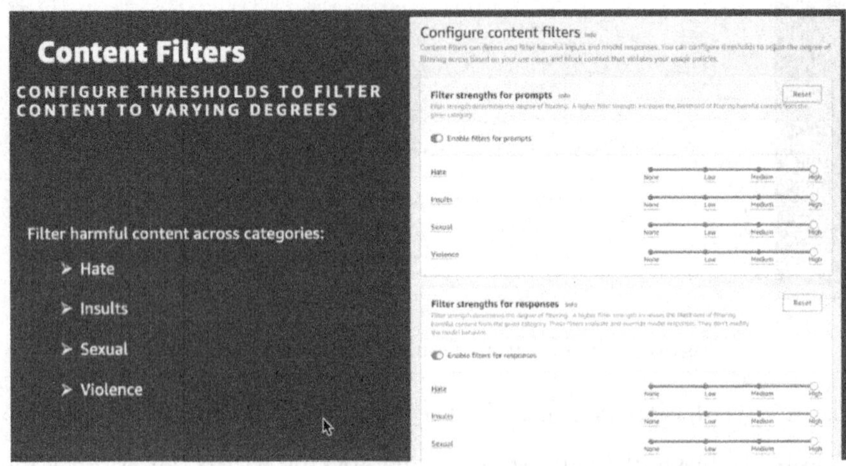

Figure 4.13: Guardrails content Filtering Configuration

Figure 4.13 depicts how easy it is to configure security filters, and as with any other AWS service, all this flexibility and ease of use is not only available from the AWS browser-based console but also available using API's for programmatic use.

While all that's covered in this section under responsible AI outlines a high level of what customers need to handle to ensure they are building an enterprise-grade, secure AI application, they often can get lost in the details. Some of the most commonly asked for detailed guidance are for the following topics.

- Data quality and bias
- Privacy and data protection
- Ethical considerations and social impact
- Monitoring and improving generative AI applications

Data Quality and Bias

Unstructured data like text, images, and audio pose unique challenges for data quality and bias when used to train generative AI models. Since this data comes from the real world, it can reflect societal biases and disparities in representation. It is critical that processes are put in place to assess and mitigate potential biases during data collection, curation, and preparation for model training and inference.

The data collection methodology itself must be carefully examined for sources of bias. If text data is scraped from the internet, for example, it may over-represent content from more privileged groups that have greater access to publishing online. Image and video data collected from public sources may contain stereotypical portrayals or lack representation of certain demographics. Human annotation processes used to label the data can also introduce bias. A diverse and representative team of data labelers should be employed and scrutinized for annotation disparities across groups.

Once collected, the training data should undergo rigorous analysis to identify skews in representation across races, genders, ages, and other demographic dimensions. This includes examining occupations portrayed, sentiment polarity across groups, and other potential indications of bias, discrimination, or harmful stereotyping. Similar demographic audits should be performed on the output generated by the AI system to quantify and mitigate biases propagating from the training data.

Beyond just demographic factors, the subject matter and semantic content of the unstructured data must also be inspected for potential biases and harms. Text about sensitive topics like violence or hate speech requires extra care, as do datasets related to politicized issues that have diverse perspectives to represent fairly. A robust content moderation process aligned with ethical AI principles should be in place to filter out inappropriate content.

Throughout the data lifecycle, processes should incorporate feedback loops to identify blind spots and continuously improve data quality and representativeness over time. This could involve crowd feedback mechanisms, third-party audits, and working closely with experts and representatives of impacted communities. Documenting the origins, filtering criteria, and limitations of each dataset is also crucial for transparency and governing its appropriate use by AI systems.

Tackling bias and ensuring high-quality training data is an interdisciplinary challenge spanning data science, ethics, social science, and cultural expertise. However, it is a critical governance imperative as generative AI systems become increasingly prominent and influential based on the unstructured data we feed them.

Data quality when using an RAG source

Ensuring high-quality, representative, and relevant unstructured data is essential for retrieving accurate context and avoiding misinformation when responding to user prompts. In an RAG use case, the generative AI model relies heavily on the unstructured data corpus to retrieve relevant information and context. If the corpus contains low-quality, biased, or misleading data, the model's responses may be inaccurate, incomplete, or even spread misinformation. Therefore, rigorous data quality measures must be implemented to ensure the integrity and representativeness of the unstructured data.

Several techniques can be employed to implement rigorous data quality measures in a Retrieval-Augmented Generation (RAG) use case:

Data Cleansing and Preparation: Before feeding unstructured data into the RAG model, it is essential to clean and preprocess the data. This involves removing irrelevant or redundant information, handling missing values, and addressing inconsistencies or errors.

Text Standardization: Unstructured data often contains various textual formats, such as different capitalization styles, abbreviations, and misspellings. Techniques like lemmatization and stemming can be applied to convert the text into a consistent and standardized form, improving the quality of the data fed into the RAG model.

Named Entity Recognition (NER) is a natural language processing method that aims to detect and categorize named entities like people's names, organizations, locations, and dates from unstructured text data. This technique aids in extracting pertinent information and maintaining data quality by identifying and eliminating irrelevant entities.

Duplicate Removal: Unstructured data sources may contain duplicate or near-duplicate information. Deduplication techniques, such as document fingerprinting or similarity-based clustering, can be used to identify and remove redundant data, improving the quality and diversity of the information fed into the RAG model.

Topic Analysis and Relevance Scoring: Techniques like Latent Dirichlet Allocation (LDA) or non-negative matrix factorization (NMF) can be employed to identify the main topics or themes present in the unstructured data. This information can be used to filter out irrelevant or off-topic content, ensuring that the RAG model focuses on the most relevant information.

Human Validation: While automated techniques can improve data quality, involving human experts in the validation process is often beneficial. This can be done through manual review and curation of the unstructured data, as well as evaluating the outputs of the RAG model to identify and address any quality issues.

Iterative Refinement: Data quality measures should be implemented as part of an iterative process, where the RAG model's outputs are evaluated, and feedback is used to refine the data quality techniques and improve the overall performance of the system.

In this section, you have learned specific techniques that will depend on the nature of the unstructured data, the requirements of the RAG use case, and the available computational resources. Additionally, a combination of these techniques may be necessary to achieve the desired level of data quality. Now, let's look at how privacy and data protection methodology can strengthen your governance.

Privacy and Data Protection

Ensuring proper governance of unstructured data for generative AI systems has become a pressing concern in the era of generative AI. Unstructured data sources, encompassing text, images, and videos, may inadvertently contain sensitive or personally identifiable information, posing substantial risks if mishandled. Addressing these governance challenges necessitates a comprehensive strategy that harmonizes technical solutions with robust policies and procedures. There are 3 techniques that come to mind that help you manage data privacy and protection on unstructured data.

One way to safeguard individual privacy while enabling meaningful data analysis is through the adoption of privacy-preserving technologies such as differential privacy. This mathematical approach involves strategically introducing controlled randomization or noise into the data, effectively masking individual-level information while still allowing for valuable insights to be gleaned from the aggregated data. Such techniques can be particularly beneficial for generative AI models trained on extensive text corpora, where there exists a heightened risk of inadvertently reproducing sensitive or personal information.

Data anonymization is another powerful tool in the privacy-preserving arsenal. This process involves removing or obfuscating personally identifiable information (PII) from the data, such as names, addresses, and identification numbers. Advanced anonymization techniques, like k-anonymity and l-diversity, can further enhance privacy protection by ensuring that individuals cannot be re-identified based on combinations of quasi-identifiers.

Protecting data is a top priority for organizations, and encryption plays a crucial role in achieving this goal. By encrypting data at rest and in transit, companies can strengthen their defenses against unauthorized access and ensure that sensitive information remains unreadable to unauthorized individuals. Even if data is intercepted or a breach occurs, strong encryption algorithms, when implemented correctly, create an impenetrable barrier, making the data indecipherable without the necessary decryption keys. Modern encryption techniques, when implemented with precision, offer an unmatched level of security, effectively preventing malicious actors from deciphering the data.

By implementing a comprehensive governance strategy that combines privacy-preserving technologies, robust access controls, and compliance with data protection regulations, organizations can effectively manage the risks associated with unstructured data in generative AI systems. This holistic approach not only protects individual privacy but also fosters trust and confidence in the responsible use of AI technologies.

Privacy and Protection in a RAG Implementation

Data privacy and anonymization are crucial aspects when dealing with unstructured text data, especially in a retrieval-augmented generation use case. This process involves ensuring that sensitive information is protected while still allowing for effective data analysis and model training. Here's a step-by-step approach to achieving data privacy and anonymization for unstructured text data:

Ensuring data privacy and anonymization for unstructured text data in a Retrieval-augmented Generation (RAG) approach is crucial to protecting sensitive information and maintaining user privacy. Here's a step-by-step approach you can follow using an example scenario:

Example Scenario: You have a dataset of customer support conversations containing personal information, such as names, addresses, and phone numbers. Your goal is to train an RAG model to assist in generating responses to customer queries while preserving data privacy and anonymization. Following is the sequence of steps you need.

Data Collection and Preprocessing - Collect the unstructured text data (customer support conversations) from various sources. - Preprocess the data by removing any irrelevant information, such as HTML tags, special characters, or unnecessary formatting.

Data Anonymization - Identify and mark sensitive information in the text data, such as names, addresses, phone numbers, email addresses, and other personally identifiable information (PII). - Replace the identified sensitive information with placeholders or pseudonyms using techniques like tokenization, substitution, or masking. - Ensure that the anonymized data maintains the context and meaning necessary for training the RAG model.

Data Splitting - Split the anonymized dataset into two parts: a training set and a retrieval corpus. - The training set will be used to train the generation component of the RAG model. - The retrieval corpus will be used to retrieve relevant information during the generation process.

Model Training - Train the generation component of the RAG model using the anonymized training set. - Ensure that the model does not memorize or reconstruct any sensitive information from the training data. - Train the retrieval component of the RAG model using the anonymized retrieval corpus.

Inference and Response Generation - During inference, when a user query is received, it is passed through the RAG model. - The retrieval component will retrieve relevant information from the anonymized retrieval corpus. - The generation component will then use the retrieved information to generate a response while preserving data privacy and anonymization.

Post-processing and Verification - After generating the response, perform post-processing steps to ensure that no sensitive information has been inadvertently included in the output. - Implement verification mechanisms, such as regular expressions or named entity recognition models, to identify and remove any remaining sensitive information.

Continuous Monitoring and Improvement - Continuously monitor the performance of the RAG model and the effectiveness of the anonymization techniques. - Periodically update the anonymization rules and techniques based on feedback and evolving privacy requirements. - Retrain the RAG model with updated anonymized data as needed. By following these steps, you can achieve data privacy and anonymization for unstructured text data in a Retrieval-augmented Generation approach, ensuring that sensitive information is protected while maintaining the ability to generate relevant and contextualized responses.

Ethical Considerations and Social Impact

Assessing the potential ethical implications and social impact of an AI system is a critical responsibility that requires a multifaceted approach and collaboration with diverse stakeholders. It involves carefully examining factors such as fairness, accountability, transparency, and potential harm or misuse. Here's a detailed overview of how this process can be approached:

Fairness Assessment: Fairness is a fundamental ethical consideration in AI systems, as biases can perpetuate and amplify existing societal inequalities. A comprehensive fairness assessment should be conducted to identify potential sources of bias in the data, algorithms, and decision-making processes. This can involve techniques such as disparate impact analysis, counterfactual evaluation, and causal reasoning. Additionally, it is crucial to engage affected communities and underrepresented groups to understand their perspectives and ensure that the system does not disproportionately impact or discriminate against them.

Accountability and Governance: Establishing clear accountability mechanisms and governance structures is essential for ensuring the responsible development and deployment of AI systems. This includes defining roles and responsibilities, establishing oversight bodies, and implementing processes for monitoring, auditing, and addressing potential issues or unintended consequences. Stakeholders from various disciplines, such as legal experts, policymakers, and industry representatives, should be involved in developing robust governance frameworks and accountability measures.

Transparency and Explainability: AI systems, particularly those used in high-stakes decision-making processes, should be transparent and explainable to the greatest possible extent. This involves developing interpretable models, providing clear and understandable explanations of the system's decisions, and enabling external audits and scrutiny. Engaging domain experts, users, and affected communities in the development process can help ensure that the system's behavior and decision-making processes are comprehensible and aligned with ethical principles.

Risk Assessment and Mitigation: A comprehensive risk assessment should be conducted to identify potential harms or misuses of the AI system. This can include risks related to privacy, security, safety, and unintended consequences. Once potential risks are identified, mitigation strategies should be developed in collaboration with relevant stakeholders, such as cybersecurity experts, privacy advocates, and domain-specific subject matter experts. This may involve implementing technical safeguards, developing guidelines and best practices, and establishing monitoring and response mechanisms.

Societal Impact Assessment: AI systems can have far-reaching societal implications, both positive and negative. It is crucial to engage a diverse range of stakeholders, including ethicists, social scientists, policymakers, and community representatives, to assess the potential social impact of the system. This assessment should consider factors such as the system's alignment with societal values, its potential impact on employment, education, healthcare, and other critical domains, as well as its broader implications for human rights, democracy, and social justice.

Continuous Monitoring and Adaptation: The ethical considerations and societal impact of AI systems are not static; they evolve as the technology develops and societal contexts change. Therefore, it is essential to establish ongoing monitoring and adaptation processes that involve diverse stakeholders. This can include regularly reviewing the system's performance, soliciting feedback from affected communities, and adapting the system or its deployment strategies as needed to mitigate emerging risks or address unforeseen consequences. By engaging in this comprehensive and collaborative process, organizations can strive to develop and deploy AI systems that are ethical, accountable, transparent, and socially responsible. It requires a commitment to ongoing dialogue, continuous learning, and a willingness to adapt and evolve in response to societal needs and ethical considerations.

Monitoring and Improving Generative AI Applications

There are many architecture options to build a generative AI application on AWS between various patterns of general use of LLM's, RAG, and fine-tuning. Even if we scope down to a RAG pattern, which is the most widely used pattern, there is no one gold standard for architecture due to the many choices available that are purpose-built for your use cases. However, at a high level, they all come down to the following reference architecture in Figure 4.14 for an RAG pattern.

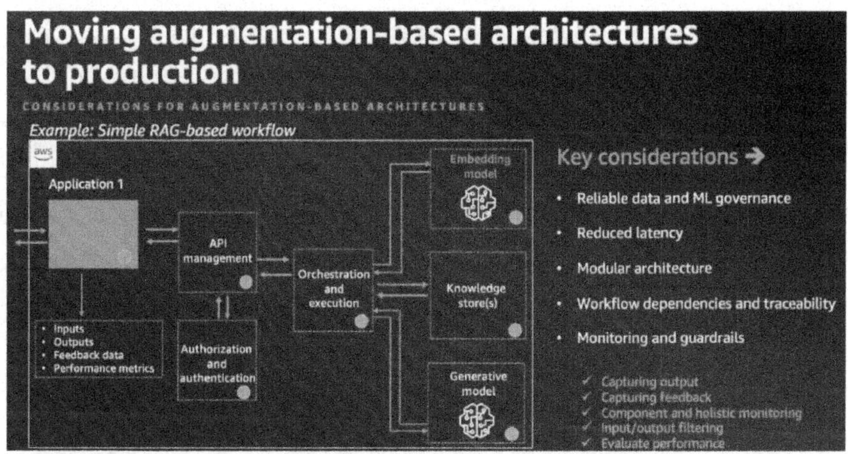

Figure 4.14: Typical RAG Architecture

These architecture factors in key considerations are showcased in Figure 4.14, and you have AWS service options that fit each block in the diagram. For example, 1/ API management can be handled at AWS API Gateway service, 2/ service level authorization is managed using IAM roles, while the app authentication is managed using your preferred identity provider using AWS Identity Center service. 3/ Orchestration is handled using either Bedrock agents, AWS lambda, or even a container application in Amazon EKS service. 4/ Inferences to embedding model and LLM models can be done using either Amazon Bedrock or Amazon Sagemaker. 5/Vector store can be Amazon openSearch or other vector store choices AWS offers.

Regardless of which services you choose in the above architecture example, from a monitoring standpoint, there are logs available in Amazon Cloudwatch that will help you understand the key attributes of your genAI application, such as performance SLA's, tokens used, input prompts, the context as well as the output generated.

We recommend you build an observability framework using these logs and create a visual dashboard using your choice of BI tool, such as

Amazon Quicksight, that can showcase important KPI's such as costs, tokens per minute, SLA's, and more.

Evaluate your foundation model (FM) using metrics.

When evaluating AI applications for the right foundation model(s), you need to prioritize speed, cost, and quality/precision and try to pick the best two with the tradeoff for the third. This is depicted in Figure 4.15 below.

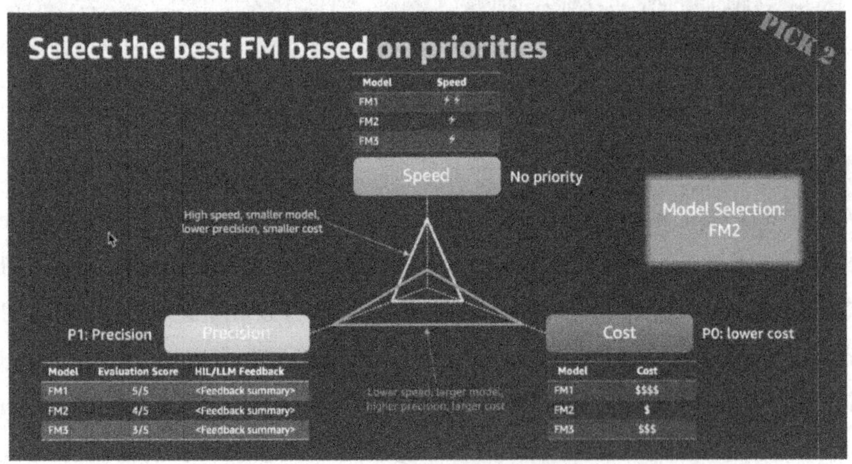

Figure 4.15: Gen AI App Eval Criteria

Speed

Speed of the foundation model (FM) often refers to the time it took between the input prompt tokens (augmented prompt) being submitted to the LLM and when all the tokens are generated by the FM. This information is available within CloudWatch logs when using Amazon Bedrock models.

If you are using a playground in Amazon Bedrock within the AWS Console, then you can also see the model metrics immediately for each of your prompt responses.

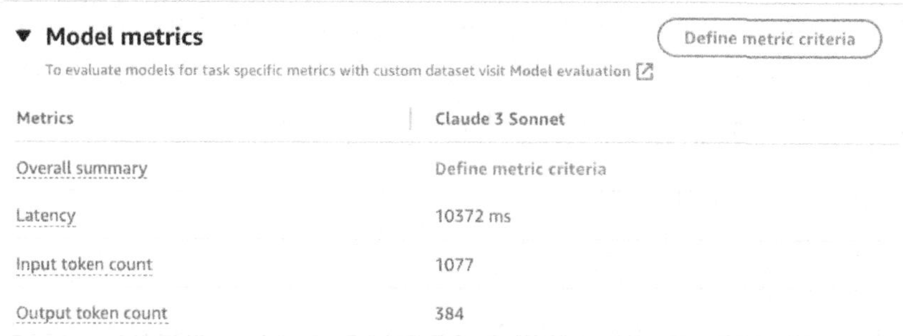

Model metrics
Define metric criteria
To evaluate models for task specific metrics with custom dataset visit Model evaluation
Metrics
Claude 3 Sonnet
Overall summary
Define metric criteria
Latency
10372 ms
Input token count
1077
Output token count
384

Figure 4.16: Amazon Bedrock Playground in AWS Console

Again, the information presented in Figure 4.16 is also available in AWS Cloudwatch logs for use within your BI tool of choice.

Cost

Amazon Bedrock offers various pricing options to cater to different needs when utilizing its foundation models (FMs). The On-Demand mode allows you to pay as you go without any long-term commitments, while the Batch mode is designed for large-scale parallel inference tasks, with outputs stored in Amazon S3. Both modes are billed based on the number of input and output tokens involved, with output tokens typically charged at a higher rate compared to input tokens.

If you require guaranteed throughput, Provisioned Throughput allows you to purchase model units for either a 1-month or 6-month term. Customizing models through fine-tuning or continued pre-training incurs charges based on the size of the training data and model storage. Inference on custom models requires Provisioned Throughput.

Model evaluation can be done automatically, with the cost of inference, or through human evaluation, where you pay for inference plus a fee per human task. AWS also offers customized private evaluation engagements for those who require it. Overall, Bedrock's pricing structure provides flexibility, allowing you to align costs with your specific FM usage requirements, whether you need on-demand or batch processing, guaranteed throughput, model customization, or various evaluation options. For more detailed pricing, refer to the Amazon Bedrock pricing page in the product documentation.

Output Quality/Precision

There are several evaluation techniques that help you evaluate the FM output precision, which is sometimes also referred to as output quality. These evaluation techniques measure a combination of metrics such as Faithfulness, answer relevancy, context precision, context recall, and many more. For more information on the best practices for evaluating the FM output quality of different models, including some reusable git code for your use, we recommend watching a 4-part YouTube series titled, "***Best practices building GenAI applications on AWS***," an AWS launched series for its customers. Part 4 GitHub code covers the most comprehensive eval criteria. Besides the automated metric evaluation, you also need to keep Humans in the loop evaluation where a human can score the model output based on ground truth response.

When deploying your application into production for chatbot-type use cases, we recommend you display a confidence score or relevancy % and accuracy % to the end user when responding to each user prompt. This allows a human to stay in control of how the responses can be used further, where this level of transparency can, in turn, build user trust in your application.

Once your application is deployed into production, we recommend you build a feedback mechanism to allow users to rate or vote on the quality of responses. When using Amazon Bedrock models, this information, in combination with the cloudwatch logs that contain prompt, context, and FM output, provides you the ability to periodically improve the performance of your overall application.

Summary

This chapter covers Guardrails for Amazon Bedrock, a feature that allows users to implement additional safeguards on user prompts and model responses. It explains how these guardrails can be configured to filter content, redact sensitive information, and enforce responsible AI policies.

The text also addresses important topics such as data quality and bias, privacy and data protection, ethical considerations, and monitoring of generative AI applications. It emphasizes the importance of rigorous data preparation, anonymization techniques, and privacy-preserving technologies like differential privacy.

For Retrieval-Augmented Generation (RAG) implementations, the passage outlines specific steps to ensure data privacy and quality, including data cleansing, standardization, and continuous monitoring.

The document concludes with guidance on monitoring and improving generative AI applications, presenting a typical RAG architecture and discussing evaluation criteria for foundation models, including speed, cost, and output quality/precision. It recommends building an observability framework and implementing user feedback mechanisms to continuously improve application performance.

Overall, the text provides a thorough examination of the security and governance aspects of deploying generative AI applications on AWS, emphasizing the importance of a multi-faceted approach that combines technical solutions with robust policies and procedures.

5. Data Mesh on AWS

A data mesh is an architectural framework for managing data at scale. In this chapter, we will introduce you to what a data mesh is and outline the core components of a data mesh from the lens of AWS. By the end of this chapter, you will understand what a data mesh is and how you can use it for an enterprise-wide decentralized data strategy. We are going to cover the following main topics:

- Data Mesh Organization Principles
- Difference between Data Lake and Data Mesh Architectures
- Data Mesh Core concepts
- Data Organization

Data Mesh Organization Principles

Data mesh is an architectural framework to manage data across the organization in a way where the data assets are developed using a distributed and decentralized ownership yet providing a federated way to discover and govern data centrally. In a typical organization, there are disparate data sources across the lines of businesses that must be brought together for analytics, such as business intelligence, data discovery, and data science. Data mesh architecture provides a unified view of these multiple siloed data sources and integrates them together using governance enforcement that is managed centrally, making it easy to share data and democratize analytics. Business units and their functions can govern and control how access to shared data objects is operated and monitor centrally who accessed their data and in what formats it's accessed. It is apparent that while data mesh architecture adds complexities to the operating model for both building and managing data, it has also been shown to bring efficiency that simplifies data access and security and democratizes data scale.

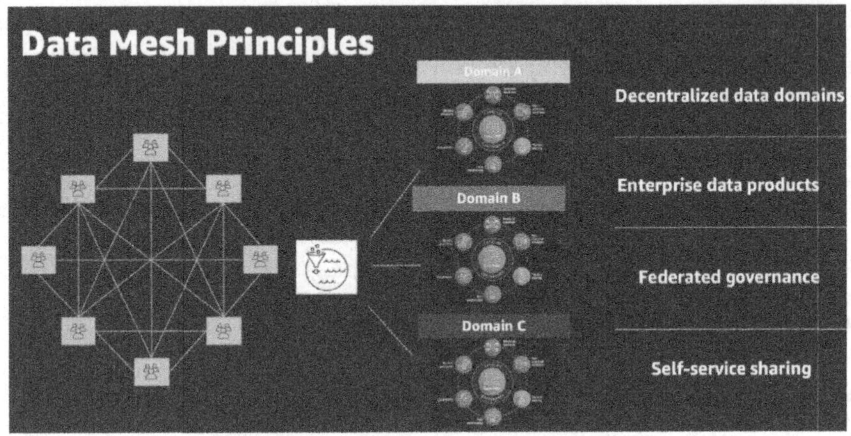

Figure 5.1: Data Mesh Principle

Data mesh empowers all personas in your organization by creating decentralized ownership with central governance using four principles outlined in Figure 5.1.

Decentralized Data Domains

In simple terms, in a data mesh architecture, the responsibility of managing data is organized to stay closely with the business functions, which can also be called data domains. In a typical organization, you can think of a domain for HR, another for finance, and so on and so forth. Another such example is if you think of a retail company that sells clothes. The retailer can have a clothing domain that entails how data is produced, organized, and consumed all for clothing products, another domain for stores and website behavior data, and another domain for customers to the store and website. Multiple teams exist within the business unit, each responsible for managing their own data. This data management includes collecting data from sources, transforming the data to adhere to enterprise standards, and preparing the data in a usable format for their particular business functions. Rather than having all domain data flow into a central data platform, each team hosts and provides access to their own datasets in a readily consumable manner.

Enterprise Data Products

In a data mesh implementation, the domain team must apply a product mindset to all data objects they are producing. Data as a product consideration allows the data assets to conform to the business domains. Treating the rest of the company business, as well as data teams, as the customers of data producers make it seamless for the data producers to focus on producing the data relevant to the product consumers.

To optimize and elevate the user experience, domain data products require certain essential attributes. The products should be easily discoverable through registration with a centralized data catalog, allowing users to conveniently find and access them. Each data product necessitates a unique, standardized address that enables programmatic retrieval by data consumers following organizational naming conventions. Furthermore, data products must establish trustworthiness by defining service-level objectives about data accuracy reflecting documented events. For instance, the domain of the order could publish information solely after verifying critical customer details like address and contact number. Additionally, all data products mandate comprehensively described syntax and semantics adhering to organizational naming standards for optimal understanding. Following these vital guidelines will ensure domain data products deliver an exceptional, seamless user experience.

Federated Data Governance

When utilizing data mesh architectures, implementing robust security necessitates a collective organizational responsibility. The leadership establishes overarching standards and policies applicable universally across all domains. Simultaneously, the decentralized nature of the data architecture permits substantial self-governance over standards and policy execution within each individual domain. With shared accountability, universal guidelines, and autonomous implementation, data mesh security integrates centralized guidance and decentralized control for a comprehensive approach.

Self-service Sharing

When designing and building a self-serve data platform, it is imperative to make it as generic as possible so that any individual or team within your organization can leverage it to easily and rapidly build new domain-specific data products tailored to their needs. However, in providing this flexibility, the platform should also hide and encapsulate the underlying technical complexity from users, presenting them with self-service infrastructure components and services for accessing, processing, managing, and sharing data through well-defined interfaces.

Some important capabilities to include in a robust self-serve data platform are:

- End-to-end data encryption to ensure security and privacy flexible data product schema definitions and validations
- Fine-grained governance controls and access policies
- Data discovery mechanisms like catalog registration and metadata publishing
- Logging and monitoring for auditing data product usage
- Caching for improved performance of common queries

Additionally, investing time upfront in automation, such as pre-defined configurations and scripts, can significantly reduce the lead time required for users to set up new data products on the platform. Overall, focusing on usability, flexibility, scalability, and security will enable widespread adoption and maximize the value of the self-serve data platform.

In this section, you have learned about the 4 core principles of a data mesh and how they all come together in improving your governance posture. There have been a lot of investments in a data lake across many customers we have seen, and they are often unclear about the value of a data lake and how it is related to a data mesh. In the next section, you will see how they are related and complement each other.

Difference between a data mesh and data lake architectures

A data lake is a large data repository where an organization can accumulate and consolidate structured data, such as data from databases or other organized sources, as well as unstructured data from sources like social media, documents, sensor data, photos, videos, email, and really any other type of digital information, all in their original formats and without needing to preprocess or organize the data prior to storing it. Data lakes allow data to be stored at any scale without limits on size. In traditional centralized data management systems and platforms, the data lake serves as the foundational and critical technology for amassing and retaining data originating from all potential sources inside and outside of a company. Data lakes act as a single source of truth that the producers and consumers can often turn to for creating, enriching, and consuming data between raw sources identical to trusted published data and everything in between. Though an organization can have multiple different data lakes, more often than not, organizations have centralized their data into one large data lake. In cases where there are multiple data lakes, organizations adopt a hub-spoke model for each data lake, making it a central data store for that data without any integration between the rest of the data lakes. From a consumer perspective, they need to access each data lake separately. This introduces a lot of complexity, as depicted in the diagram below.

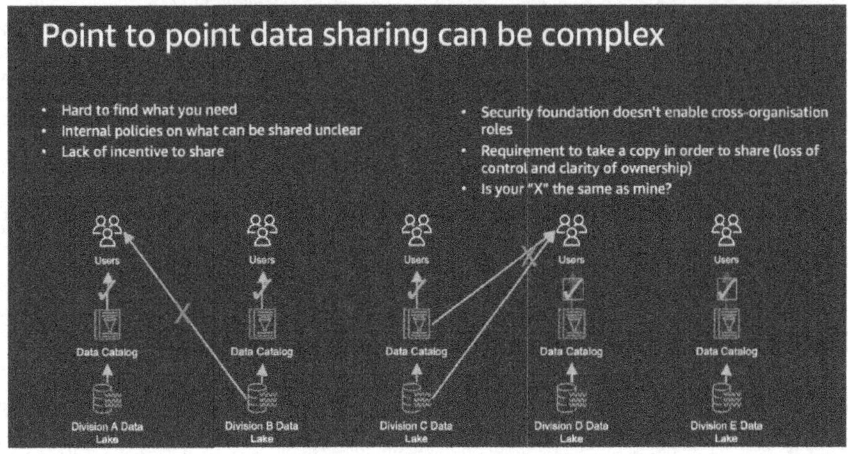

Figure 5.2: Data Sharing

In contrast, a data mesh architectural approach utilizes data lakes differently and does not rely on a single centralized data lake as the most important component governing data management. With a data mesh, a data lake is not necessarily the central piece of the overall data architecture. Rather, data lakes may be leveraged to implement specific data products or services or could be part of a self-service data infrastructure, but they do not serve as the core centralized repository. The data mesh paradigm distributes data management across domains in a decentralized fashion but then federates these data lakes into a unified data repository that allows producers and consumers to have a one-place-stop shop for all their data needs. In short, one or more data lakes can be a part of a data mesh architecture. The following diagram depicts this.

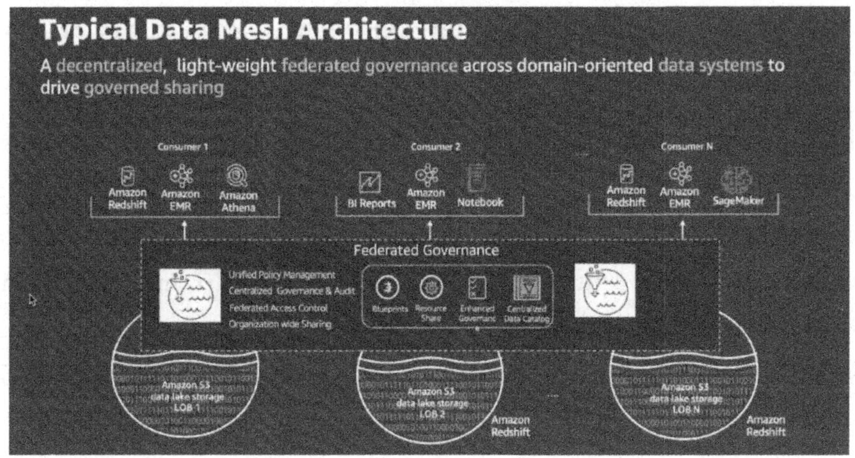

Figure 5.3: Data Mesh Architecture

A data mesh can be an ensemble of different data stores, all with a connected tissue, as shown in Figure 5.3. Notice how federated data governance is in a data mesh is created using AWS Data Lake backed by S3 in one account, a combination of S3 data lake and Redshift in another account, and it can also be your on-prem and external data store not on AWS as long as they can be brought together using the data mesh principles outlined earlier in this chapter.

Difference between Data Mesh and Data Fabric

When speaking to customers, there was also a lot of confusion as to the difference between a data mesh and a data fabric.

The modern data fabric architecture employs automation as well as machine learning in order to accomplish end-to-end integration of the various cloud environments and data pipelines. You are able to conceptualize the data fabric as a layer of technology that exists above the foundational infrastructure and which cohesively assimilates and exhibits data in a manner that is comprehensible and accessible to personnel lacking in technical expertise. For example, decision-makers have the capability to view all of their data consolidated in a solitary location and identify connections spanning disparate datasets by utilizing the data fabric.

Both the data fabric architecture and the data mesh architecture possess analogous objectives of unified and effective data governance. As an illustration, envision a scenario in which you employ AWS services to ingest data into a centralized data lake while concurrently relying on legacy infrastructure to transform data. Your data fabric would seamlessly incorporate both of these systems and present a unified perspective without necessitating modifications to the existing pipeline.

Therefore, the data fabric employs technological solutions to operate in conjunction with your extant infrastructure. Conversely, implementing a data mesh necessitates altering the foundational infrastructure itself. You must transition your data management from a centralized push-and-ingest model to a distributed serve-and-pull model across your business domains.

In this section, you have learned the difference between data lake and data mesh architectures and also how data mesh differs from a data fabric. Let's dive deeper into some of the core concepts of a data mesh in the next section to help you gain more clarity on how to apply it in your organization.

Data Mesh Core Concepts

Data mesh is an architectural paradigm for data management that recognizes that data is a product in and of itself, like any business domain. It should be managed as such with distributed ownership and domain-oriented design. Data Mesh is an architectural pattern that embraces the distributed nature of data ownership and enables domain-driven and self-serve data infrastructure.

The data mesh paradigm breaks up data platforms into self-contained domains called data domains, which have their own teams, technology stacks, and methods of managing data. This decentralized approach allows each data product to use the technologies best suited for its use case. These teams may already have a data pipeline and data management components that can be integrated with a data governance model. There is no centralized data warehouse or lake. Instead, data products expose their data and functionality to other teams through well-documented APIs and schemas that allow the data to be discovered and consumed in a standardized way.

Data mesh is a paradigm shift that provides autonomy to data producers to build high-quality data products with multiple endpoints. This enables data producers to focus on building data products and not worry about infrastructure management. Data mesh simplifies data sharing and minimizes data movement using a federated governance model that provides capabilities like self-service workflow, data marketplace, and single pane for glass for policy management.

Data mesh advocates for thinking of data as a critical asset and first-class citizen, putting it on par with business domains and products from an organizational perspective. Teams own the entire data lifecycle for their domain rather than just doing analysis or engineering work on centralized data. Implementing a data mesh involves cultural and organizational shifts around decentralized data ownership as well as the architectural changes of breaking up existing data platforms. Adopting these principles aims to make organizations more data-centric, agile with data, and able to support advanced analytics.

The four data mesh principles are outlined below:

<u>Decentralized Data Platform and Governance:</u> There is no monolithic, centralized data platform. Technology and governance standards ensure interoperability between domains.

- **Domain-Oriented Self-Serve Data Infrastructure:** Domain teams can access, manipulate, enrich, and serve data through infrastructure services tailored to their domain context. This facilitates agility.

- **Federated Computational Governance:** Things like metadata, data quality, security policies, etc, are defined and managed federally, but implementation is decentralized across domains.

- **Discoverability and Reusability:** Domain data products are appropriately documented and exposed through catalogs and APIs to encourage reuse and reduce duplication across domains.

So, in summary, data mesh introduces decentralization across key data dimensions like ownership, computing, governance, etc., but it federates aspects like standards and policies to enable organization-wide visibility and economies of scale where relevant. The domain focus facilitates agility while the federated aspects maintain coherence. In summary, data mesh is a paradigm shift in how organizations manage distributed data at scale, both organizationally and technically. It emphasizes decentralized data ownership within domains while upholding consistency and reliability across those domains.

Let's now look at the core components of a data mesh in detail, namely:

- Data Domain

- Data as a product

- Data producer

- Data consumer
- Federated governance
- Data Sharing

Data Domain

Data domains are a key concept in the data mesh architecture, which is a decentralized approach to data management and sharing. In a data mesh, data domains are the areas of responsibility for different teams or organizations within an organization. Each team or organization owns and manages its own data and shares it with other teams or organizations as needed.

Data domains are defined based on the business context and the data needs of the organization or organizational structure or sometimes based on a set of use cases. For example, a company may have separate data domains for customer data, product data, and health-related data. Each data domain would have its own set of external data needs, data models, data pipelines, and data infrastructure managed by the team or organization responsible for that domain.

The data mesh approach allows for more efficient and effective data management, as each team or organization can focus on its own data domain and ensure that its data is accurate and up-to-date. It also allows for more collaboration and sharing of data across the organization, as teams can easily access and use data from other domains as needed. In summary, data domains in a data mesh refer to the areas of ownership and responsibility for different data sets within an organization.

This decentralized approach enables better collaboration, data sharing, and alignment between teams and business units, leading to improved decision-making and insights generation.

Data domains are aligned with organizational entities, but they can also be aligned with other dimensions like use cases-based approaches, teams, and environments, among others.

Basic domain design in data governance includes the following components:

- Data sources, which include all the different sources of data within an organization

- Data owners are a team of people who own the data assets and are responsible for defining data policies, managing data quality, and accessing workflows and approvals.

- Data engineers and operations cover the operational aspects and data pipelines to transform data assets.

- Data products are a set of data assets built and cataloged for consumers to find and access. Data products are matured and high-quality data assets.

- Data privacy and compliance ensures that the organization's data collection, use, and sharing practices comply with relevant data privacy regulations. This domain defines and enforces data privacy policies, conducts privacy impact assessments, and manages data subject rights requests.

Using these design components, you can develop a data domain which not only ensures tight affiliation of domain-specific data but also enables your teams to be more effective.

Data as a Product

Companies are increasingly treating data as a monetizable asset or product. With the rise of AI, big data, and analytics, large datasets can provide valuable insights and competitive advantages.

Companies like Google, Facebook, and others build their entire businesses around collecting user data and selling access to that data, targeted advertising, etc. The data itself is the core product. Other companies package and sell access to proprietary datasets they have developed or collected to business customers who can use them to enhance their analytics, AI/ML models, business intelligence, and more.

There are an increasing number of "data marketplaces" emerging where companies can directly access and purchase a wide variety of datasets from data providers to use for various business purposes. The data acts like any other commodity. Structured, accurate, relevant, and timely data has value for business, research, and other applications. Well-organized and clean datasets require effort to develop and maintain so they can command high licensing fees and prices. There are still many open questions about data ownership, privacy, and monetization models as data's role as a digital product continues to evolve. However, "data as a product" looks to be a long-term trend across industries. The data itself is the thing being bought and sold.

Data marketplaces catalog both internal and external data products and provide a self-service workflow to request access to data. Data products need to be accompanied by good business metadata that can help consumers find the data products. Data products also need to maintain high quality and lineage along with technical and business metadata.

Companies offer data access via APIs that application developers can leverage by paying API access fees based on usage levels. The underlying data has value.

Data is packaged into proprietary analytics products, reports, and benchmarks that are sold to business customers for strategic decision-making. In essence, data is an asset that can be monetized in many ways - one underlying commodity but multiple monetization avenues based on licensing access, building services on top, or packaging for various customer needs. Data's value as an asset keeps increasing.

Companies directly package and sell access to raw datasets they have collected or aggregated. The intrinsic value is in the data itself, such as in training AI models.

Using this data as a product approach provides a tight coupling of different data sets for that product and reduces data duplication.

Data Producer

Data producers are the teams or business units that generate and own specific data domains or data products within an organization. They are responsible for the full lifecycle of the data they produce. In a data mesh architecture, each data producer team operates in a self-served manner, building domain-oriented data products to serve their applications and analytical needs.

Data producers provide APIs and data products that encapsulate their data, data pipelines, transformations, validations, etc. Other teams can discover and consume these well-documented data products rather than directly accessing raw data. Data producers are aligned to business domains rather than technology divisions.

For example, the "clinical real-world data" team would be the data producer for real-world data with clinical related data products. Data producers implement appropriate data governance, metadata management, schemas, data quality checks, etc., for their domain. Data stewards and data product owners are responsible for checking the metrics for data products, and they work with the central governance teams on metadata audibility and access flow, among other data product management activities.

Central data governance teams provide overall standards and oversight across domains. The autonomous nature of data producers facilitates agility and innovation as teams build data products suited to their domain requirements. Encapsulation and APIs/services prevent unintended breakages. So, in summary, data producers drive the decentralization, domain-orientation, and self-service aspects of data mesh to better serve their data needs while also enabling organizational data to be discovered and reused.

Data Consumer

Data consumers are any applications, services, or people that need to use data to perform their functions. This includes downstream analytics applications, ML models, business intelligence tools, etc.

In a data mesh, data is produced and managed by domain-oriented data product teams. Data consumers discover and access the data products they need through a data marketplace supported by a business data catalog and using self-service methods.

There is meant to be a clean separation between data producers (the data product teams) and data consumers. Consumers access data products through well-defined interfaces and contracts without needing direct access or visibility into the production systems. - Data mesh emphasizes decentralized data ownership and aims to give data product teams autonomy over data quality, governance, evolution, etc, for their own domain's data assets. However, these teams still need to consider and collaborate with consumer needs.

Data producers can also be consumers, and data consumers can be data producers as well. A data producer building data products might need data from other domains to merge with their data assets. Similarly, a data consumer might build a data product initially for a specific need but later want to publish it to the catalog for others to use. The data mesh paradigm simplifies the publishing and subscribing of data and enables data consumers and data producers to share data products.

The onboarding experience for new data consumers is important. Discovery, self-service access, documentation, and reliability help attract and retain data users to feed into the mesh. So, in summary, data consumers fuel the broader data ecosystem, but in a decentralized data mesh, their main contact point is with domain data products via interfaces and the data catalog, not the underlying production. Data product teams still need to properly support consumer needs.

Federated Governance

Federated governance means governance is also decentralized. Rather than having centralized data governance, each domain team implements its own governance for the data products they manage.

Domain teams operate autonomously but collaborate and coordinate as needed. There are still some central platform teams that provide infrastructure, tooling, and services to enable the domains, but they do not govern or control the domain data products. Domain teams own the full lifecycle of their data products, including requirements, development, documentation, quality, security, privacy, lifecycle management, consumption, and more.

Benefits include increased agility, reduced bottlenecks, improved data quality, and empowered domain teams. Challenges include a potential lack of standards, coordination issues, and platform maturity.

In summary, data mesh federated governance decentralizes data management to autonomous domain teams with loose federation agreements for coordination. This empowers domain teams while enabling organization-wide data scalability.

Data Sharing

Data sharing is built on trust between data producers and data consumers, where consent and transparency are non-negotiable components. Make sure you have appropriate consent before collecting or sharing personal data, and clearly disclose your data practices and anonymize data where possible. Personally identifiable information needs to be removed from datasets to protect privacy. Data sharing trust needs to be established with techniques like aggregation, encryption, data access workflow, and Implementing security controls. Encrypt data in transit and at rest, implement access controls, and take measures to prevent unauthorized access or leaks.

This adds statistical noise to datasets to prevent the identification of individuals while still preserving overall statistical validity. Only share the minimum amount and relevant data needed for the intended purposes. Avoid sharing extraneous attributes about individuals and establish data-sharing agreements.

Data mesh and a federated data governance model provide a platform where data producers and consumers can easily implement controls and workflow that are transparent and customizable based on the consent requirements of data producers. Data-sharing contractual agreements can define restrictions on data use, retention policies, liability, etc. Allow people to access the data you have about them and opt out of data collection/sharing if they choose.

Adhere to relevant regulations like GDPR when handling personal data in the EU. Also, consider established ethical guidelines for your domain.

When physically transferring data, use secure courier services, encryption, access controls on devices, and track data provenance.

Review data-sharing practices internally on a regular basis and perform external audits to ensure proper controls are in place. The key is balancing innovation enabled by data sharing with individual privacy, security, and ethical considerations. Adopting practices like the above can help strike that balance.

Here are a few key things to know about data sharing in a data mesh architecture:

- Data mesh promotes decentralized data ownership and aims to give domain teams more control and responsibility over data. This includes sharing and accessing data.

- Data is shared through self-service data platforms that domain teams operate. Teams publish their datasets to a platform catalog that allows discovery and access. Data meshes often use a "data product" approach where domains package datasets with documentation, SLAs, etc, to make sharing easier. Products provide APIs and various other endpoints for access.

- There is usually a strong focus on the discoverability of datasets. Catalogs, data marketplaces, and metadata management help connect data producers with internal data consumers. Domain teams have the ability to control access and set usage guidelines. However, there is an overall culture that promotes appropriate sharing of data across the organization.

- Technical measures like data access controllers, encryption, and anonymity can also be built into platforms to share sensitive data safely. Shared data is made available to other domains through data pipelines and APIs. Streaming/pub-sub infrastructure helps efficiently transport and update shared datasets. In summary, while decentralized, teams are still expected to appropriately share key data products across their organization's data mesh to mutually benefit from broader analytics. Self-serve platforms reduce friction in discovery and access.

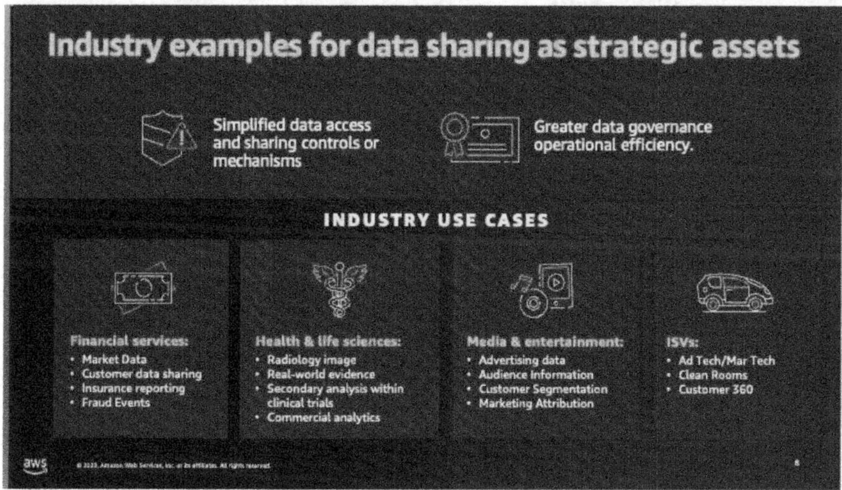

Figure 5.4: Industry Examples of Data Sharing

Data sharing patterns can be broadly categorized as internal vs external data sharing. However, it is important to note that data governance guidelines for secure data sharing apply to both external and internal data assets, so we need to have a unified strategy that works for various data products.

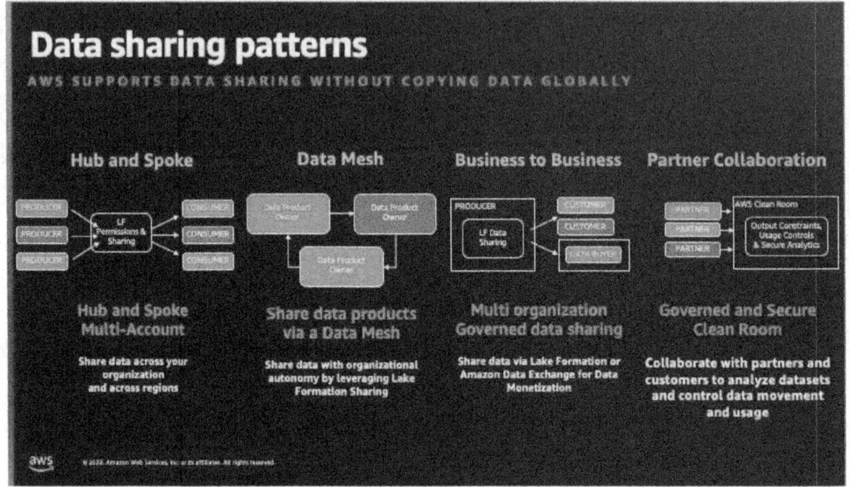

Figure 5.5: Data Sharing Patterns

In this example above in Figure 5.5, we have a hub and spoke and a data mesh pattern to build a data collaboration and data sharing environment in a federated data ecosystem. Both these patterns enable multi-account data sharing for internal data assets across organizations. Data mesh requires people to process changes along with technology to manage federated assets. For external data sharing, the most common patterns are business-to-business and partner collaboration, where data products are shared across different organizations.

In this section, you have learned the core components of a data mesh and understood how they are related to each other to share data across organizations in a secure way.

Data Organization

There are multiple personas with distinct role responsibilities in a data mesh architecture.

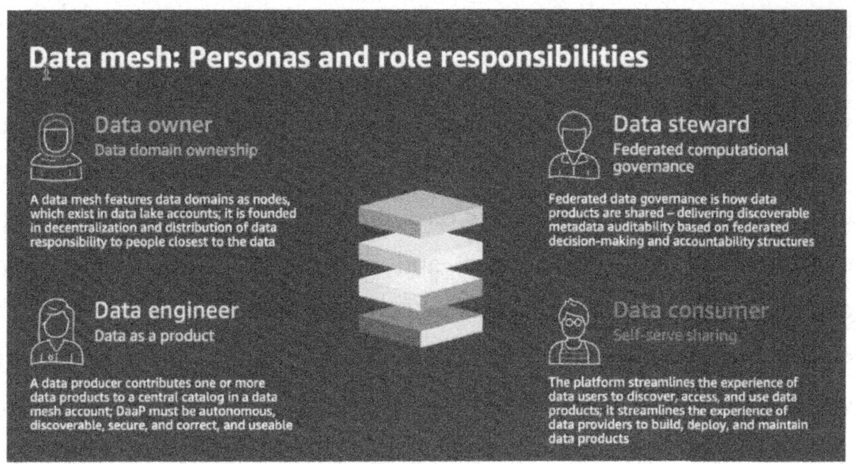

Data mesh: Personas and role responsibilities
Data owner
Data domain ownership
A data mesh features data domains as nodes, which exist in data lake accounts; it is founded in decentralization and distribution of data responsibility to people closest to the data
Data steward
Federated computational governance
Federated data governance is how data products are shared – delivering discoverable metadata auditability based on federated decision-making and accountability structures
Data engineer
Data as a product
A data producer contributes one or more data products to a central catalog in a data mesh account; DaaP must be autonomous, discoverable, secure, and correct, and useable
Data consumer
Self-serve sharing
The platform streamlines the experience of data users to discover, access, and use data products; it streamlines the experience of data providers to build, deploy, and maintain data products

Figure 5.6: Data Mesh Personas and Roles

A domain owner in a data mesh is responsible for governing and curating a specific domain data product. They act as the product manager for their domain's data, overseeing its overall lifecycle from sourcing, integration, preparation, and access. Domain owners delineate business logic and context about their domain that informs how the data is modeled and used. They also define service level agreements and availability requirements for the domain's data products to meet business needs. Additionally, domain owners establish data standards, ownership, quality metrics, and usage policies regarding the data product. They facilitate collaboration across other domains and IT to enable the integration and responsible use of their data products through the wider data mesh. Overall, the domain owner plays a critical role in decentralizing data governance and enabling domain-oriented autonomous data product development that is aligned with business priorities.

In a data mesh architecture, data engineers play a critical role in enabling decentralized data ownership and self-serve data infrastructure. Rather than building centralized pipelines, data engineers focus on creating reusable data building blocks and platforms that empower domain teams to easily build, manage, and share their own data products. This includes developing foundational data infrastructure like storage, messaging, scheduling, and observability that domain teams can self-serve. Data engineers also create frameworks and templates that domain teams can use as starting points for their data products, handling cross-cutting concerns like security, privacy, and governance. Additionally, data engineers support domain teams by providing coaching and reviews to ensure best practices are followed in developing data products. Their deep technical skills in areas like data modeling, data pipelines, and data quality are leveraged through consultative partnerships rather than top-down mandates. Ultimately, data engineers in a data mesh enable decentralization and autonomy through developer platforms and advisory partnerships.

A data steward in a data mesh is responsible for governing, curating, and overseeing specific domains of data products. Rather than having centralized data governance, data meshes empower domain teams to be accountable for managing their own data products end-to-end, from sourcing to transformation to consumption. As such, data stewards within each domain team oversee data quality, security, compliance, metadata, access control, and usage monitoring for their domain's data assets. They define policies and best practices for their domain, which align with the overarching data mesh principles and architecture. Data stewards also serve as the point of contact for their domain data consumers to field queries, requests, issues, and feedback. Through decentralized data governance, data stewards in a mesh enable autonomous domain teams to provide reliable self-serve data products to consumers organization-wide.

A data consumer is an essential actor within a data mesh architecture. Data consumers utilize data products published by domains to gain valuable business insights. Rather than relying on a centralized data team for all analytics needs, data consumers can discover and directly access domain-owned data products through the data mesh platform catalog. This self-service access empowers data consumers to build reports, analytics, and applications utilizing the highest quality data directly from the domain experts. Data consumers provide feedback on data products to domain owners, enabling continuous improvement. Overall, data consumers act as a driving force for domains to provide fit-for-purpose data products in a data mesh. With easy discovery and access to distributed data products, data consumers gain agility and democratization of data at scale.

Summary

Data mesh is an architectural framework for decentralized, domain-oriented data management to empower analytics at scale. It breaks up data platforms into autonomous domains called data products, owned by teams aligned to business functions. These domains expose their data assets to the organization through self-service interfaces. Data mesh also enables federated governance where standards are defined centrally but implemented locally. Key concepts include decentralized data ownership within domains and treating data as a product with SLAs. Data mesh ultimately aims to make organizations more data-centric and agile by blending organizational decentralization with just enough technical standardization across domains to enable trust and widespread data access.

6. Approach to Building a Data Mesh on AWS

Organizations are facing challenges in managing and deriving insights from vast and diverse datasets. Traditional centralized data architectures often struggle to keep pace with the growing complexity and volume of data, leading to bottlenecks in data access, governance, and analytics. Data mesh architecture has emerged as a promising approach to address these challenges by decentralizing data ownership, fostering domain-oriented data governance, and empowering domain teams to manage their data assets effectively. Leveraging cloud computing platforms like Amazon Web Services (AWS) provides organizations with the scalability, flexibility, and agility needed to implement a data mesh architecture successfully.

Data mesh architecture represents a paradigm shift in data management, emphasizing decentralized ownership, domain-oriented data governance, and self-serve data platforms. In a data mesh architecture, data is treated as a product, and each domain or business unit within an organization is responsible for its own data assets, governance, and analytics. This approach breaks down silos and empowers domain teams to manage and derive insights from their data autonomously.

AWS's scalable and flexible infrastructure enables organizations to build data platforms that can scale seamlessly to handle growing data volumes and user demands. Harness AWS analytics and machine learning services like Amazon Athena, Amazon SageMaker, and Amazon QuickSight to derive insights from data and build predictive analytics models. These services provide powerful capabilities for data exploration, modeling, and visualization, empowering domain teams to drive data-driven decision-making.

Building a data mesh architecture on AWS offers organizations a powerful approach to managing and deriving insights from their data assets effectively. By leveraging AWS's building blocks for data mesh, organizations can break down data silos, empower domain teams, and drive innovation and growth in the digital age.

Building block services on AWS

Amazon Web Services (AWS) plays a pivotal role in enabling organizations to implement a data mesh architecture effectively. As a leading cloud computing platform, AWS offers a wide range of services and capabilities that are essential for building scalable, flexible, and secure data mesh solutions.

Here are several key ways in which AWS facilitates the implementation of data mesh architecture:

- **Managed Services for Data Processing:** AWS offers managed services for data processing and orchestration, such as Amazon EMR (Elastic MapReduce) and AWS Glue. These services enable organizations to ingest, transform, and analyze data at scale without the need to manage underlying infrastructure. With Amazon EMR, organizations can run distributed data processing frameworks like Apache Spark and Apache Hadoop, while AWS Glue provides fully managed ETL (Extract, Transform, Load) capabilities with serverless data integration and transformation.
- **Data Management:** AWS offers a variety of data storage and management services that are integral to implementing a data mesh architecture. Amazon S3 serves as a highly scalable and

durable object storage service, suitable for building data lakes and storing large volumes of structured and unstructured data. Additionally, services like Amazon RDS (Relational Database Service), Amazon DynamoDB, and Amazon Redshift provide managed database solutions for storing and managing structured data, while services like AWS Lake Formation simplify the setup and management of data lakes on AWS.

- **Analytics and Machine Learning:** AWS provides a comprehensive suite of analytics and machine learning services that enable organizations to derive insights from their data and build intelligent applications. Services like Amazon Athena, Amazon SageMaker, and Amazon QuickSight empower organizations to perform ad-hoc querying, machine learning model training and deployment, and data visualization and business intelligence, respectively. These services integrate seamlessly with other AWS services, allowing organizations to leverage their data mesh architecture for advanced analytics and AI-driven insights.

- **Real-Time Data Streaming:** AWS offers real-time data streaming services like Amazon Kinesis, which enable organizations to ingest, process, and analyze streaming data in real-time. Amazon Kinesis provides capabilities for both data ingestion (Kinesis Data Streams, Kinesis Data Firehose) and real-time analytics (Kinesis Data Analytics), allowing organizations to build scalable and responsive data streaming applications on AWS.

The AWS services play the role of building blocks, which are crucial components in the implementation of a data mesh architecture. These services offer a foundation upon which organizations can build scalable, resilient, and efficient data ecosystems. AWS provides a comprehensive set of services and capabilities that are essential for implementing a data mesh architecture. By leveraging AWS services for scalable infrastructure, managed data processing, storage and management, analytics and machine learning, and real-time data streaming, organizations can build flexible, resilient, and cost-effective data mesh solutions that drive innovation and deliver value to their business.

Let's introduce some of the following building blocks: **Amazon S3, Amazon Redshift, AWS Glue, AWS Lake Formation, and Amazon DataZone.**

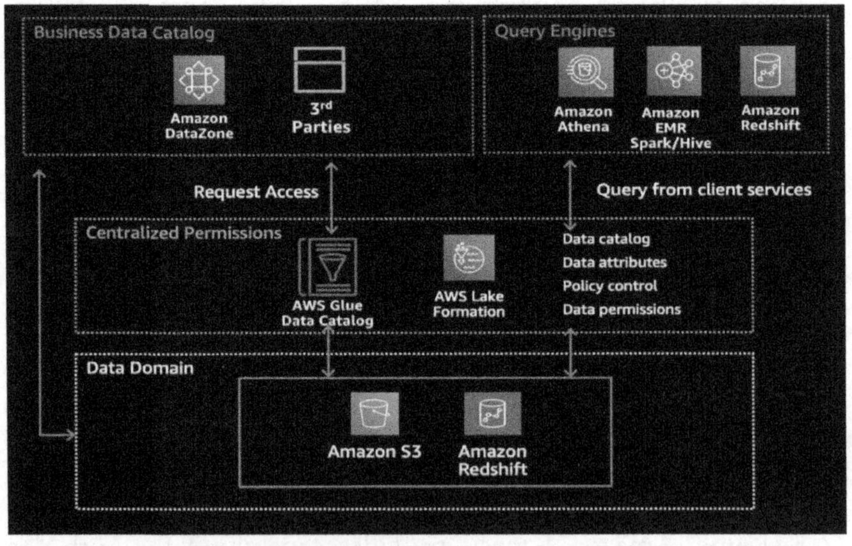

Figure 6.1: The main services for building a Data Mesh

Amazon S3 and Amazon Redshift

Data storage and management are foundational components of any data mesh architecture, and Amazon Web Services (AWS) offers a comprehensive suite of services to address the diverse storage and management needs of organizations. These services are essential for building scalable, durable, and cost-effective data ecosystems within a data mesh architecture.

Amazon S3 is a highly scalable and durable object storage service that allows organizations to store and retrieve any amount of data securely. Amazon S3 serves as the foundation for many data-driven applications on AWS. Its virtually unlimited storage capacity, high availability, and robust security features make it an ideal choice for storing and managing large volumes of data. Amazon S3 provides features such as versioning, encryption, and lifecycle policies to ensure data integrity, confidentiality, and compliance.

With Amazon S3, organizations can build data lakes, store raw and processed data, and enable seamless integration with other AWS services for data analytics and processing.

Amazon Redshift is a fully managed data warehouse service that allows organizations to analyze large volumes of data using SQL queries. Amazon Redshift is optimized for data warehousing and analytics workloads, with features such as columnar storage, parallel query processing, and automatic compression. It offers exceptional performance, scalability, and cost-effectiveness, making it a powerful tool for data-intensive workloads, such as business intelligence, data warehousing, and analytics.

Amazon Redshift integrates seamlessly with other AWS services and enables seamless data exchange with Redshift data sharing. Organizations can build end-to-end analytics solutions with ease.

AWS offers a wide range of services for data storage and management, providing organizations with the flexibility, scalability, and reliability needed to build robust data ecosystems within a data mesh architecture.

AWS Glue

AWS Glue is a fully managed extract, transform, and load (ETL) service that makes it easy to prepare and load data for analytics. It simplifies the process of building, managing, and monitoring ETL workflows, allowing organizations to extract data from various sources, transform it into a format suitable for analysis, and load it into data lakes, data warehouses, or other storage destinations.

The key features and capabilities of AWS Glue:

- AWS Glue includes a **centralized metadata repository** called the Data Catalog, which stores metadata information about datasets, tables, and schemas. The Data Catalog provides a unified view of data assets across different sources, making it easy to discover, understand, and manage data.
- AWS Glue allows users to **define ETL jobs using a visual interface or by writing custom scripts in Python**. ETL jobs can be scheduled to run on a recurring basis or triggered by events such as data arrival. AWS Glue automatically provisions the necessary compute resources to execute ETL jobs, ensuring scalability and reliability.
- AWS Glue provides **support for dynamic DataFrames**, which allows users to work with semi-structured and unstructured data formats such as JSON, Parquet, and Avro. This flexibility enables users to process diverse datasets without requiring schema changes or preprocessing.
- AWS Glue includes **data crawlers** that automatically scan data sources such as Amazon S3, Amazon RDS, and Amazon Redshift to infer schema and populate the Data Catalog. Data crawlers eliminate the need for manual data discovery and

schema inference, saving time and effort in data preparation.

- AWS Glue **integrates seamlessly with other AWS services**, such as Amazon S3, Amazon Redshift, Amazon RDS, Amazon DynamoDB, and Amazon EMR. This allows users to leverage the capabilities of these services in conjunction with AWS Glue to build end-to-end data pipelines and analytics solutions.
- AWS Glue is built on a **serverless architecture**, which means that users don't have to provision or manage the underlying infrastructure. AWS Glue automatically scales resources up or down based on workload requirements, allowing users to focus on data transformation logic rather than infrastructure management.

Overall, AWS Glue simplifies the process of data preparation and ETL by providing a fully managed service with built-in automation, scalability, and integration with other AWS services. It enables organizations to accelerate time-to-insight and derive value from their data assets more efficiently.

AWS Lake Formation

AWS Lake Formation is a fully managed service that simplifies the process of building, securing, and managing data lakes on Amazon Web Services (AWS). Data lakes are centralized repositories that allow organizations to store and analyze large volumes of structured and unstructured data at scale. AWS Lake Formation provides a set of capabilities to streamline the setup and management of data lakes, enabling organizations to accelerate time-to-insight and derive value from their data more efficiently.

The key features of AWS Lake Formation:

Data Catalog: AWS Lake Formation includes a centralized metadata repository called the Data Catalog, which stores metadata information about datasets, tables, and schemas within the data lake. The Data Catalog provides a unified view of data assets across different sources, making it easy to discover, understand, and manage data within the data lake.

Data Security and Access Control: AWS Lake Formation offers granular access controls to govern access to data within the data lake. Organizations can define permissions at the table and column level, ensuring that only authorized users have access to sensitive data. AWS Lake Formation integrates with AWS IAM (Identity and Access Management) for authentication and authorization, allowing organizations to enforce security policies and comply with regulatory requirements.

Data Transformation and Preparation: AWS Lake Formation integrates seamlessly with AWS Glue, allowing organizations to perform data transformation and preparation tasks within the data lake environment. Data can be cleansed, normalized, and enriched using Glue's built-in ETL (Extract, Transform, Load) capabilities, enabling organizations to prepare data for analysis and machine learning.

Data Governance and Compliance: AWS Lake Formation provides features for data governance and compliance, including data lineage, auditing, and encryption. Organizations can track the lineage of data from source to destination, audit access to sensitive data, and encrypt data at rest and in transit to ensure data integrity, confidentiality, and compliance with regulatory requirements.

Integration with AWS Services: AWS Lake Formation integrates seamlessly with other AWS services, such as Amazon S3, Amazon Redshift, and Amazon Athena, allowing organizations to leverage the capabilities of these services within the data lake environment. Data stored in the data lake can be analyzed using SQL queries, machine learning algorithms, or business intelligence tools, enabling organizations to derive insights and make data-driven decisions.

AWS Lake Formation simplifies the process of building, securing, and managing data lakes on AWS, enabling organizations to unlock the value of their data assets more efficiently. By providing capabilities for data ingestion, cataloging, security, transformation, and integration, Lake Formation empowers organizations to accelerate innovation, drive business agility, and gain a competitive edge in the digital age.

Amazon DataZone

Amazon DataZone is a new AWS service that provides a comprehensive solution for building and managing data mesh. It enables organizations to decentralize their data ownership, governance, and operations.

With Amazon DataZone, you can:

Define data domains and data assets: Amazon DataZone enables you to organize your data assets within data domain(s). A data domain represents a logical grouping of related data assets.

Establish data ownership: by defining data asset(s) within a project or a domain unit.

Discover and access data products across the organization: data consumers are able to easily discover and access the data products they need, regardless of their location or ownership.

Monitor the data quality: Amazon DataZone is fully integrated with AWS Glue Data Quality; it provides a view of data quality scores and rules.

You can leverage Amazon DataZone connected with other AWS services to build a robust, scalable, and well-governed data mesh within your organization.

We have explored the essential building block services provided by Amazon Web Services (AWS) for implementing a data mesh architecture.

Amazon S3 and Amazon Redshift provide scalable, durable, and cost-effective storage solutions for structured and unstructured data, suitable for building data lakes, data warehouses, and transactional databases.

AWS Glue is a fully managed extract, transform, and load (ETL) service that simplifies the process of data preparation and loading for analytics. It includes a Data Catalog for storing metadata information. AWS Glue integrates seamlessly with other AWS services for data processing, analytics, and machine learning.

AWS Lake Formation is a fully managed service for building, securing, and managing data lakes on AWS. With Lake Formation, organizations can accelerate time-to-insight and ensure data governance, compliance, and security within their data mesh architecture.

Amazon DataZone is a data management service that makes it faster and easier for customers to catalog, discover, share, and govern data stored across AWS, on-premises, and third-party sources.

AWS provides a comprehensive suite of building block services for implementing a data mesh architecture. By leveraging these services, organizations can accelerate innovation, drive business agility, and derive value from their data assets.

Architecture reference patterns for Data Mesh on AWS

The Data Mesh pattern is natively supported by AWS. Mainly, a data mesh is a security architecture that allows data to be shared securely across producer and consumer accounts, standardizes data classification and tag-based security, and distributes security rules between AWS Accounts. When creating a data mesh, AWS follows a set of general design guidelines and offers a range of services to support best practices in the development of scalable data platforms, ubiquitous data sharing, and self-service analytics on AWS.

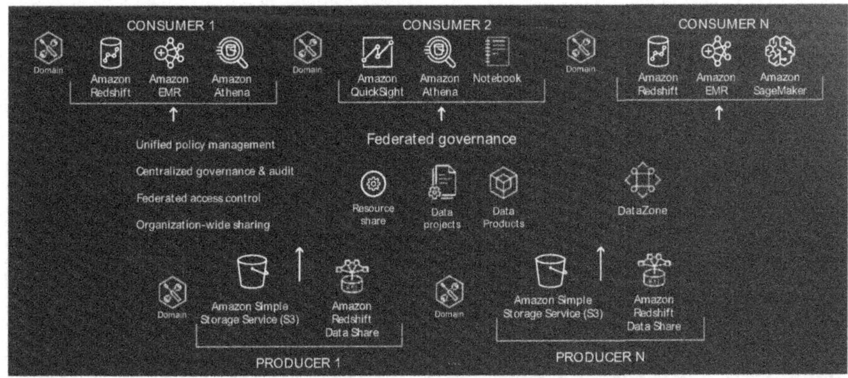

Figure 6.2: Data mesh reference architecture

Fig 2 represents a high-level, logical architecture of a data mesh design in an AWS environment. With a separate data and technology stack from the others, each data domain owns and runs a number of different data products. Data domains can be consumer domains, like a product recommendation service that uses data from other domains to create the product recommendations displayed on an e-commerce website, or purely producer domains, like a finance domain that only produces sales and revenue data for domains to consumers. Producers of data domains make datasets available to the entire company by registering them with a central catalog. They have the freedom to decide what to share, with whom, and for how long. One unified data catalog provides easy access to all data assets. The datasets registered by data domain producers are included in the data catalog together with auxiliary metadata like ownership details, history, data quality measures, and business context. A unified data catalog not only facilitates sharing but also helps users locate available information more quickly. It also enables data owners to set access rights and track usage across business divisions. It's important to note that sharing is done through metadata linking alone. Data isn't copied to the central account, and ownership remains with the producer. The source modalities of data product sharing lead to different data mesh reference architecture patterns such as:

1. Sharing data products from a data lake
2. Sharing data products from a data lake and a data warehouse

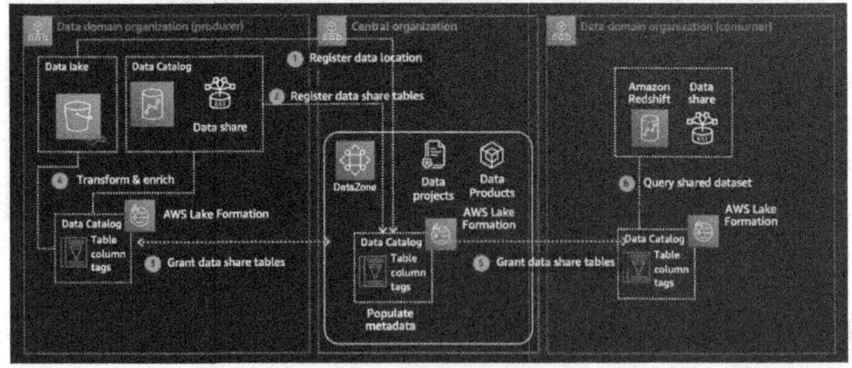

Figure 6.3: Data mesh reference architecture for sharing data products from a data lake (Amazon S3)

As described in the high-level design earlier, you have the three constructs in this architecture pattern, including a producer domain, a consumer domain, and a central governance account. A transformed, enriched, and ready-to-share data product based on a data lake is hosted in the producer domain. The producer domain catalogs all pertinent metadata in the governance account catalog and registers the data product in the central governance account. AWS Lake Formation and

Amazon DataZone enable the domain ownership setup that involves a cycle of all data transformation and metadata updates being reflected from the producer domain account to the central governance account. Following this configuration, domain owners can provide potential customers access to the data products and share them with them. These customers can then create their own catalog and subscribe to the data products. There is no data duplication or copying; instead, the producer domain expands consumer access to its data through federated means. Consumers can then specify the rights required for their users to subscribe to and utilize various engines, like Amazon Athena.

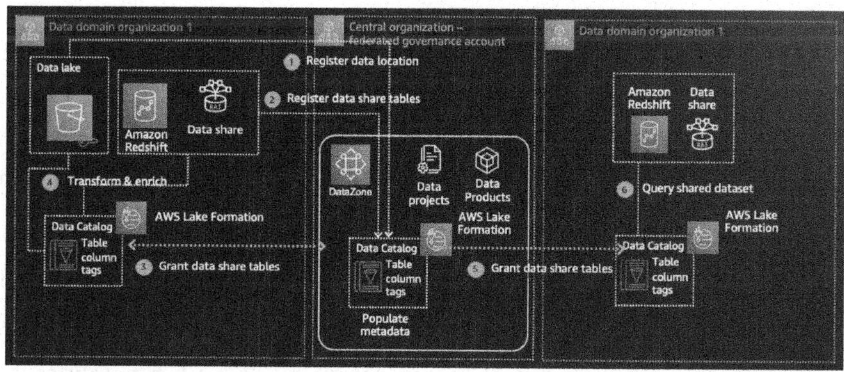

Figure 6.4: Data mesh reference architecture for sharing data products from a data lake (Amazon S3) and a data warehouse (Amazon Redshift)

In this architecture pattern, we look at sharing data products from a data lake and an Amazon Redshift data warehouse. You can share real-time data between Amazon Redshift data warehouses through data sharing. By centrally managing permissions for data sharing throughout the company using AWS Lake Formation, Amazon Redshift facilitates more straightforward governance of Amazon Redshift data sharing. On the tables and views in the Redshift data shares, you may audit permissions, manage permission grants, and check access controls. As with the previous pattern, register the data lake data product, fill in the central catalog, and onboard your data lake into the central account. In a similar vein, establish an AWS Glue Data Catalog federated database that is run by AWS Lake Formation in order to share the Redshift datashare tables with the governance account. Redshift Managed Storage (RMS) provides real-time data sharing; it is not copied or relocated to Amazon S3. Data consumers are able to instantly identify the data in AWS Lake Formation and begin querying data shares from both the warehouse and the data lake.

The above data mesh reference architectures are primarily driven by AWS Lake Formation and Amazon DataZone. We'll cover these services in more detail in the next sections.

Introduction to AWS Lake Formation

Organizations are increasingly recognizing the value of data lakes as a central repository for storing and analyzing large volumes of structured and unstructured data. AWS Lake Formation, a fully managed service offered by Amazon Web Services (AWS), simplifies the process of building, securing, and managing data lakes on the cloud. It provides organizations with a comprehensive set of tools and capabilities to accelerate time-to-insight and derive value from their data assets more efficiently.

AWS Lake Formation serves as a foundational component in building a data mesh architecture, which is a decentralized approach to data management that emphasizes domain-oriented, self-serve data platforms. By providing capabilities for cataloging, security, and access control, AWS Lake Formation enables organizations to establish robust and scalable data ecosystems within a data mesh architecture.

In this section, we will explore the key features and benefits of AWS Lake Formation and its role in simplifying data lake management. AWS

Lake Formation empowers organizations to unlock the full potential of their data assets.

Understanding AWS Lake Formation

AWS Lake Formation is a comprehensive service offered by Amazon Web Services (AWS) designed to simplify and accelerate the process of setting up, securing, and managing data lakes in the cloud. AWS Lake Formation is a powerful service that can serve as the foundation for building a robust data mesh on AWS. By providing a centralized control plane for data lake management, Lake Formation simplifies the creation and administration of a secure, governed data lake.

Data lakes are centralized repositories that allow organizations to store and analyze vast amounts of structured and unstructured data at scale. AWS Lake Formation streamlines the creation and management of data lakes, providing organizations with the tools and capabilities needed to leverage their data effectively for analytics, machine learning, and other data-driven initiatives. The figure below highlights the main challenges solved by AWS Lake Formation.

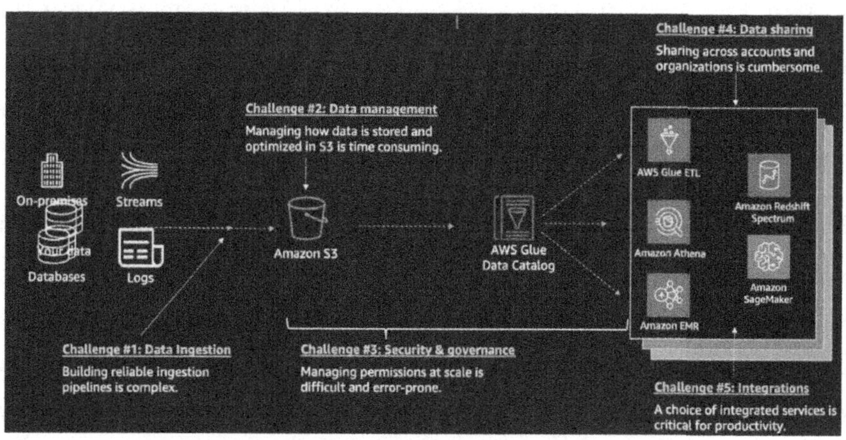

Figure 6.5: Challenges solved by AWS Lake Formation

At its core, AWS Lake Formation provides a set of capabilities for building, securing, and managing data lakes on AWS. These capabilities include:

Data Lake Creation: AWS Lake Formation allows organizations to quickly and easily set up data lakes on AWS using a simple and intuitive interface. Organizations can define their data lake architecture, specify data sources and storage options, and configure security and access controls.

Data Cataloging and Metadata Management: AWS Lake Formation includes a centralized data catalog that automatically catalogs and indexes metadata from various data sources, making it easy to discover, understand, and access data assets within the data lake. The data catalog provides a unified view of data across different formats and sources, enabling organizations to derive insights from diverse datasets.

Security and Access Control: AWS Lake Formation provides robust security features to protect data within the data lake. Organizations can define granular access controls and permissions, ensuring that only authorized users and applications can access sensitive data. AWS Lake Formation integrates with AWS Identity and Access Management (IAM) and AWS Key Management Service (KMS) to enforce encryption, authentication, and authorization policies.

Data Ingestion and Integration: AWS Lake Formation supports seamless data ingestion and integration from a wide range of data sources, including databases, data warehouses, streaming data sources, and object storage services. Organizations can use AWS Glue, a fully managed ETL (Extract, Transform, Load) service, to automate data ingestion, transformation, and loading processes, reducing the time and effort required to prepare data for analysis.

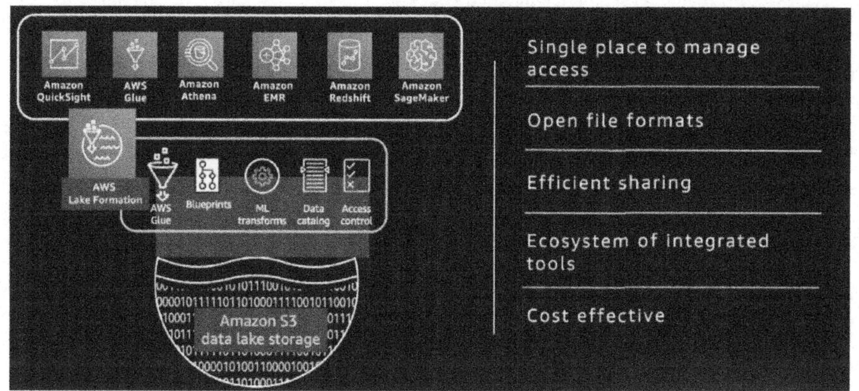

Figure 6.6: Main functionalities of AWS lake Formation

AWS Lake Formation is a powerful service that simplifies and accelerates the process of building, securing, and managing data lakes on AWS. By providing a comprehensive set of capabilities for data lake creation, cataloging, security, and integration, AWS Lake Formation empowers organizations to unlock the full potential of their data assets and drive greater business value through data-driven insights and decision-making.

Implementing a DataMesh with AWS Lake Formation

Implementing a data mesh architecture with AWS Lake Formation involves structuring data lakes and associated data management processes in a way that aligns with the principles of domain-driven data ownership, federated data governance, and self-serve data platforms. This section provides a detailed guide on how to implement a data mesh using AWS Lake Formation, covering the setup, configuration, and management of data lakes and associated data management processes.

1. Setting Up Data Lakes and Data Catalogs

AWS Lake Formation enables the creation of data lakes in the AWS cloud. Define the storage location, data lake architecture, and associated

AWS services (e.g., Amazon S3 buckets) to store data assets securely and durably.

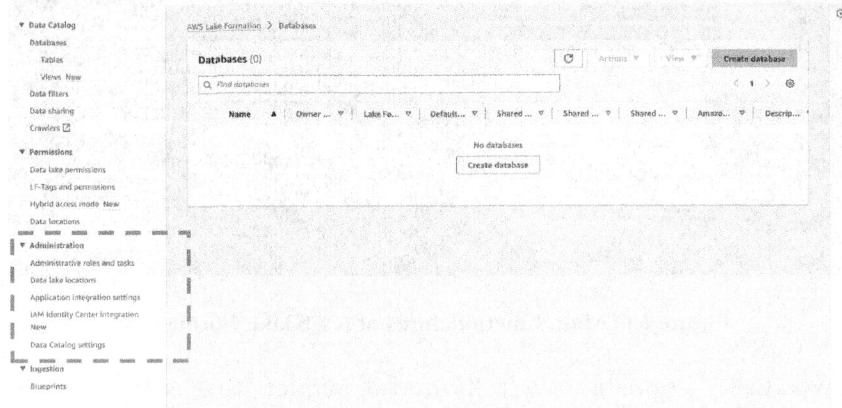

Figure 6.7: AWS Lake Formation console – data lake administration

The first step in building a data mesh is to define clear data domains that align with your organization's business capabilities and ownership. These domains will serve as the building blocks of your data mesh, with each domain responsible for managing and governing its own data assets.

AWS Lake Formation's database and table constructs provide a logical separation of data, allowing you to delegate ownership and access control at the domain level.

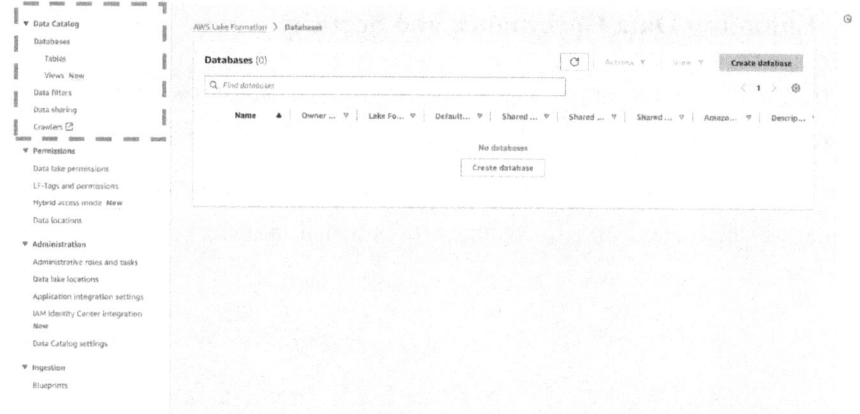

Figure 6.8: AWS Lake Formation console – data catalog

Create domain-specific data catalogs within AWS Lake Formation to organize and manage metadata from diverse data sources. Define schemas, tables, and partitions to catalog metadata and facilitate data discovery and exploration.

For example, let's say your organization has three primary data domains: finance, marketing, and sales. You can create three separate databases in Lake Formation, each representing a distinct data domain: *finance_db*, *marketing_db,* and *sales_db.*

Within each database, you can then create tables that correspond to the specific data assets owned by that domain. This domain-driven approach ensures that data ownership and governance are aligned with your business structure. As data is ingested, Lake Formation automatically catalogs the metadata, including the data's origin, schema, and other relevant information. This centralized data catalog provides a unified view of all the data assets across your data mesh, making it easier for domain teams to discover and access the data they need.

2. Enforcing Data Governance and Security

Configure fine-grained access controls and permissions within AWS Lake Formation to enforce data governance policies and restrict access to sensitive data. Use IAM roles and policies to grant or revoke access to data assets based on user roles and responsibilities.

Figure 6.9: AWS Lake Formation console – permission management

Using Lake Formation's fine-grained access control, you can grant specific permissions to users and groups within each data domain. This allows domain teams to manage access to their data assets independently without compromising the overall security and compliance of the data mesh.

AWS Lake Formation provides the fine-grained access control at different levels:

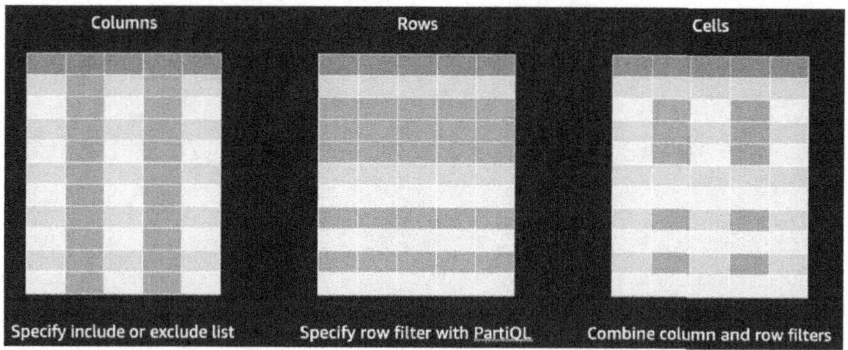

Figure 6.10: Fine Grained Access Control in AWS Lake Formation

Enable encryption-at-rest and encryption-in-transit for data stored in the data lake using AWS KMS and AWS encryption features. Implement encryption policies and key management practices to protect data confidentiality and integrity.

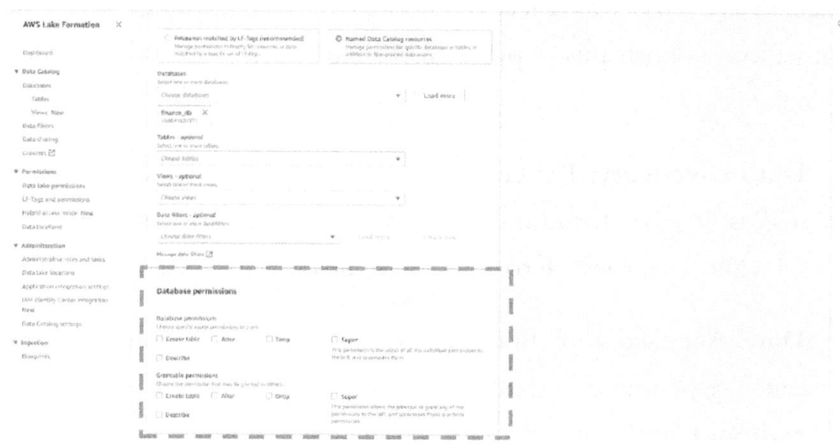

Figure 6.11: AWS Lake Formation console – permission management

3. Building Data Ingestion and Integration Pipelines

Schedule and automate data ingestion pipelines using AWS Glue triggers and workflows. Define data ingestion schedules, dependencies, and error-handling mechanisms to ensure reliable and timely data delivery.

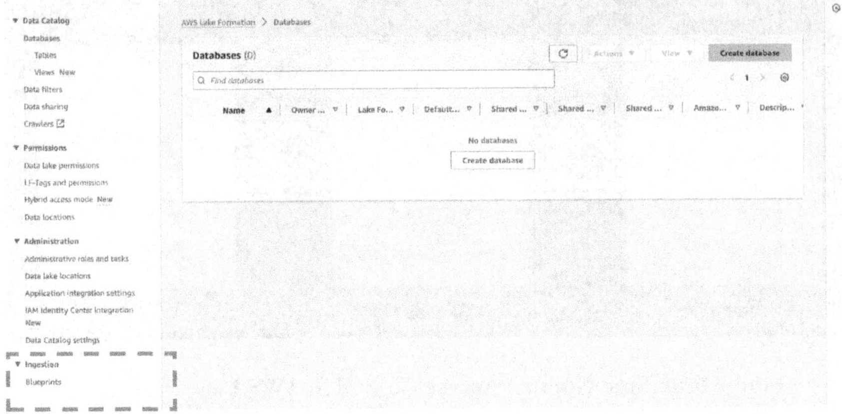

Figure 6.12: AWS Lake Formation console – data integration

4. **Empowering data or business analysts with Self-Serve Data Platforms**

Enabling self-service data access is a core tenet of data mesh. AWS Lake Formation supports this by providing a range of self-service capabilities, including:

- **Data Discovery:** The centralized data catalog in Lake Formation makes it easy for domain teams to search for and discover relevant data assets across the data mesh.

- **Data Access:** With fine-grained access control, domain teams can independently grant and revoke access to their data assets without relying on a centralized data team.

- **Data Transformation:** Lake Formation integrates with AWS Glue, allowing domain teams to create and manage their own data transformation workflows to prepare data for analysis.

Enable domain teams to explore and analyze data using self-serve data exploration tools such as Amazon Athena and Amazon Redshift Spectrum. Grant permissions and access controls to allow domain teams to query and analyze data within their respective data domains.

5. **Monitoring and data quality checks**

AWS monitoring and logging tools, such as Amazon CloudWatch and AWS CloudTrail, are used to monitor data lake performance, resource utilization, and system health. Set up alerts and notifications to proactively detect and respond to performance issues and anomalies.

AWS Glue Data Quality can be used to implement automated data quality processes. Define data quality rules and policies and configure AWS Glue jobs to perform data quality checks as part of data ingestion and transformation pipelines.

We explored the implementation of a data mesh architecture using AWS Lake Formation. AWS Lake Formation is a comprehensive service that simplifies the creation, management, and security of data lakes in the cloud. It provides capabilities for data lake creation, data cataloging, security, data ingestion, and integration. Implementing a data mesh with AWS Lake Formation involves a combination of the following activities:

- Designating data ownership to domain-specific teams promotes accountability and responsibility for managing and curating data assets within each domain. Domain teams are empowered to make data-driven decisions and drive innovation within their areas of expertise.
- Implementing role-based access controls and domain-specific data governance policies ensures that data is managed and accessed according to predefined rules and regulations. This promotes compliance with regulatory requirements and organizational standards.
- Offering self-serve data exploration and analysis tools enables domain teams to access, analyze, and derive insights from data autonomously. This promotes collaboration, innovation, and

agility in data-driven decision-making.

- Implementing data quality assurance processes and automation ensures that data ingested into the data lake meets predefined quality standards. This improves data integrity, reliability, and trustworthiness for downstream analytics and decision-making.
- Continuously monitoring data lake performance and optimizing data processing workflows ensures efficient resource utilization and timely data delivery. This helps maintain the high availability, scalability, and performance of the data lake infrastructure.

By following these key points and best practices, organizations can successfully implement a data mesh architecture using AWS Lake Formation, enabling them to build scalable, agile, and resilient data architectures that empower domain teams to unlock the full potential of their data assets and drive business innovation and growth.

Introduction to Amazon Redshift for Data Sharing

Amazon Redshift is a fully managed, petabyte-scale data warehouse service in the AWS cloud. It is designed to handle large-scale datasets and complex queries with high performance and scalability. Built on top of a massively parallel processing (MPP) architecture, Amazon Redshift distributes data and queries across multiple nodes for parallel processing, enabling fast query performance even on large datasets. The service is deeply integrated with AWS database, analytics, and machine learning services to employ Zero-ETL approaches, build machine learning models in SQL, and enable Apache Spark analytics using data in Redshift.

Sharing Data with Amazon Redshift

Amazon Redshift data sharing operates on the principle of data isolation and access control. The data owner maintains full control over the shared datasets, including data access permissions, while consumers can access the shared data for analysis and reporting. With Amazon Redshift data sharing, you can safely provide access to real-time data between Amazon Redshift clusters, workgroups, AWS accounts, and AWS Regions without physically transferring or copying the data.

Data sharing in Amazon Redshift involves the following key components:

- **Data Providers:** These are users or accounts that own and share datasets with data consumers. Data providers define the shared datasets and manage data access permissions for consumers.

- **Data Consumers:** These are users or accounts that consume shared datasets for analysis and reporting. Data consumers can access shared datasets as read-only views, allowing them to query the data without modifying it.

- **Shared Datasets:** These are datasets shared by data providers with data consumers. Shared datasets are stored in the provider's Amazon Redshift cluster and can be accessed by authorized data consumers through cross-account queries.

Amazon Redshift clusters that share data can be in the same or different AWS accounts or different AWS Regions, so you can share data across organizations and collaborate with other parties. Consumer cluster administrators receive the datashares that they are granted usage for and review the contents of each datashare. To consume shared data, the consumer cluster administrator creates an Amazon Redshift database from the datashare. The administrator then assigns permissions for the database to users and roles in the consumer cluster. After permissions are granted, users and roles can list the shared objects as part of the standard metadata queries, along with the local data on the consumer cluster.

A datashare is the unit of data sharing. Datashare objects are objects from specific databases on a cluster that producer cluster administrators can add to datashares to be shared with data consumers. Datashare objects are read-only for data consumers. Examples of datashare objects are tables, views, and user-defined functions.

There are several types of datashares:

1. Standard Datashares

You can share data between AWS accounts, AWS Regions, Availability Zones, serverless workgroups, and provisioned clusters using standard datashares. Sharing is possible between different kinds of clusters, such as provisioned clusters and Amazon Redshift Serverless.

2. AWS Data Exchange Datashares

A unit of licensing for sharing your data through AWS Data Exchange is called an AWS Data Exchange datashare. Licensed access to your Amazon Redshift data can be easily obtained using AWS Data Exchange for Amazon Redshift. AWS Data Exchange automatically adds a customer as a data consumer on all AWS Data Exchange datashares included with the product when a client subscribes to a product with AWS Data Exchange datashares. Likewise, it also removes all customers from AWS Data Exchange datashares when their subscription ends. AWS Data Exchange automatically manages billing, invoicing, payment collection, and payment distribution for paid products with AWS Data Exchange datashares. Providers can license data in Amazon Redshift at a granular level, such as schemas, tables, views, and user-defined functions. You can use the same AWS Data Exchange datashare across multiple AWS Data Exchange products. Any objects added to the AWS Data Exchange datashare are available to consumers. Producers can view all AWS Data Exchange datashares managed by AWS Data Exchange on their behalf using Amazon Redshift API operations, SQL commands, and the Amazon Redshift console.

3. AWS Lake Formation-managed datashares

You can limit user access to items within an Amazon Redshift datashare and centrally establish and enforce access rights at the database, table, column, and row levels with AWS Lake Formation. You can specify permissions in Lake Formation using column-level filters or tags and apply them to any datashare and its objects by sharing data through Lake Formation. An example of an AWS Lake Formation-managed datashare is the preceding reference architectural pattern for sharing data products from a data lake and a data warehouse.

Accessing Datashares

Amazon Redshift enables the discovery of shared data through standard SQL interfaces, JDBC/ODBC drivers, and the Data API. You can query data with high performance using familiar business intelligence and analytics tools. Redshift allows you to query objects from other local and remote Redshift databases for which you have access permissions by staying connected to local databases in your cluster. You can create consumer databases from datashares to consume shared data and query using external schema links to the consumer database schemas. A single query can reference objects from both the connected database and nonconnected databases, including consumer databases created from datashares.

It also provides metadata views that enable cluster administrators to discover datashares. These views list datashares created within a cluster as well as datashares received from other clusters in the same AWS account, other accounts, or other AWS Regions. The views display information such as:

- Datashares that are shared from and received by clusters.
- Contents of database objects in the datashares, including basic share metadata, objects like tables or schemas, and information about consumer clusters accessing the datashares.

The metadata views help administrators track both the data shares their cluster has sent to others and the data their cluster uses from external sources. By detailing the database objects and consumers involved with each datashare, the following views give visibility into how datashares are being accessed and utilized across clusters.

SVV_DATASHARES: to view a list of all datashares created in your outbound cluster and shared with inbound.

SVV_DATASHARE_CONSUMERS: to view a list of data consumers.

SVV_DATASHARE_OBJECTS: to view a list of objects in all datashares created in your outbound cluster and shared with inbound.

Best Practices for Data Sharing in Amazon Redshift

To maximize the benefits of data sharing in Amazon Redshift, organizations should follow these best practices:

1. **Define Clear Data Access Policies:** Clearly define who can access shared datasets and what level of access they have.
2. **Monitor Data Usage and Performance:** Monitor data sharing activity and query performance to identify bottlenecks and optimize resource utilization.
3. **Optimize Data Distribution and Storage:** Use appropriate

distribution keys and sort keys to optimize data distribution and improve query parallelism.

4. **Secure Data Sharing Across Accounts:** Use AWS Identity and Access Management (IAM) roles and policies to control access to shared datasets and encrypt data in transit and at rest.
5. **Audit Access Policies:** Regularly review and update data access policies to reflect changes in organizational requirements and compliance regulations. Conduct periodic audits of data access permissions to ensure that only authorized users have access to shared datasets.

Amazon Redshift is a fully managed data warehouse service on AWS designed to handle large-scale datasets and complex queries. It uses a massively parallel processing (MPP) architecture to distribute data and queries across multiple nodes, enabling fast performance. Amazon Redshift's data-sharing capabilities allow data owners (data providers) to securely share real-time data with authorized data consumers without physically copying or transferring the data. This is based on the principle of data isolation and access control.

Summary

This chapter has presented the Amazon Web Services (AWS) approach to building a data mesh architecture, which represents a paradigm shift in data management. In a data mesh, data is treated as a product, and each domain or business unit within an organization is responsible for its own data assets, governance, and analytics. This decentralized approach empowers domain teams to manage and derive insights from their data autonomously, breaking down traditional data silos.

AWS plays a pivotal role in enabling organizations to implement a successful data mesh architecture. The chapter highlights several key AWS services that serve as building blocks for a data mesh, including:

- **Amazon S3 and Amazon Redshift:** Scalable and durable storage solutions for structured and unstructured data, enabling the creation of data lakes and data warehouses.

- **AWS Glue:** A fully managed extract, transform, and load (ETL) service that simplifies data preparation and loading for analytics.

- **AWS Lake Formation:** A comprehensive service that streamlines the process of building, securing, and managing data lakes on AWS, providing capabilities for cataloging, security, and access control.

- **Amazon DataZone:** A new AWS service that offers a comprehensive solution for building and managing data mesh architectures, enabling organizations to decentralize data ownership, governance, and operations.

The chapter explores two key reference architecture patterns for implementing a data mesh on AWS:

- **Sharing data products from a data lake:** A producer domain hosts a transformed, enriched, and ready-to-share data product based on a data lake and registers the metadata in a central governance account.

- **Sharing data products from a data lake and a data warehouse:** In addition to the data lake, data products are also shared from an Amazon Redshift data warehouse, leveraging Redshift's data-sharing capabilities.

The chapter delves deeper into the implementation of a data mesh using AWS Lake Formation, covering the setup of data lakes and data catalogs, enforcing data governance and security, building data ingestion and integration pipelines, and empowering domain teams with self-serve data platforms. By leveraging the comprehensive suite of AWS services, organizations can build scalable, agile, and well-governed data mesh architectures that drive innovation, business agility, and data-driven decision-making.

7. Services to power your Data Mesh: Capabilities to Build, Manage, and Share Data Products

In this chapter, we delve into the array of AWS services essential for constructing data products and explore their diverse capabilities. We'll examine how AWS Managed services can be harnessed to create a data mesh and implement federated data governance solutions on the AWS platform. The chapter highlights the comprehensive suite of managed services offered by AWS, which can be leveraged to build a robust and scalable data mesh architecture. This approach empowers organizations to develop high-quality data products and establish effective federated data governance frameworks. We'll explore how these services seamlessly integrate to form a secure, efficient, and scalable data platform, providing a solid foundation for modern data management and analytics. By understanding these tools and their interplay, readers will gain valuable insights into architecting sophisticated data solutions that meet the evolving needs of today's data-driven enterprises.

Various ways to build a data product in AWS

To build successful data products, you need to align people, processes, and technology. Establishing a data product owner role responsible for building data products is crucial, and they need to be supported by a team of data engineers and experts who actually build the product. The data product build needs to implement the organization's data quality rules and implement data lineage. Once the data products are built, they need to be cataloged with business metadata. A good metadata management practice requires a data steward to audit the metadata and work with data product owners to build high-quality metadata.

Here are some key patterns for building data products in a data mesh:

- **Self-serve data infrastructure** - Provide data infrastructure, tools, and platforms that make it easy for teams to access, understand, and build on top of data in a self-serve manner. This includes data catalogs, data pipelines, etc. One of the key patterns for building a data mesh platform is to empower data producers and consumers by providing an infrastructure with the right tools and platforms to build high-quality data products that can be shared in a self-serve way.

- **Domain-oriented decentralization** - Organize data products around domains rather than technology or organizational structure. Domain teams have autonomy and ownership to build data products to serve their domain's needs. The organization of data products should be defined based on domains to ensure better alignment with business needs and enable domain teams to have autonomy and ownership.

- **Mindset** - Optimize for data engineers, data scientists, and other developers who need to build data products. Provide them with APIs, SDKs, and tooling for self-serve access and the ability to build on data.

- **Observability and discoverability** - Make it easy to find, understand, and monitor data products via comprehensive metadata, data catalogs, and observability tools. Support discoverability and collaboration. This includes providing data lineage to capture provenance and dependencies.

- **Product-minded culture** - Take a product approach to building data assets. Focus on understanding customer/user needs, iterate based on feedback, and treat data as a product.

- **Automated governance** - Automate data quality, security, compliance, and other data governance aspects as much as possible via pipelines, validation frameworks, etc. Make governance invisible but embedded.
- **Interoperable standards** - Standardize how data assets are described, accessed, protected, and integrated to promote seamless interoperability between data products. By following these patterns, organizations can effectively build and manage data products in a decentralized and scalable manner, enabling better collaboration, governance, and alignment with business needs.

Understand how to build and expose a data product with AWS Glue

Building a high-quality data product is a multi-step process that involves cleaning, transforming, and profiling data sets. As part of the build, it is critical to design a robust data integration pipeline that can transform the data and maintain its quality. This is where AWS Glue comes into play. AWS Glue is a serverless data integration service that simplifies the process of discovering, preparing, moving, and integrating data from multiple sources. It is designed for analytics, machine learning, and application development workloads.

AWS Glue provides a comprehensive set of tools for authoring, running jobs, and implementing business workflows, thereby enhancing productivity and enabling data operations. One of the key features of AWS Glue is its ability to discover and connect to over 70 diverse data sources, allowing users to manage their data in a centralized data catalog.

Users can visually create, run, and monitor extract, transform, and load (ETL) pipelines to load data into their data lakes. Additionally, cataloged data can be immediately searched and queried using Amazon Athena, Amazon EMR, and Amazon Redshift Spectrum. AWS Glue consolidates major data integration capabilities into a single service, including data discovery, modern ETL, cleansing, transforming, and centralized cataloging.

Being serverless, AWS Glue eliminates the need to manage infrastructure, allowing users to focus on their core tasks. With flexible support for various workloads such as ETL, ELT, and streaming, AWS Glue caters to diverse user types and workloads. One of the key advantages of AWS Glue is its seamless integration with AWS analytics services and Amazon S3 data lakes. It provides integration interfaces and job-authoring tools that are easy to use for users with varying technical skill sets, from developers to business users.

AWS Glue consists of a Data Catalog (a central metadata repository), an ETL engine that can automatically generate Scala or Python code, a flexible scheduler for job monitoring and retries, and AWS Glue DataBrew for cleaning and normalizing data with a visual interface. Together, these features automate many of the undifferentiated tasks involved in data discovery, categorization, cleaning, enrichment, and movement, allowing users to focus more on data analysis. AWS Glue catalog integrates with Amazon DataZone, where a business catalog is built on top of a technical catalog. This integration enables organizations to better understand and manage their data assets, facilitate data governance, and accelerate data-driven decision-making. Furthermore, AWS Glue connects with various data sources and runs data pipelines to conform, transform, and curate data. AWS Glue data quality enables developers to build data quality rules, ensuring the integrity and reliability of the data throughout the integration process. In summary,

AWS Glue is a comprehensive and serverless data integration service that streamlines the process of discovering, preparing, moving, and integrating data from multiple sources. It provides a centralized data catalog, ETL capabilities, data cleansing and transformation tools, and integration with AWS analytics services and data lakes. By automating many of the undifferentiated tasks involved in data integration, AWS Glue enables organizations to focus on extracting valuable insights from their data.

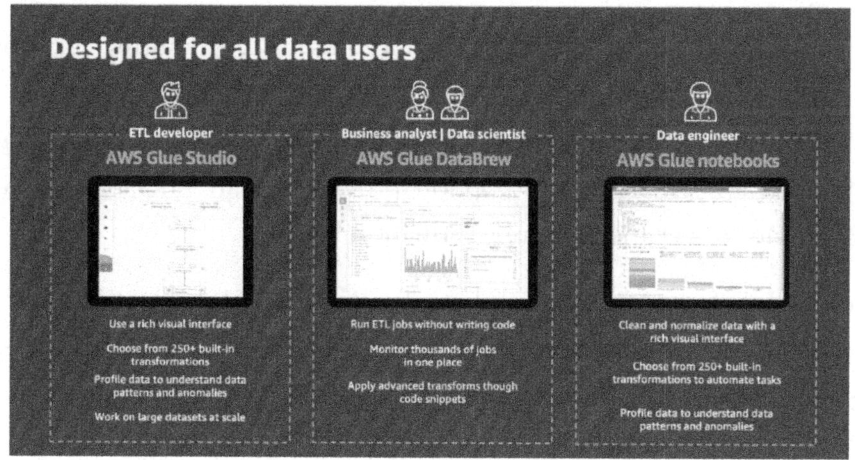

Figure 7.1: Building Data Product using AWS Glue capabilities

Building high-quality, shareable data products for research and development in the Life Sciences domain is a complex endeavor that requires robust data integration, transformation, and governance capabilities. AWS Glue, a fully managed extract, transform, and load (ETL) service provided by Amazon Web Services (AWS), offers a comprehensive set of tools and features to facilitate this process. AWS Glue provides several capabilities to streamline the creation of data products:

1. AWS Glue Studio: This visual interface enables users to build and

manage ETL workflows without writing code. It offers a drag-and-drop canvas, making it easier to design, test, and deploy data integration pipelines.

2. AWS Glue DataBrew: For users who prefer a low-code or no-code approach, AWS Glue DataBrew provides a visual environment for data preparation tasks. It includes pre-built transformations and machine learning-powered recommendations to clean, normalize, and enrich data sources.

3. AWS Glue ETL: For more advanced use cases requiring custom transformations or complex data processing, AWS Glue ETL allows users to develop Apache Spark-based ETL scripts using PySpark or Scala. This option provides greater flexibility and control over the data transformation logic.

In the Life Sciences domain, where data products play a crucial role in research and development, several types of data assets need to be processed and transformed to ensure high quality and compliance with regulatory standards.

Some examples include:

1. Clinical Trial Data Products: Clinical trial data often requires extensive cleaning, standardization, and anonymization to protect patient privacy. ETL pipelines can be built to integrate data from various sources (e.g., electronic data capture systems, lab results, imaging data), apply transformations for data quality and validation, and generate analysis-ready datasets.

2. Genomics-based Data Assets: Genomic data processing involves complex workflows, such as sequence alignment, variant calling, and annotation. AWS Glue can be used to orchestrate these workflows, integrating data from different genomic platforms

and generating curated datasets for downstream analysis.

3. Patient-based Data Assets: Integrating patient data from electronic health records, wearable devices, and other sources requires robust data governance and security measures. AWS Glue can help implement data masking, access controls, and data lineage tracking to ensure compliance with privacy regulations and enable secure sharing within the organization.

Once these clinical data products are built, AWS Glue can facilitate the deployment and sharing process. AWS Glue Data Catalog provides a centralized metadata repository, enabling data discoverability and access control. Additionally, AWS Glue can integrate with other AWS services like Amazon Athena, Amazon Redshift, and Amazon SageMaker for downstream analytics, machine learning, and reporting tasks. By leveraging the capabilities of AWS Glue, Life Sciences organizations can streamline the creation of high-quality, shareable data products, enabling accelerated research, development, and collaboration while maintaining compliance with industry standards and regulations.

AWS Glue Studio provides a user-friendly visual interface that simplifies the process of creating Extract, Transform, and Load (ETL) jobs, enabling seamless data integration and transformation. This interface empowers users to design and configure their data integration workflows without the need for extensive coding expertise.

However, for more advanced use cases or specific customizations, AWS Glue Studio also offers the flexibility to leverage the power of scripting and notebooks within the same environment. To embark on creating a new ETL job in AWS Glue Studio, users can navigate to the dedicated Jobs page.

This centralized hub serves as a comprehensive management console, allowing users to monitor and oversee all their existing jobs, as well as initiate the creation of new ones. Upon initiating the process of creating a new job, the visual interface guides users through a streamlined series of steps, enabling them to specify the data sources they wish to extract from, define the transformations to be applied, and designate the target destinations for the transformed data.

The visual interface in AWS Glue Studio presents a user-friendly experience, abstracting away the complexities of underlying code and enabling users to focus on the logical flow of their data integration processes. Users can leverage pre-built connectors and transformations or create custom ones, all within the visual canvas. This approach empowers users to quickly prototype, iterate, and refine their ETL jobs without the need for extensive coding.

However, for users who require more advanced capabilities or seek to leverage specific customizations, AWS Glue Studio seamlessly integrates with a script editor and notebook environment.

This powerful combination allows users to write and execute code directly within the AWS Glue Studio environment, enabling them to leverage the full breadth of AWS Glue's functionality and extend their ETL jobs with custom logic or advanced transformations.

The script editor and notebook environment within AWS Glue Studio supports various programming languages, such as Python and Scala, enabling users to leverage their existing coding skills and the vast ecosystem of libraries and frameworks available for data processing and analysis.

This empowers users to tackle complex data integration challenges, implement custom algorithms, and extend the capabilities of their ETL jobs beyond the visual interface. By combining the user-friendly visual interface with the power of scripting and notebooks, AWS Glue Studio caters to a broad range of user skill sets and requirements.

Whether users prefer a code-free experience or require the flexibility of coding, AWS Glue Studio provides a comprehensive and integrated environment for building and managing robust data integration pipelines.

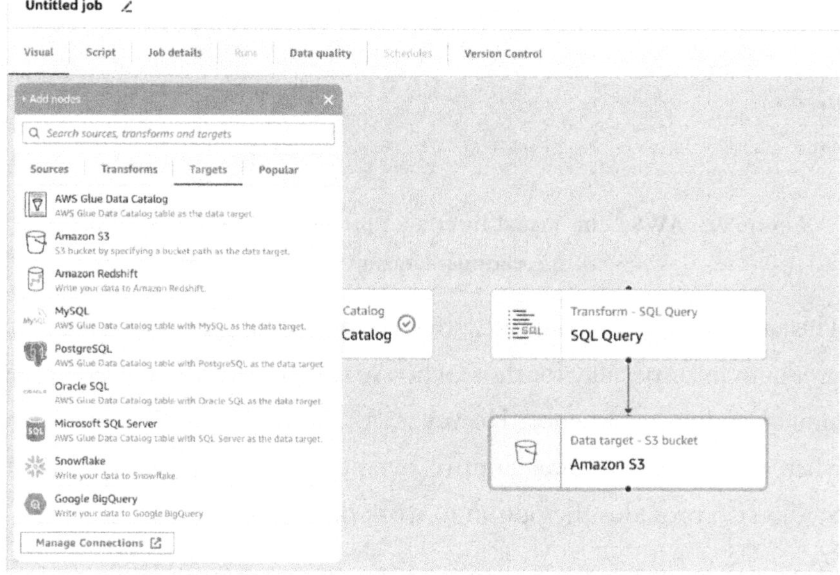

Figure 7.2: Visual interface provides a list of targets

One of the key advantages of the visual interface is its intuitive nature, which makes it accessible to users with varying levels of technical expertise. You can easily drag and drop components, configure parameters, and define data transformations using a user-friendly graphical representation.

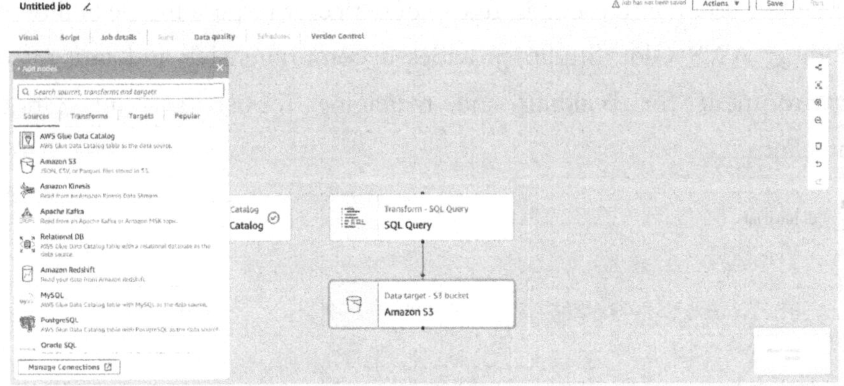

Figure 7.3: AWS Glue Visual Interfaces provides an option to connect to various data sources

This approach can significantly reduce the learning curve and increase productivity, especially for those who are new to data integration or have limited coding experience. However, for more advanced scenarios or when you require greater control over the ETL process, AWS Glue Studio also provides the option to work directly with code.

Within the same Studio environment, you can access a script editor or a notebook interface. The script editor allows you to write and edit Python or Scala scripts that define the logic and transformations for your ETL jobs.

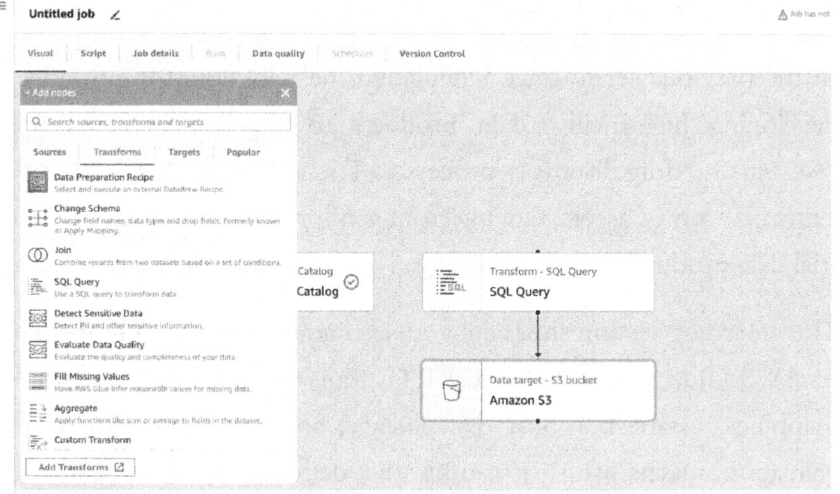

Figure 7. 4: AWS Glue Visual Interfaces provides an option to select transformation jobs like detecting sensitive data to accelerate the data management and pipeline

This approach provides greater flexibility and customization capabilities, enabling you to leverage the full power of programming languages and libraries. Additionally, AWS Glue Studio supports the use of notebooks, which are interactive coding environments that combine code, visualizations, and documentation. Notebooks can be particularly useful for data exploration, prototyping, and debugging ETL jobs.

They allow you to execute code cells, analyze intermediate results, and iterate on your transformations in an interactive manner. By combining the simplicity of the visual interface with the power of scripting and notebooks, AWS Glue Studio caters to a wide range of user preferences and skill levels. Whether you prefer a more visual approach or prefer to work directly with code, AWS Glue Studio provides the tools and flexibility to create and manage your ETL jobs effectively.

AWS Glue DataBrew and Data Profiling

In the previous section, we highlighted the paramount importance of developing high-quality data products to expedite and streamline research and drug discovery processes. These data products encompass a diverse array of assets, ranging from genomic data resources to clinical trial data products.

The preceding section sheds light on leveraging the powerful capabilities of AWS Glue Studio and visual ETL tools to construct intricate data mappings, establish robust data lineage, and implement robust data validation mechanisms. Ensuring the delivery of high-quality data products necessitates a thorough assessment of key metrics, encompassing frequency distributions and value counts. Frequency distributions provide invaluable insights into the distribution of data values within a dataset, enabling the identification of potential anomalies, outliers, or missing data points.

These distributions offer a visual representation of how data is distributed across different categories or ranges, allowing for a deeper understanding of the data's characteristics and potential issues. Value counts, on the other hand, offer a quantitative measure of the occurrences of specific values within a dataset. This metric is particularly useful for identifying potential data quality issues, such as erroneous or inconsistent entries, as well as for uncovering patterns or trends within the data. Among the key metrics to be evaluated are the number of null values, distinct values, and unique values. Null values represent missing or unavailable data points, which can have profound implications for downstream analysis and modeling processes. Identifying and addressing null values is crucial to ensure the completeness and reliability of the data.

Distinct values refer to the count of non-null values that are unique and different from one another within a dataset. This metric is particularly useful for assessing the diversity of data points and identifying potential duplicates or redundant entries, which can skew analysis results and lead to erroneous conclusions. Unique values, conversely, represent the count of values that occur only once within a dataset, with no duplicates or repeated occurrences.

This metric is crucial for identifying potential data quality issues, such as erroneous or inconsistent entries, and ensuring the integrity and reliability of the data. By rigorously assessing these key metrics, researchers and data scientists can gain a comprehensive understanding of the data quality and make informed decisions regarding data cleaning, transformation, and preprocessing steps. Addressing data quality issues through techniques such as data imputation, deduplication, and standardization can significantly enhance the reliability and usability of the data products.

Ultimately, this meticulous process of data quality assessment and remediation enhances the reliability and usability of the data products, facilitating more accurate and insightful analyses. This, in turn, accelerates the pace of research and drug discovery endeavors, enabling researchers and pharmaceutical companies to make informed decisions, identify promising drug candidates, and potentially bring life-saving treatments to market more efficiently.

Data profiling is an essential process in data analytics and data engineering that involves examining and understanding the characteristics, structure, quality, and statistical properties of datasets. AWS Glue is a fully managed extract, transform, and load (ETL) service provided by Amazon Web Services (AWS) that includes a powerful data profiling feature.

Here's how you can perform data profiling using AWS Glue:

1. Create an AWS Glue Crawler: The first step is to create an AWS Glue Crawler, which is a program that connects to a data store, extracts metadata, and generates a Data Catalog. When creating the Crawler, you can specify the data source (e.g., Amazon S3, Amazon RDS, Amazon Redshift, etc.) and configure the Crawler to automatically run on a schedule or on-demand.

2. Run the Crawler: After creating the Crawler, run it to extract the metadata from your data source. The Crawler will populate the AWS Glue Data Catalog with the schema information, data types, and other metadata about your datasets.

3. View Data Profiles: Once the Crawler has completed its run, you can view the data profiles for your datasets in the AWS Glue Console. Navigate to the "Data Catalog" section and select the table or partition for which you want to view the data profile.

    a) Analyze Data Profiling: AWS Glue's data profile feature stands as a beacon of insight, illuminating the depths of your dataset with unprecedented clarity. This powerful tool unfurls a panoramic view of your information, presenting a meticulously detailed table schema alongside a wealth of statistical revelations—from row counts and extreme values to distributions and distinct value frequencies. Armed with this comprehensive analysis, data professionals can navigate the intricacies of their datasets with confidence, making informed decisions that optimize processing, enhance quality, and unlock the full potential of their data assets.

    b) Compliance: Identifies potential data quality issues, such as null values, duplicates, and data type mismatches.

c) Bloom Filter: Provides a probabilistic data structure that can be used to efficiently check if a value is present in a dataset or not.

d) Customize Data Profiling: AWS Glue also allows you to customize data profiling by creating and scheduling AWS Glue Jobs. These Jobs can be written in Apache Spark or Python, and you can use them to perform advanced data profiling operations, such as custom data quality checks, data transformations, and generating custom reports.

By leveraging the data profiling capabilities of AWS Glue, organizations can gain valuable insights into their data, uncover potential data quality issues, and make informed decisions about data cleaning, transformation, and integration processes.

Integrate with Other AWS Services

The data profiles generated by AWS Glue can be easily integrated with other AWS services. For example, you can export the data profiles to Amazon Athena for querying and analysis or use them as input for AWS Glue ETL jobs to perform data cleansing and transformation tasks. By leveraging the data profiling capabilities of AWS Glue, you can gain valuable insights into your data, identify data quality issues, and make informed decisions about data cleansing, transformation, and analysis tasks. This can help improve the overall quality and reliability of your data analytics pipelines.

AWS Glue DataBrew

AWS Glue DataBrew is a visual data preparation tool that allows you to perform data profiling and data quality analysis on your datasets. It is a part of the AWS Glue service, which is a fully managed extract, transform, and load (ETL) service offered by Amazon Web Services

(AWS). Here are some key features and use cases of AWS Glue DataBrew for data profiling:

- Data Profiling: DataBrew provides a wide range of data profiling capabilities that includes a panoramic view of various data types, statistics (min, max, mean, etc.), null values, and patterns for individual columns in a table.

- Data Quality Analysis: DataBrew allows you to define and enforce data quality rules to ensure data integrity. You can create rules based on various conditions, such as allowed values, data formats, and range checks. DataBrew will highlight any data quality issues, making it easier to address them before further processing.

- Data Visualization: DataBrew provides interactive data visualizations, such as histograms, scatter plots, and box plots, to help you explore and understand your data better.

- Data Transformation: While data profiling is the primary focus of DataBrew, it also offers data transformation capabilities. You can perform operations like filtering, joining, and basic transformations directly within the DataBrew interface.

- Integration with AWS Glue: DataBrew is tightly integrated with AWS Glue, allowing you to easily import data from various sources, such as Amazon S3, Amazon Athena, Amazon RDS, and more. The profiling results and transformations performed in DataBrew can be seamlessly incorporated into your AWS Glue ETL jobs.

Collaboration and Governance:

AWS Glue DataBrew is an exceptional and all-encompassing data preparation tool that empowers users to efficiently process, refine, and enhance data for subsequent analysis and machine learning operations. Its remarkable features streamline the intricate process of data preparation, providing a secure and collaborative platform for teams to collaborate seamlessly.

One of DataBrew's most significant strengths lies in its robust collaborative capabilities. It allows teams to work harmoniously on data preparation tasks, with multiple users capable of accessing and contributing to datasets concurrently. This feature encourages effective teamwork and cross-functional cooperation, expediting the data preparation journey through the allocation of tasks and the exchange of insights among team members. Moreover, DataBrew's user-friendly interface ensures inclusivity, facilitating seamless collaboration among data engineers, analysts, and business stakeholders, regardless of their technical proficiency.

Data security and governance are other key priorities for DataBrew. Administrators can configure granular permissions through access control mechanisms, thereby ensuring that data access and modifications are restricted to authorized users. Comprehensive audit logs are implemented to meticulously track user activities, enabling organizations to maintain a detailed audit trail and meet critical compliance standards. This level of security and governance is paramount for organizations operating in regulated industries or managing sensitive data.

DataBrew offers a comprehensive range of transformation and enrichment capabilities, empowering users to clean, normalize, and enrich their data through a variety of built-in and customizable transformations. These transformations can be applied both interactively and through automated coding, allowing for agile and efficient iterations.

Furthermore, DataBrew seamlessly integrates with an array of AWS services, including Amazon S3, Amazon Athena, and Amazon Redshift. This integration facilitates smooth data ingestion and establishes a harmonious connection with existing data ecosystems. As a result, organizations can seamlessly incorporate DataBrew into their existing data infrastructure, thus simplifying end-to-end data pipelines.

In summary, AWS Glue DataBrew is a formidable and comprehensive data preparation solution that empowers organizations to efficiently manage and refine their data. Through its collaborative nature, robust security and governance frameworks, advanced data quality assessment tools, and extensive transformation capabilities, DataBrew enables teams to unlock the full potential of their data, thereby driving informed decision-making and precise analytical insights across a multitude of industries and use cases.

AWS Glue Data Quality

AWS Glue Data Quality is an incredible feature within the AWS Glue suite that revolutionizes the way organizations manage and monitor the quality of their data. It provides a comprehensive and automated approach to data quality measurement, monitoring, and improvement, making it easier than ever to ensure trust in your data-driven decisions.

One of the standout features of AWS Glue Data Quality is its automatic rule recommendation. It analyzes data in your data lakes and pipelines, identifying potential data quality issues and suggesting rules to address them. This not only reduces the manual effort involved in data quality management but also ensures that potential issues are identified and dealt with promptly. Of course, you also have the flexibility to customize these rules to your specific needs.

You can modify the automatically generated rules, add additional rules from the wide range of built-in rule types, and even create custom rules using the Data Quality Definition Language (DQDL). DQDL is a powerful domain-specific language designed specifically for data quality rules, providing a robust and flexible way to define the quality constraints that matter most to your organization.

To take it a step further, AWS Glue Data Quality also enables you to integrate these data quality rules into your data pipelines. You can include rules in AWS Glue data pipelines and schedule them to run at specific intervals.

This ensures a continuous validation of your data, providing regular assessments of your data quality scores. What's more, the data quality scores calculated by AWS Glue Data Quality aren't just for technical teams. With the integration of Amazon DataZone, these scores can be seamlessly incorporated into your business catalog.

This makes it easy for data consumers and producers to understand the quality of the data they're working with, fostering collaboration and ensuring everyone is on the same page when it comes to data quality.

By leveraging AWS Glue Data Quality, organizations can transform their approach to data management. With accurate and timely assessments of data quality, as well as a comprehensive framework for defining and enforcing data quality rules, organizations can make more informed decisions, optimize their operations, and unlock the full potential of their data. It's a game-changer for any business that relies on the quality and reliability of its data assets.

AWS Glue Data Catalog

AWS Glue consists of a Data Catalog that automates much of the undifferentiated heavy lifting involved with discovering, categorizing, cleaning, enriching, and moving data so you can spend more time analyzing your data.

For instance, a clinical data product comprises various data assets, such as patient records and encounter details. As we develop these data products, we incorporate essential elements like data lineage, data quality measures, transformation pipelines, and data profiling. An AWS Glue catalog plays a crucial role in this process by providing a centralized metadata repository to describe the data product and associate lineage and quality information with the individual assets and their respective columns.

The AWS Glue catalog acts as a comprehensive data catalog, storing metadata about the structure, schema, and properties of the data assets within the data product. This metadata includes information about the data sources, data types, partitioning schemes, and any transformations applied to the data.

Additionally, the catalog allows for the tracking of data lineage, which provides visibility into the origin and transformation history of each data element. By leveraging the AWS Glue catalog, data engineers can document and maintain the lineage of the data assets, enabling them to trace the flow of data from its source through various transformations and processing steps. This lineage information is invaluable for understanding the provenance of the data and ensuring its integrity and reliability.

AWS Glue Crawler

AWS Glue crawler is a powerful tool that simplifies the process of building and maintaining a data catalog, which is a critical component of any data lake or data warehouse architecture.

A data catalog is a centralized repository that stores metadata (data about data) such as table and column names, data types, schemas, and other relevant information about the data sources within an organization.

The AWS Glue crawler is designed to automatically discover and catalog data sources, whether they are stored in Amazon S3, Amazon RDS, Amazon Redshift, or other supported data stores. It can crawl through these data sources, infer their schemas, and extract the relevant metadata, which is then stored in the AWS Glue Data Catalog. One of the key benefits of using the AWS Glue crawler is that it reduces the manual effort required to maintain the data catalog.

Without a crawler, data engineers would need to manually define and update the metadata for each data source, which can be a time-consuming and error-prone process, especially in environments with a large number of data sources or frequent schema changes.

The AWS Glue crawler can be scheduled to run periodically or triggered on demand, ensuring that the data catalog stays up-to-date with the latest changes in the data sources. This feature is particularly valuable in scenarios where data sources are frequently updated, or new data sources are added to the environment.

In addition to automated metadata discovery and cataloging, the AWS Glue crawler can also perform data quality checks, such as identifying and cataloging partitions within data sources. This capability can greatly simplify data processing tasks by allowing users to easily filter and access specific partitions of data rather than having to process the entire data set. Overall, the AWS Glue crawler plays a crucial role in enabling effective data management and governance within AWS data environments.

Automating the process of building and maintaining a comprehensive data catalog empowers data analysts, scientists, and engineers to easily discover, understand, and access the data they need, ultimately facilitating more efficient and informed data-driven decision-making.

GenerativeAI capabilities in AWS Glue

Amazon Q data integration in AWS Glue, a capability of Amazon Q Developer, enables you to build data integration pipelines using natural language. Describe your intent through a chat interface, and Amazon Q data integration in AWS Glue will generate a complete job. You can test the job and put it into production with a single click.

ETL pipelines and data engineering processes often involve complex transformations, data cleansing, and data integration tasks. Generative AI capabilities can be leveraged to assist and streamline various aspects of these processes.

1. Data Classification and Cataloging: AWS Glue can leverage generative AI models to automatically classify and catalog data sources based on their content and metadata.

2. Data Transformation and Mapping: GenAI models can assist in understanding the structure and semantics of data sources, which can help in automating the data transformation and mapping processes.

3. Data Quality and Anomaly Detection: GenAI models can be trained to detect data quality issues, anomalies, and inconsistencies in data sources.

4. Documentation and Metadata Generation: GenAI models can be used to automatically generate documentation and metadata descriptions for data sources, transformations, and workflows within AWS Glue.

5. Natural Language Querying: AWS Glue can integrate with genAI models to enable natural language querying of data sources and ETL workflows. This can make it easier for non-technical users to interact with and understand the data integration processes.

Understand how to build and expose a data product with Amazon EMR

Building high-quality data products in a data mesh architecture using Amazon EMR (Elastic MapReduce) involves several steps and considerations. A data mesh architecture involves decentralized data ownership and management, enabling domain-specific teams to build and maintain their own data products while adhering to organizational standards.

Data products can be built as source-based assets or created and processed data products. Multiple stages of data products can be built using Amazon EMR, which can expose a consumer to multiple endpoints that can be easily found and used to build analytics.

1. Data Ingestion and Storage: Identify the various data sources (databases, data lakes, streaming data, etc.) that will feed into your data mesh. Leverage AWS services like Amazon S3 (data lake), Amazon Kinesis (streaming data), and Amazon DynamoDB (NoSQL database) to ingest and store raw data from different sources.

2. Data Processing and Transformation: Provision Amazon EMR

clusters for distributed data processing and transformation tasks. Utilize open-source frameworks like Apache Spark or Apache Hive running on EMR to clean, transform, and enrich raw data into consumable data products.

3. Data Governance and Quality: Define and implement data quality rules, policies, and metrics to ensure the integrity, consistency, and trustworthiness of data products. Establish data governance frameworks, including data access controls, data lineage tracking, and compliance with relevant regulations (e.g., GDPR, HIPAA).

4. Self-Service Data Platform: Build a self-service data platform using AWS Lake Formation, Amazon Athena, and Amazon QuickSight to empower data consumers (analysts, data scientists, etc.) to discover, access, and analyze data products.

5. Continuous Integration and Deployment: Set up a CI/CD pipeline using AWS CodePipeline, AWS CodeBuild, and AWS CodeDeploy to automate the build, testing, and deployment of data products.

6. Monitoring and Observability: Implement monitoring and logging solutions using AWS CloudWatch, AWS CloudTrail, and AWS Lambda functions to monitor the performance, health, and resource utilization of EMR clusters and other AWS services.

7. Collaboration and Communication: Foster collaboration and communication among data producers, data consumers, and data stewards within the data mesh.

8. Continuous Improvement: Building a data mesh architecture with Amazon EMR and other AWS services is an iterative process that requires close collaboration between different teams

and stakeholders. It's essential to align your implementation with your organization's specific needs, goals, and data governance requirements while fostering a decentralized, domain-driven approach to data management and product development.

Amazon EMR simplifies the process of running and scaling open-source distributed data processing frameworks like Apache Hadoop, Apache Spark, and others. Amazon EMR offers a range of capabilities that make it well-suited for data processing and analysis.

Amazon EMR enables distributed computing, allowing organizations to process and analyze vast amounts of data efficiently. Amazon EMR enables distributed computing, allowing organizations to process and analyze vast amounts of data efficiently.

Amazon EMR supports machine learning, enabling organizations to build and train machine learning models on large datasets for applications such as disease prediction, drug discovery, and personalized medicine. Amazon EMR can process real-time streaming data from sources like patient monitoring devices or telemedicine platforms using frameworks like Apache Kafka, Apache Flink, or Apache Spark Streaming, enabling real-time data analysis and decision-making.

Amazon EMR provides various security features, such as data encryption, access control, and integration with AWS Identity and Access Management (IAM), ensuring the protection and compliance of sensitive data.

Using Generative AI with Amazon EMR

EMR is primarily designed for batch processing and analytics workloads; it can also be used to integrate with and support generative AI workloads in several ways:

- Data Preprocessing: Generative AI models often require large amounts of data for training and fine-tuning. EMR can be used to preprocess and transform the data into the required formats, such as text cleaning, image resizing, or feature engineering.

- Distributed Model Training: Some generative AI models, like large language models or generative adversarial networks (GANs), can benefit from distributed training across multiple nodes. EMR's managed Spark or Hadoop clusters can be used to parallelize and distribute the training process, leveraging the scalability and performance of the EMR infrastructure.

- Inference at Scale: Once trained, generative AI models can be deployed on EMR clusters for inference at scale. EMR can handle high-throughput inference requests, enabling real-time generation or transformation of data (e.g., text generation, image synthesis) across multiple nodes.

- Data Pipelines: EMR can be integrated into data pipelines that involve generative AI models. For example, you could use EMR to preprocess data, then trigger a machine learning workflow on Amazon SageMaker for model training, and finally deploy the trained model back on EMR for inference.

- Batch Processing: While generative AI models are often used for real-time applications, EMR can also be used for batch processing of generative tasks. For instance, you could use EMR to generate synthetic data or transform large datasets using a generative model in a batch mode.

- To integrate generative AI workloads with EMR, you typically need to bring your own models or use pre-trained models from frameworks like TensorFlow, PyTorch, or Hugging Face.

Understand how to build and expose a data product with AWS Clean Rooms

AWS Clean Rooms is a secure data collaboration service that enables organizations to analyze and gain insights from combined datasets without sharing or exposing the underlying data. Here's a high-level overview of how to build and expose a data product with AWS Clean Rooms:

1. Set up AWS Clean Rooms: Begin by setting up AWS Clean Rooms in your AWS account. This involves creating a Clean Room and defining the necessary access controls and permissions.

2. Onboard Data Providers: Identify the data providers (organizations or partners) whose datasets you want to combine and analyze. Onboard these data providers to your Clean Room by creating data provider entities and inviting them to join.

3. Upload and Configure Data: Each data provider uploads their data to AWS Clean Rooms. This data remains private and isolated within the Clean Room. Configure the data by defining data types, schemas, and metadata.

4. Create Data Products: Data products are the analytical outputs derived from the combined datasets within the Clean Room. Define the data products you want to create, such as aggregated reports, statistical models, or machine learning models.

5. Define Analytics and Queries: Specify the analytics and queries you want to run on the combined datasets to generate the desired data products. You can use AWS Clean Rooms' built-in querying capabilities or integrate with other AWS services like Amazon Athena or AWS Glue.

6. Run Analytics and Generate Data Products: Once the data providers have uploaded their data and the analytics are defined, run the queries or analytical workloads within the Clean Room to generate the data products.

7. Expose Data Products: After generating the data products, you can expose them to authorized data consumers (e.g., analysts, partners, or customers) within the Clean Room. Data consumers can access and analyze the data products without having direct access to the underlying raw data.

8. Manage Access and Permissions: Use AWS Clean Rooms' access control and permission management capabilities to govern who can access the data products and what actions they can perform (e.g., view, query, export).

9. Monitor and Audit: AWS Clean Rooms provides monitoring and auditing capabilities to track usage, access, and activities within the Clean Room, helping you maintain compliance and data governance.

10. Integrate with Other AWS Services: AWS Clean Rooms can be integrated with other AWS services, such as AWS Glue, Amazon Athena, and AWS Lake Formation, to enhance data processing, querying, and lake house capabilities.

The underlying raw data remains isolated and inaccessible to unauthorized parties, while the derived data products can be securely shared and analyzed within the Clean Room environment.

8. Build a Data Product on a Big Data Platform

A data product is a technology-based solution or service designed to help users extract value from data. Data products are highly trusted, reusable, and consumable data assets that have data as their core component. They provide specific capabilities and functionalities to address customers' data-related needs, acting as a bridge between data producers and data consumers.

The goal of data products is to make data accessible, reusable, consumable, insightful, and actionable for the increasing number of stakeholders and generative AI that rely on data to inform decision-making. Data products leverage data analysis, processing, and visualization techniques to generate meaningful insights or support AI and machine learning, presenting them in an easy-to-use way.

Some key characteristics of data products include:

- **Scalability:** The data product can handle growing data volumes and user demands without compromising performance or reliability.
- **Domain-centric:** The domain model enhances data understanding and adds business context by housing the business logic of transformations, analytics calculations, metrics, and machine learning.
- **Modular and reusable:** They are built once and then reused multiple times in various use cases, so new ones can be built using existing ones.

- **Discoverable and self-service:** The data product is easily discoverable by potential users and provides self-service access and consumption capabilities.

- **Continuously improved:** Data products should undergo regular reviews, feedback collection, and iterative improvements to address user needs, adapt to changing business requirements, and leverage new data sources or technologies.

- **Interoperable:** Comprised of one or more datasets that work with each other to bring holistic, unbiased data insights.

- **Reusable:** Built of composable elements that can be used to build several data products, as well as derivative data products.

Data products are engineered to drive different business outcomes through both transactional and analytical workloads. Some common use cases include predicting customer churn, preparing datasets, tokenizing sensitive customer data, automated decision-making, publishing, and migrating customer data, recommendation systems, predictive models, and data analytics platforms.

AWS Glue/EMR/Athena to Create Data Products

We will be showcasing a step-by-step instruction on how to use Data Products as a Data Analytics platform, utilizing AWS services like S3, Glue, and Athena to collect, store, and derive insights from a CSV file data product. For this instruction, we will be showing you how you can expose some of these data products to our ETL service, Glue. We would be focusing on our big data platform, Glue, to create a central repository of our data to make it easily discoverable and reusable for different use cases.

For this, we assume you already have an AWS account. If not, the first step will be to sign up for an AWS account because you will need that to work through the steps.

Loading data into S3

We would be loading this data from our local machine into S3; this is just one of the many various ways by which you can upload data into S3. We would be exploring this option for the instructions:

- Sign in to the AWS Management Console and open the Amazon S3 console
- In the left navigation pane, choose Buckets

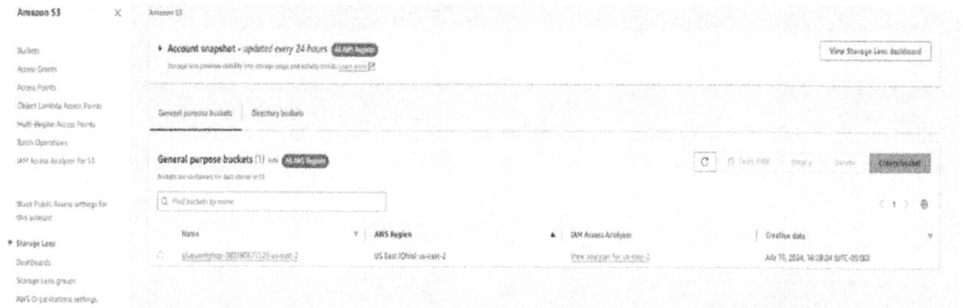

Figure 8.1: Amazon S3 buckets

- Choose Create bucket

Once you get the **Create Bucket** page:

- Under **General configuration**, view the AWS Region where your bucket will be created
- For the **Bucket name**, enter a name for your bucket, e.g., "any company."
- Under Object Ownership, to disable or enable ACLs and control ownership of objects uploaded in your bucket, choose one of the following settings: **ACLs disabled or enabled** (you can leave at

the recommended option)

- Under **Block Public Access settings for this bucket**, choose the Block Public Access settings that you want to apply to the bucket. By default, all four Block Public Access settings are enabled.

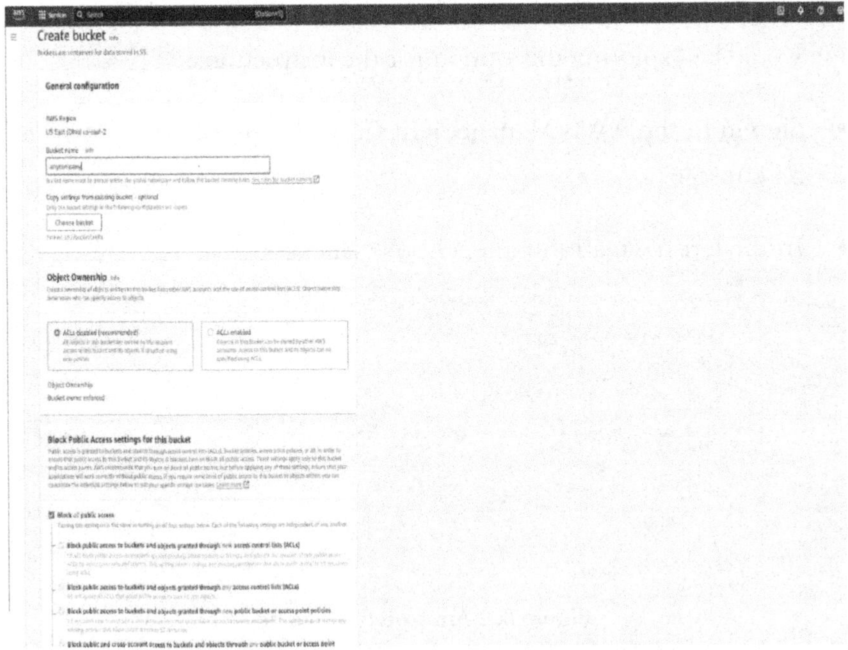

Figure 8.2: Parameters to create a new bucket

- (Optional) **Under Tags**, you can choose to add tags to your bucket. Tags are key-value pairs used to categorize storage. (To add a bucket tag, enter a Key and optionally a Value and choose Add Tag.)

- Under **Default encryption**, select an encryption type, or you can use the default selected.

- (Optional) Choose **Advanced Settings**. If you want to enable Object Lock, choose Enable, read the warning that appears, and acknowledge it

- Choose **Create bucket**.

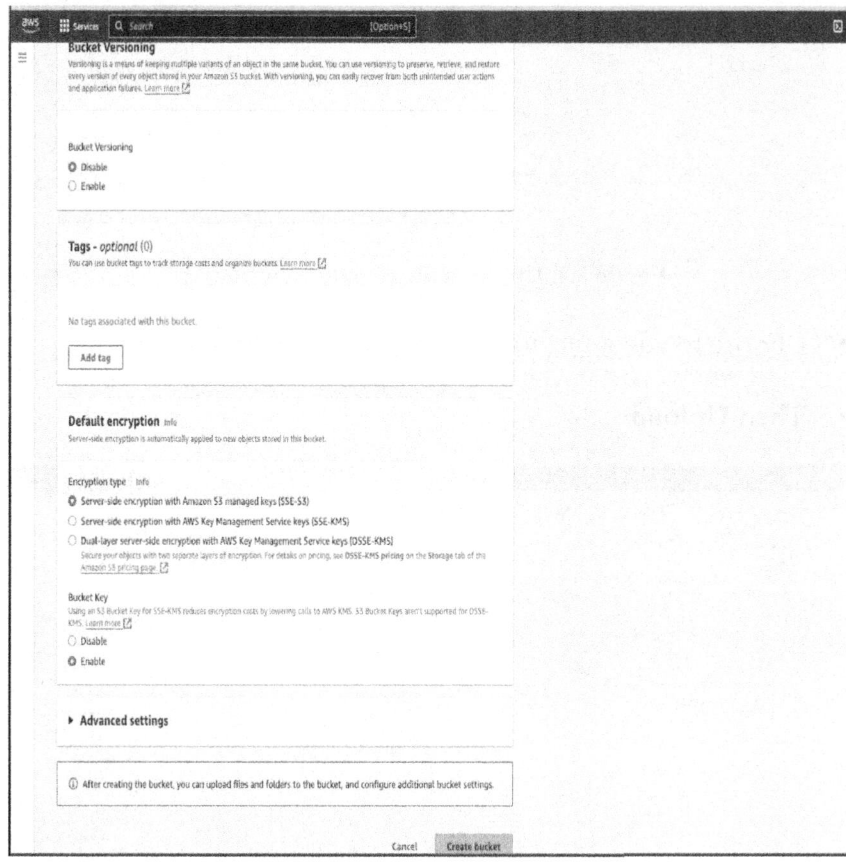

Figure 8.3: Parameters to create a new bucket

- After you have completed your bucket creation, go to the bucket (anycompanybucket1234)

- Navigate to the bucket and choose the "**Upload**" button.

Figure 8.4: Upload a file into the new bucket

- Choose to add a file, to add the file from your local drive
- Then **Upload**

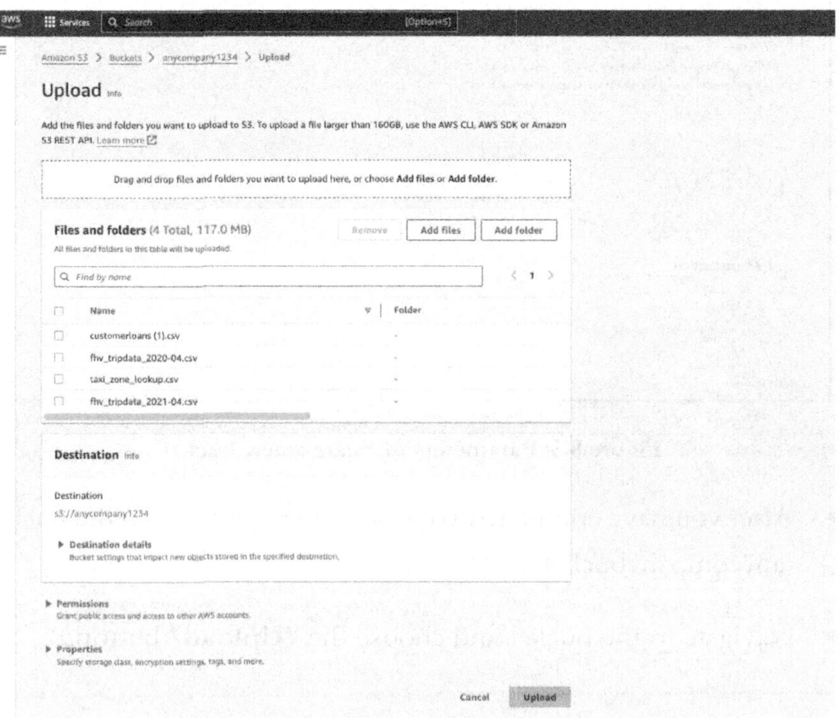

Figure 8.5: New file added in the bucket

We uploaded our CSV files into an Amazon S3 bucket, which serves as the foundation for our data lake. Amazon S3 provides a scalable and durable object storage service that can handle large volumes of data, which is one of the characteristics of a data product. This S3 data lake will now act as the data source from which we will create an AWS Glue Data Catalog.

Database creation with AWS Glue

In this step, we will be creating an AWS Glue database:

- Go to the AWS Glue console from the Console search bar
- Click **Databases** on the left under the **Data Catalog** section

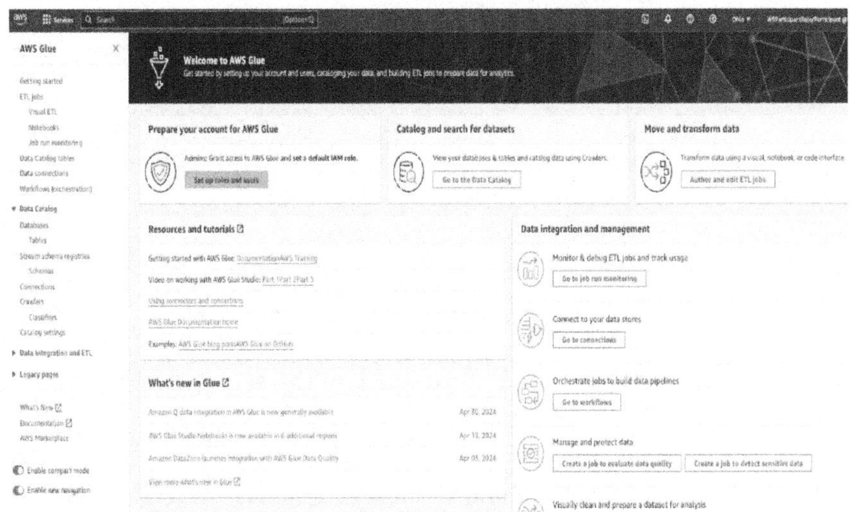

Figure 8.6: AWS Data Catalog

- Click on **Add Database** on the top right-hand side of the console.

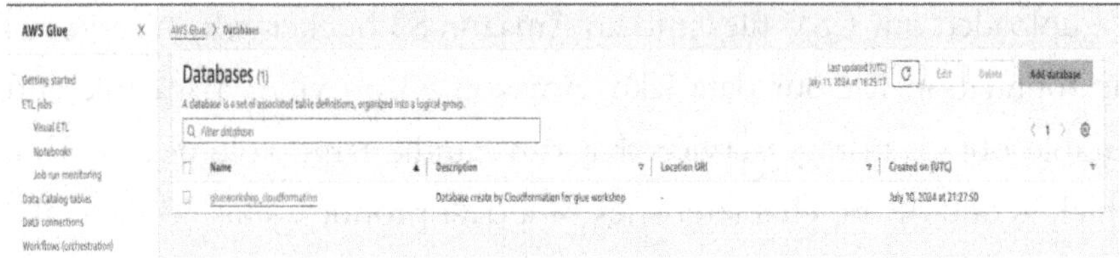

Figure 8.7: Create a new database

- Key in details of the database, such as name, location (optional), and description (optional), then **Create a database.**

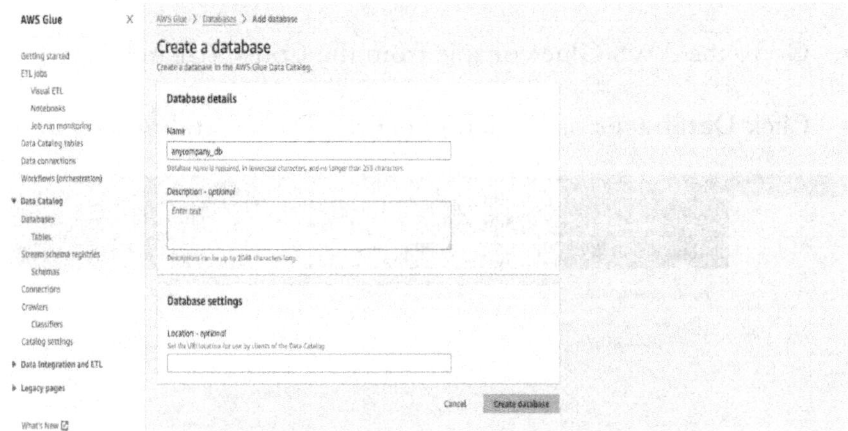

Figure 8.8: Parameters to create a database

Go back to **Databases** and confirm that you can see your newly created database.

In this section, we have been able to create a database for the AWS Glue Data Catalog. Let's use the AWS Glue Crawler to get the tables into the newly created database.

Crawling data with AWS Glue

We can use the AWS Glue Crawler to extract the metadata and to create tables:

- On the AWS Glue console, in the navigation pane, choose

Crawlers on the left under **Data Catalog** Section

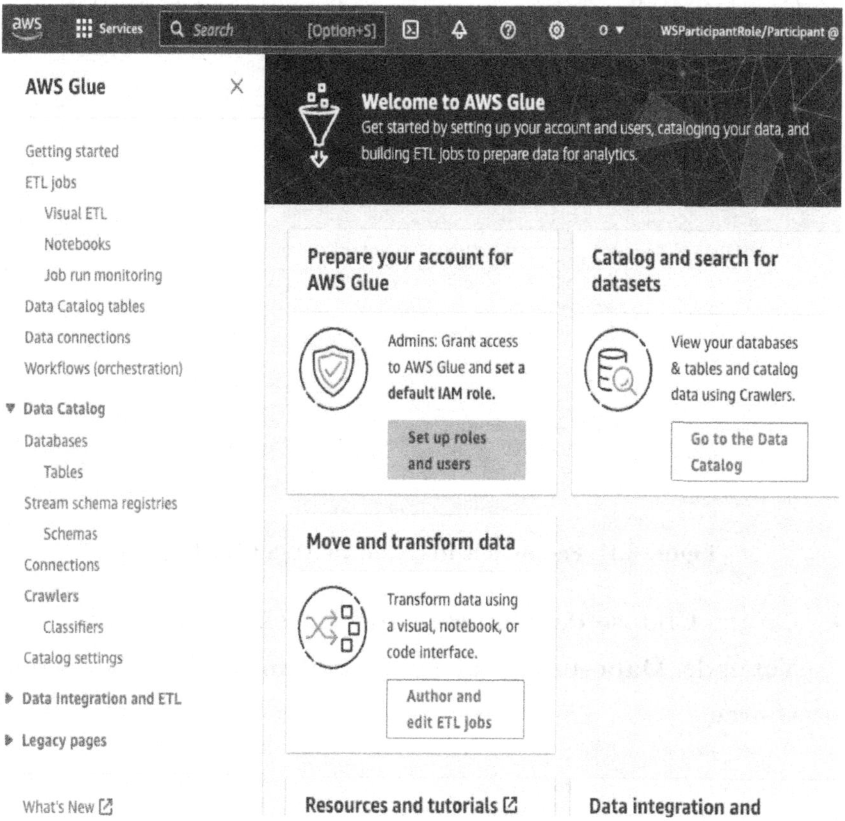

Figure 8.9: Access to AWS Glue Crawler

- Choose to Create a crawler.

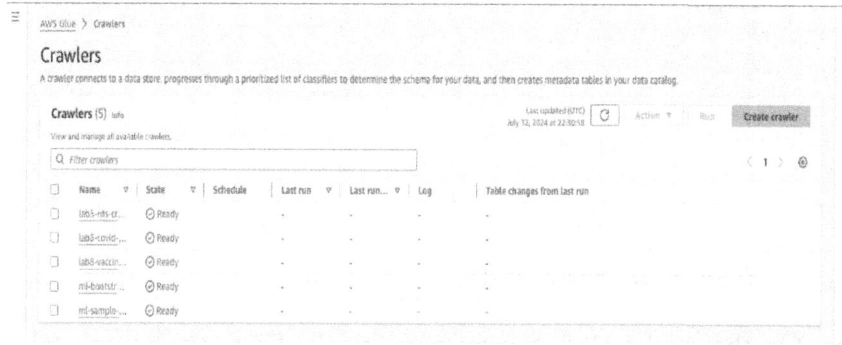

Figure 8.10: Create an AWS Glue Crawler

- On the Set crawler properties page, provide a name for the new Crawler, such as anycompany_crawler; you can leave the other options empty and click Next.

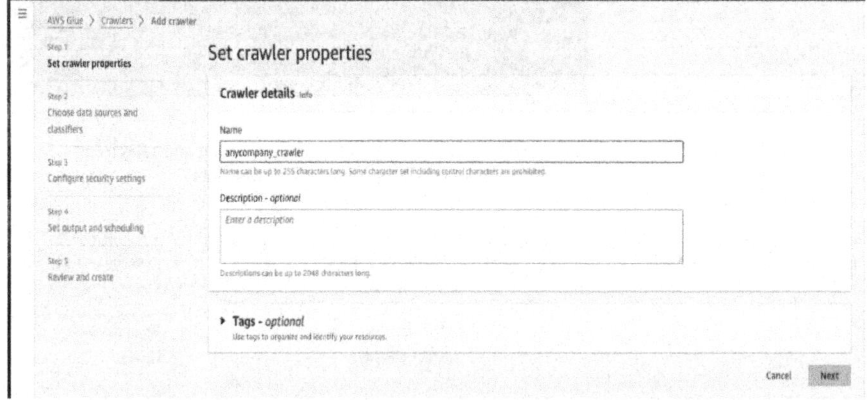

Figure 8.11: Parameters to create an AWS Glue Crawler

- On the **Choose data sources and classifiers** page, select **Not Yet** under **Data source configuration and click on Add a data source**.

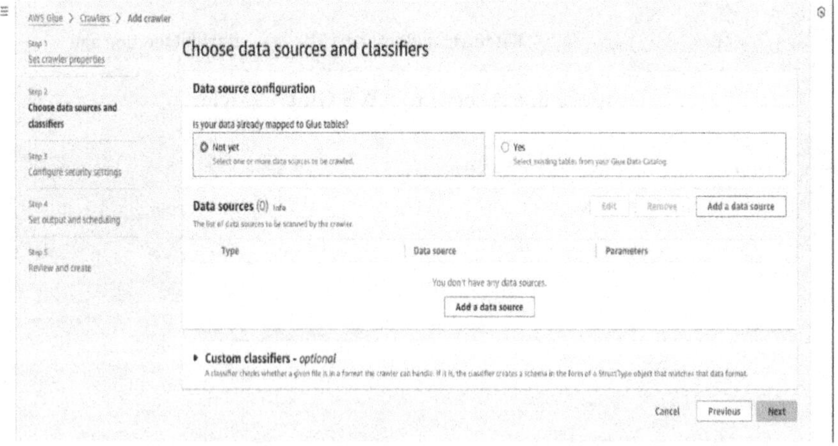

Figure 8.12: Choose the data source for the AWS Glue Crawler

- On the Add a Data Source page, in the **S3 path**, Browse S3 to choose your existing path or manually add the path that has your files.

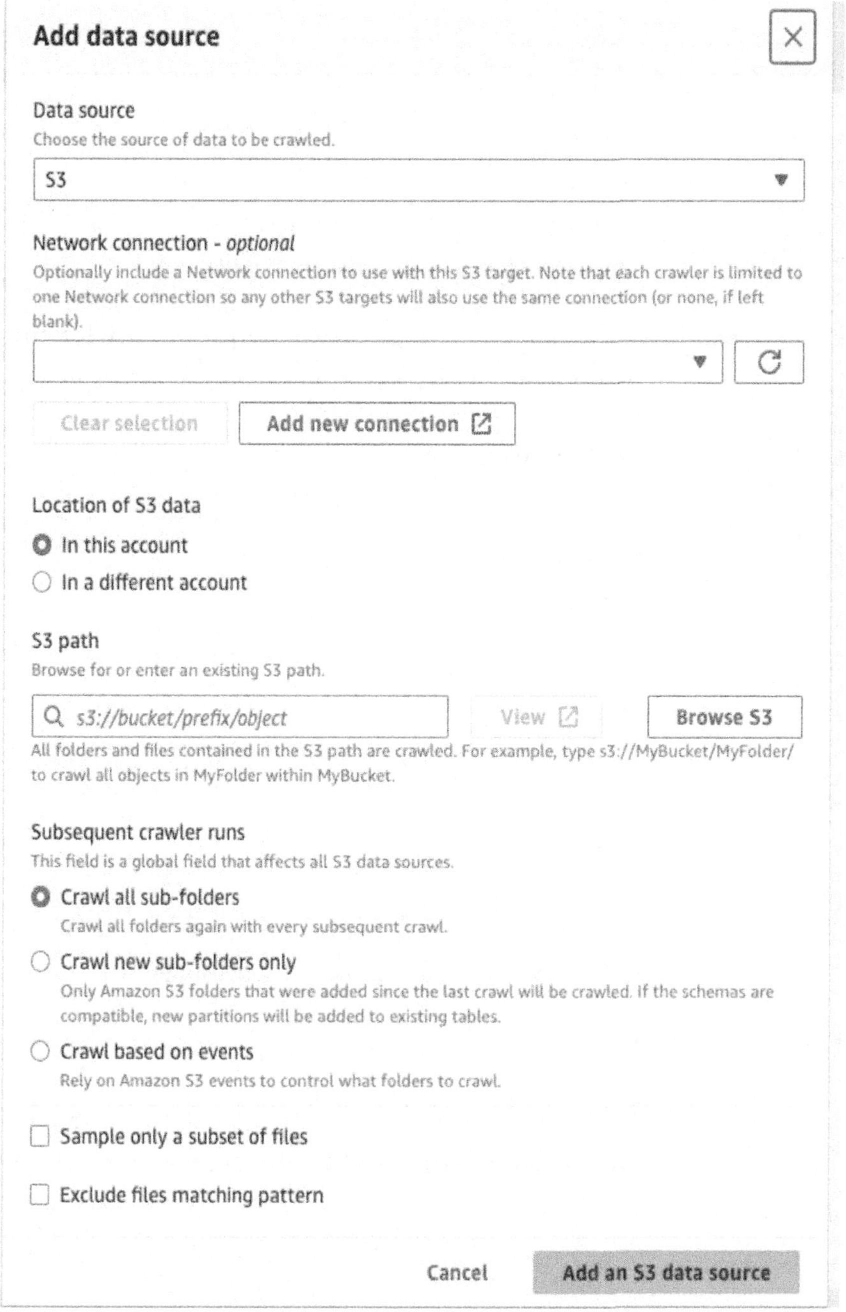

Add data source

Data source

Choose the source of data to be crawled.

S3

Network connection - *optional*

Optionally include a Network connection to use with this S3 target. Note that each crawler is limited to one Network connection so any other S3 targets will also use the same connection (or none, if left blank).

Clear selection

Add new connection

Location of S3 data

- In this account
- In a different account

S3 path

Browse for or enter an existing S3 path.

s3://bucket/prefix/object

View

Browse S3

All folders and files contained in the S3 path are crawled. For example, type s3://MyBucket/MyFolder/ to crawl all objects in MyFolder within MyBucket.

Subsequent crawler runs

This field is a global field that affects all S3 data sources.

- Crawl all sub-folders
  Crawl all folders again with every subsequent crawl.
- Crawl new sub-folders only
  Only Amazon S3 folders that were added since the last crawl will be crawled. If the schemas are compatible, new partitions will be added to existing tables.
- Crawl based on events
  Rely on Amazon S3 events to control what folders to crawl.

- [ ] Sample only a subset of files
- [ ] Exclude files matching pattern

Cancel

Add an S3 data source

Figure 8.13: Add a data source for the AWS Glue Crawler

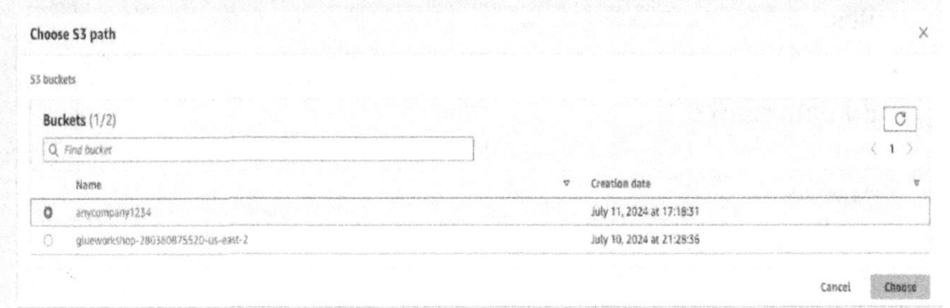

Figure 8.14: Select an Amazon S3 path

- You can leave the default settings on **subsequent crawler runs as On-demand** (identifies the repeated execution of crawler)
- Click On **Add an S3 data source**.

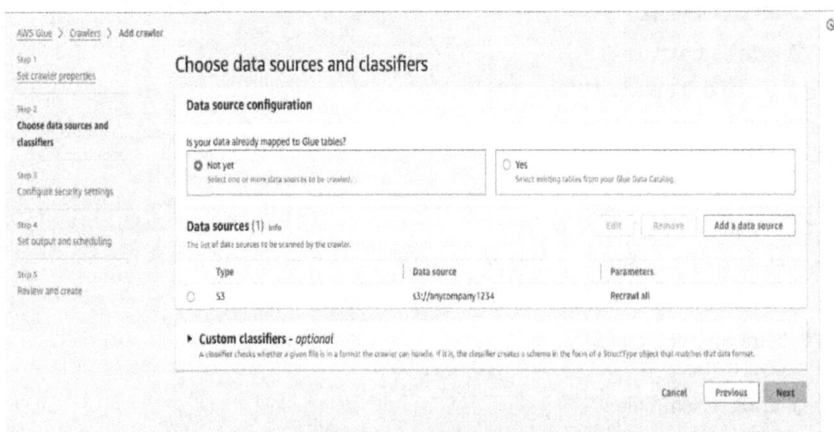

Figure 8.15: Validate the Amazon S3 data source

- Choose Next
- On the **Choose an IAM role** (Identity and Access Management) page, click **Choose an existing IAM role** and pick the role you created

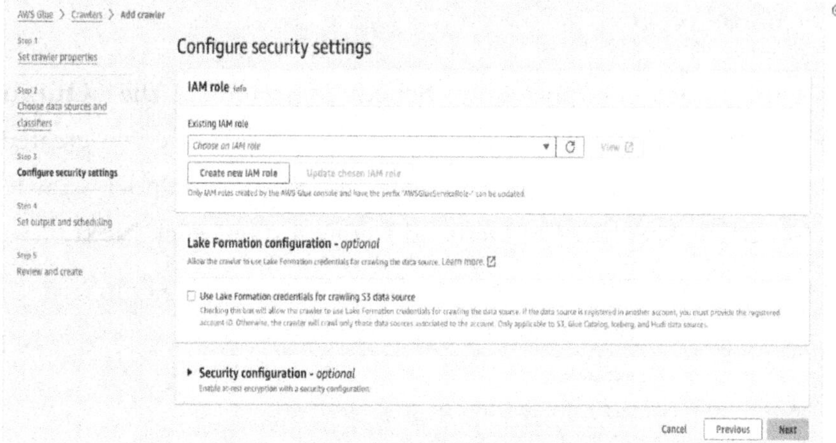

Figure 8.16: Configure the IAM role

- If you have none, then choose Create a new IAM Role.

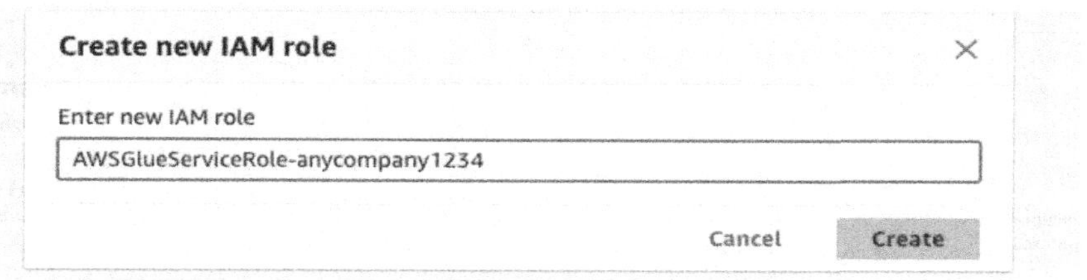

Figure 8.17: Create a new IAM role

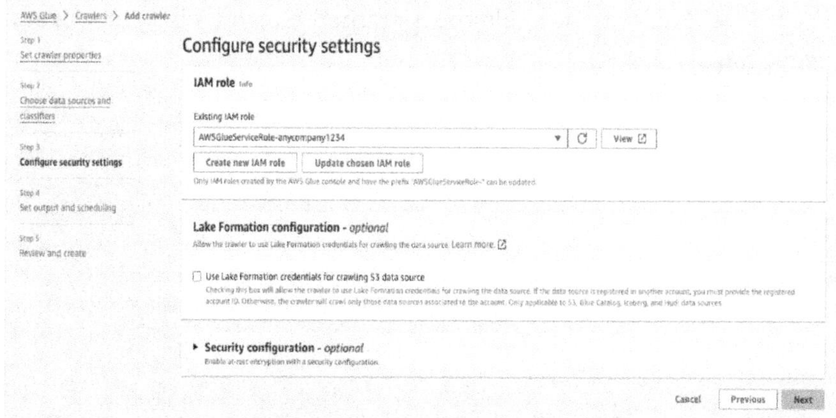

Figure 8.18: Validate the security settings

- Choose **Next**
- Under Set Output and Scheduling, under the **Output Configuration** section, specify the target database you created, or you can create one and then choose that. Under Crawler schedule, keep the On Demand frequency and click **Next**.

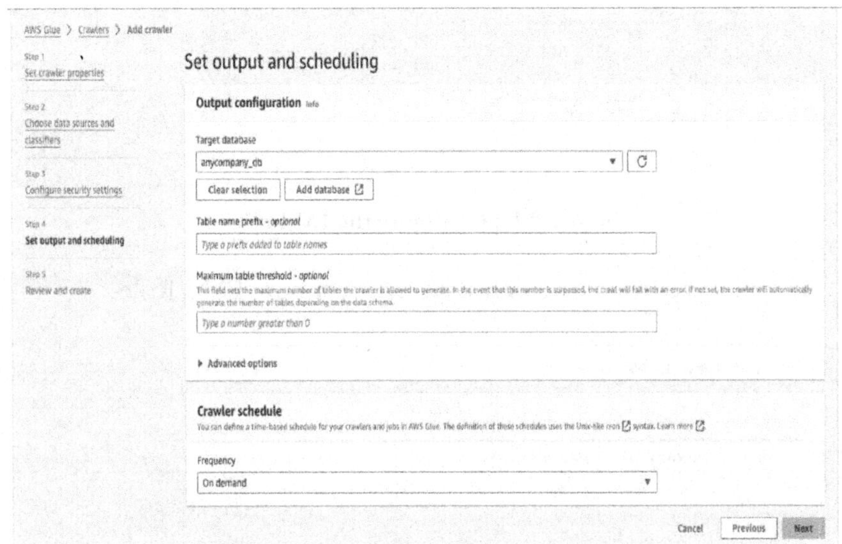

Figure 8.19: Setup the target database

- Choose Next, review all the parameters, and click on **Create Crawler**.

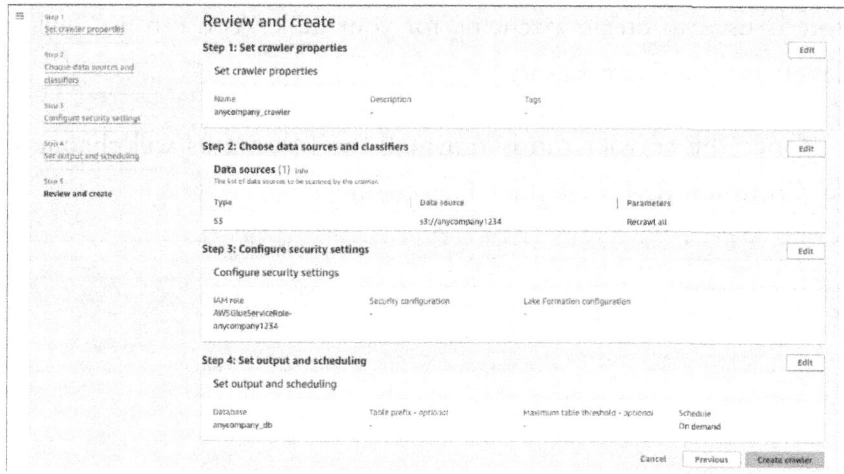

Figure 8.20: Create the AWS Glue Crawler

- Choose Create Crawler. After crawler completion, choose **Run Crawler**.

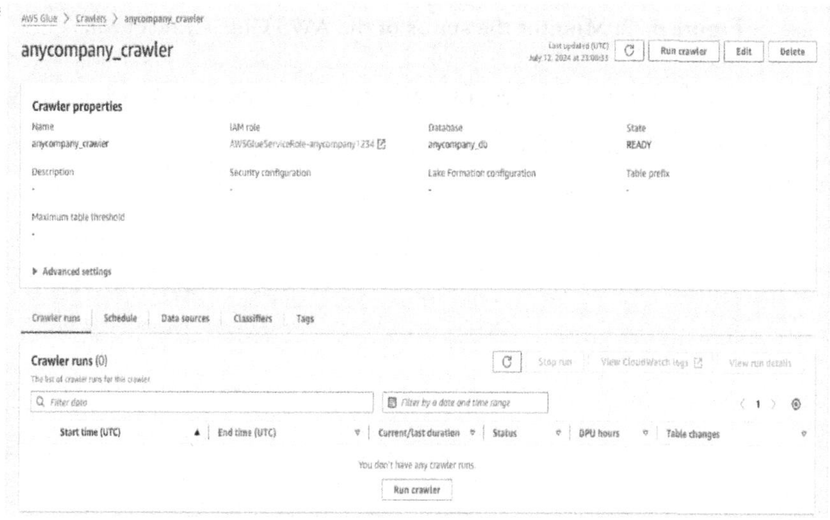

Figure 8.21: Run the AWS Glue Crawler

When you define a crawler, you choose one or more classifiers that evaluate the format of your data to infer a schema. When the crawler runs, the first classifier in your list to successfully recognize your data store is used to create a schema for your table. You can use built-in classifiers or define your own.

- Once the crawler run is finished, the Job Status will change to **Completed.** To see the tables created

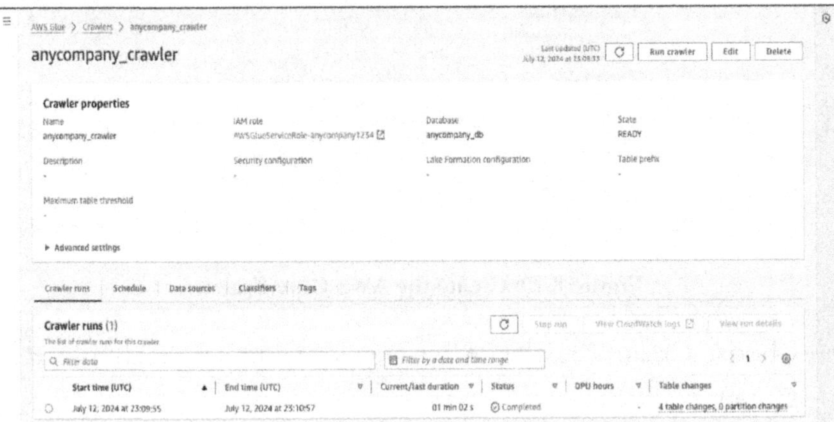

Figure 8.22: Monitor the status of the AWS Glue Crawler run

- On the left pane under **DataCatalog**, click on **Tables**; it will open the Tables page.

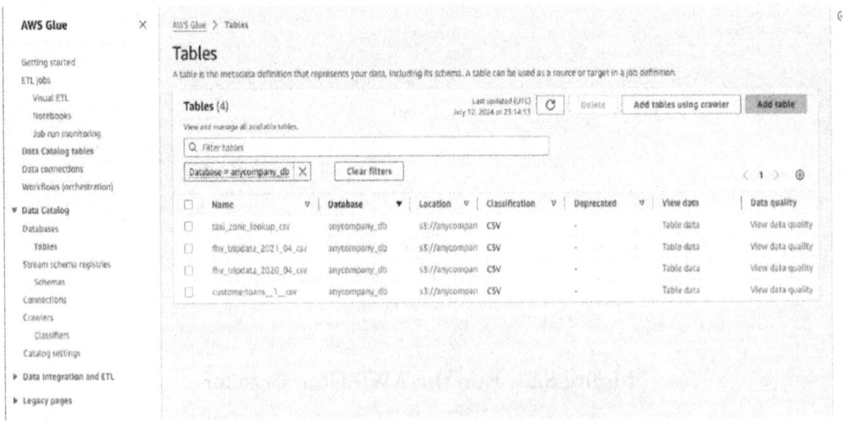

Figure 8.23: List of Tables in the AWS Glue Data Catalog

- To view the table schema automatically generated by the crawler based on the file uploaded. Click on a table created by the crawler.

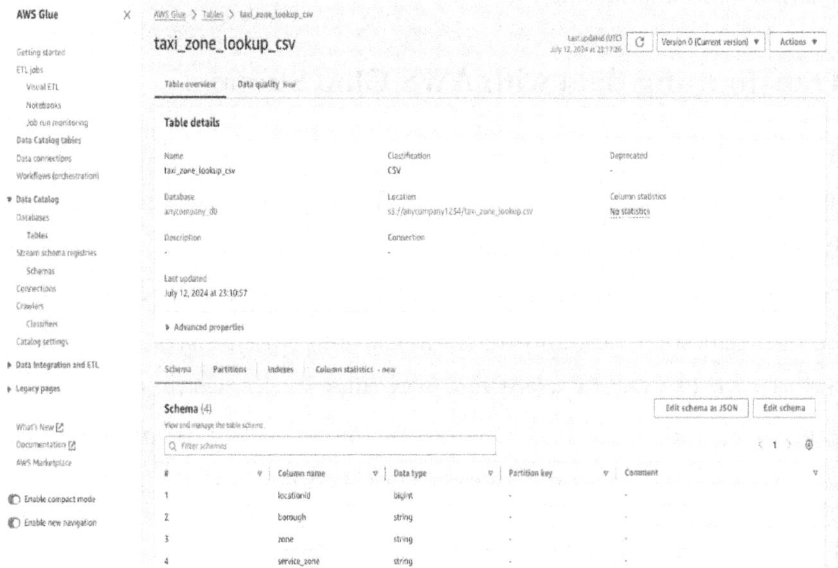

Figure 8.24: Select the new created Table

By leveraging the Glue Crawler and Data Catalog, we've shown how you can establish a reliable and scalable data infrastructure, laying the groundwork for data products that deliver consistent, high-value insights to your business. This process began with the AWS Glue Crawler, which scanned and cataloged your data sources (residing in an S3 data lake), creating a centralized and structured Data Catalog that forms the foundation for robust data products.

This Data Catalog provides a comprehensive view of your organization's data assets, enabling data discovery, governance, and self-service access to support the development of high-quality data products. Ongoing crawler runs, scheduled to run regularly, continuously update the Data Catalog, ensuring the metadata remains accurate and up-to-date – a crucial characteristic for maintaining the reliability and trustworthiness of your data products. Furthermore, the Glue Crawler's versatility in handling diverse data sources and formats allows you to build data products that seamlessly integrate with multiple systems, enhancing their flexibility and adaptability.

Transforming data with AWS Glue Studio

After loading all of our data into our AWS Glue Data Catalog, we can start consuming the "product" from our data. However, after combining data from multiple sources into a large, central repository, we still want to make sure to clean and organize the raw data and prepare it for storage, data analytics, and machine learning (ML). Extract, transform, and load (ETL) uses a set of business rules to do exactly that. Extract, transform, and load (ETL) works by moving data from the source system to the destination system at periodic intervals.

The ETL process functions in three main steps:

- Extract the relevant data from the source
- Transform the data so that it is better suited for analytics
- Load the data into the target database

From the AWS Glue Data Catalog, we can obtain a comprehensive view of our data assets, as well as accurate and our latest metadata. As the next steps, we need to apply the process of extract, transform, and load (ETL) so that individual raw datasets can be prepared in a format and structure that is more consumable for analytics purposes, resulting in more meaningful insights.

AWS Glue Studio is a graphical interface that makes it easy to create, run, and monitor extract, transform, and load (ETL) jobs in AWS Glue. You can visually compose data transformation workflows and seamlessly run them in AWS Glue's Apache Spark-based serverless ETL engine.

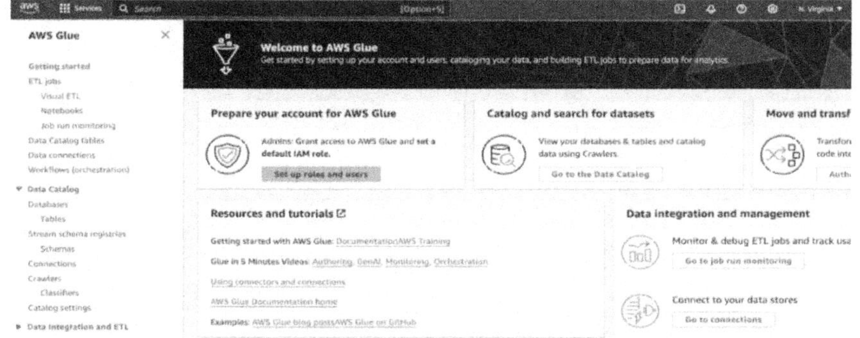

Figure 8.25: The AWS Glue Studio experience

- In order to access the service from the console, simply navigate to **AWS Glue** and click on **Visual ETL**
- From there, we are going to create a new visual job. A new window should appear with our canvas, where we can start composing our data transformation workflows.

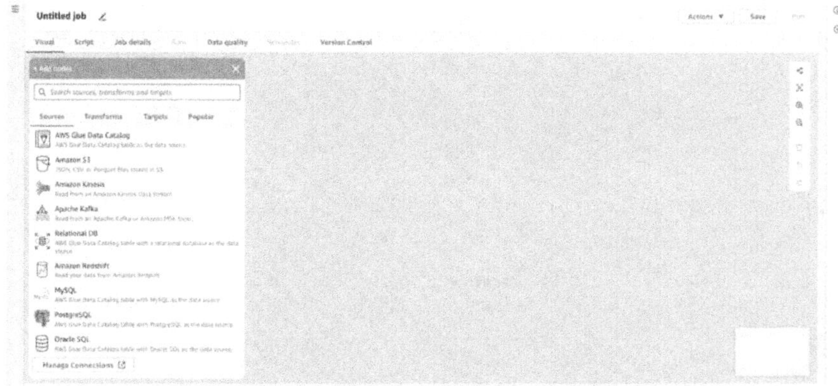

Figure 8.26: The AWS Glue Studio User Interface

- From the sources section, you can see the different options for our data sources. In this case, we are going to select Amazon S3.
- We select our S3 source type, like **an S3 location** or **Data Catalog table**.

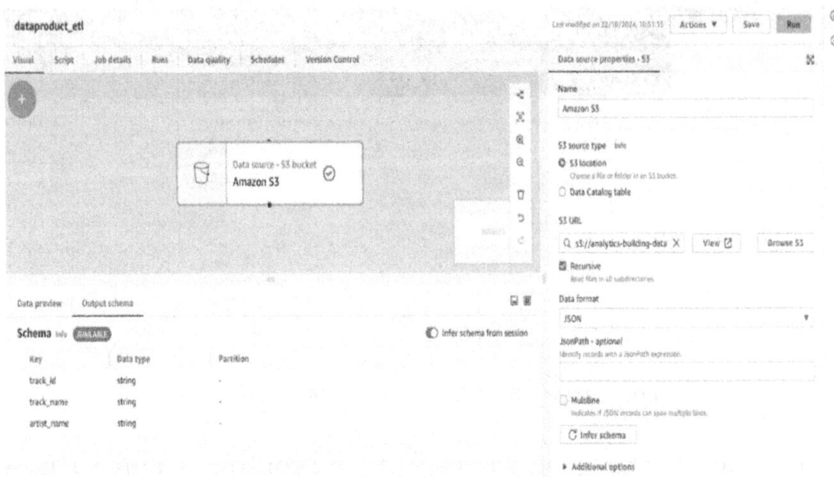

Figure 8.27: The Amazon S3 data source in the AWS Glue Studio

- In this case, we are going to perform different actions on two different data sources - directly from an S3 bucket and the **AWS Glue Data Catalog**.

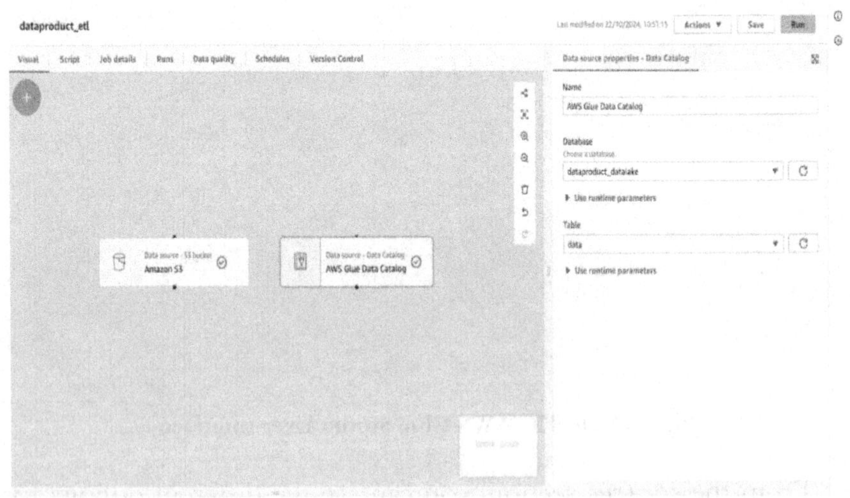

Figure 8.28: The AWS Glue Data Catalog action in the AWS Glue Studio

Next, we are going to be performing some basic transformations. From the transforms section, you can see the different options available, and you can simply drag and drop them into the visual canvas.

- For this example, we are going to apply a simple transformation by changing the schema of some key variables, like changing the data type from *string to int.*

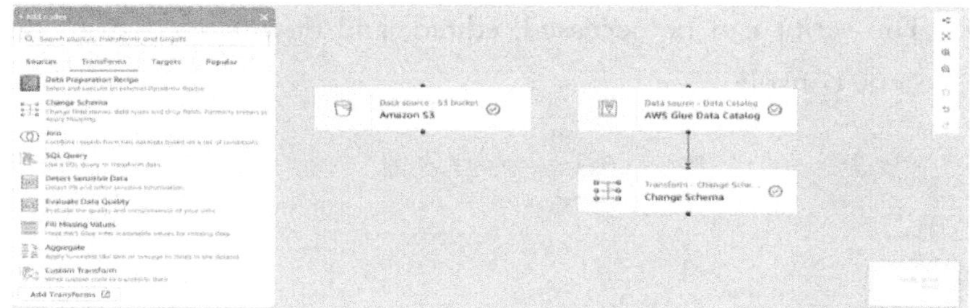

Figure 8.29: Simple transformation in AWS Glue Studio

After that, we can keep performing transformations like 'Join' to combine records from two datasets based on a set of conditions or fill in missing values in our data, all by easily dropping and connecting each building block. Once that has been done, we can put the data back into our target database.

- In this case, we are using Amazon S3 (into a bucket with all of the processed data). Furthermore, you can specify the format of the processed data.

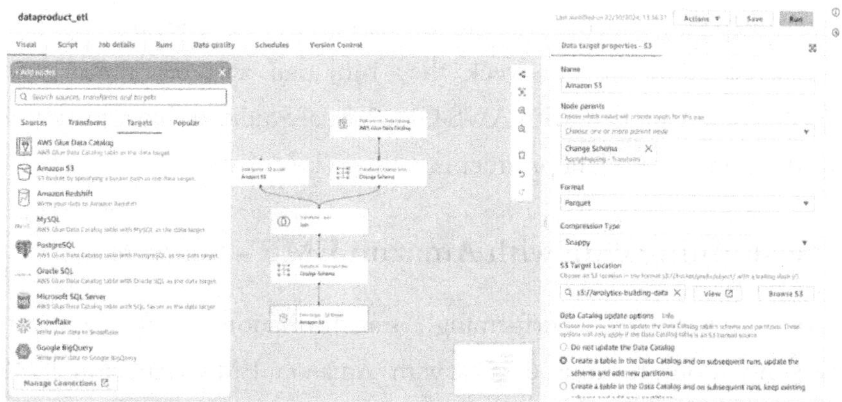

Figure 8.30: Overview of the transformation flow in AWS Glue Studio

On the other hand, as we were implementing our transformations using the building blocks, AWS Glue was automatically generating the underlying code needed to execute the job.

- The script can be accessed, edited, and downloaded from the same console.

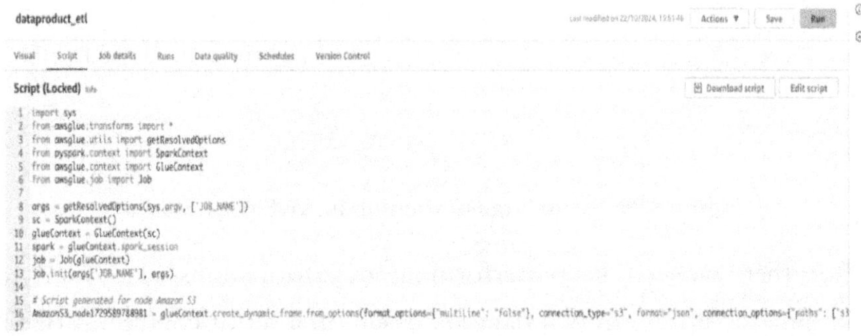

Figure 8.31: Script generated from the transformation flow in AWS Glue Studio

Once the job has successfully been executed, you can view the processed data directly from your chosen data target. By navigating to Amazon S3 or your AWS Glue Data Catalog, you can view the new, updated, processed data. Furthermore, you can schedule your jobs to automatically run at specific times.

You can specify constraints, such as the number of times that the jobs run, which days of the week they run, and at what time. After transforming your data with AWS Glue Visual Studio and loading it into our data target, our data product is ready to be consumed.

Transforming data with Amazon EMR - Serverless

Another way of performing transformations and applying transformations to your data is with Amazon EMR. Amazon EMR (previously called Amazon Elastic MapReduce) is a managed cluster platform that simplifies running big data frameworks, such as Apache

Hadoop and Apache Spark, on AWS to process and analyze vast amounts of data. Using these frameworks and related open-source projects, you can process data for analytics purposes and business intelligence workloads. Amazon EMR lets you transform and move large amounts of data into and out of other AWS data stores and databases.

Similar to AWS Glue, Amazon EMR contains a serverless option called Amazon EMR Serverless. Amazon EMR Serverless is a serverless option in Amazon EMR that makes it easy for data analysts and engineers to run batch jobs and interactive workloads using open-source big data analytics frameworks without configuring, managing, and scaling clusters or servers. This option simplifies the operation of analytics applications that use the latest open-source frameworks, such as Apache Spark and Apache Hive. Amazon EMR Serverless guides you in avoiding over/under-provisioning resources for your data processing jobs. EMR Serverless automatically determines the resources that the application needs, get these resources to process your jobs, and releases the resources when the jobs finish. With Amazon EMR Serverless, you'll continue to get the benefits of Amazon EMR, such as open-source compatibility, concurrency, and optimized runtime performance for popular frameworks.

It's important to note that the choice between AWS Glue and Amazon EMR Serverless will depend on your specific use case, workload requirements, and existing infrastructure. It's always recommended to evaluate your needs and perform cost and performance analyses before making a decision.

Accessing Amazon EMR Serverless

- After signing into the **AWS Management Console**, open the **Amazon EMR console**. From the left-hand panel, you can navigate to the **Amazon EMR Serverless** section.

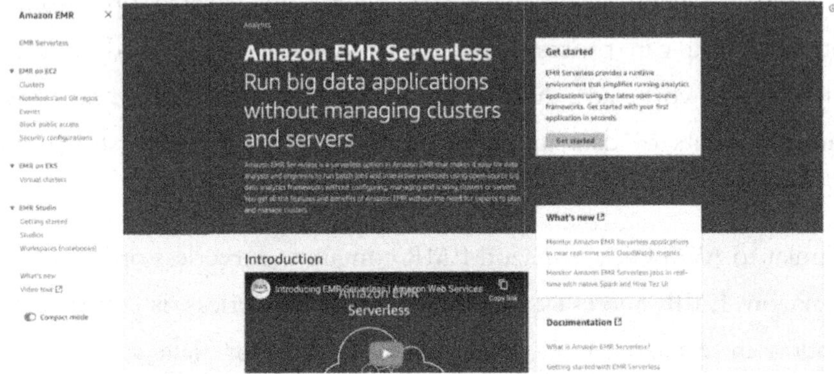

Figure 8.32: The Amazon EMR console

- Once you click on get started, you start configuring your application within Amazon EMR Studio.

EMR Studio is an integrated development environment (IDE) that makes it easy for data scientists and data engineers to develop, visualize, and debug data engineering and data science applications written in R, Python, Scala, and PySpark. EMR Studio provides fully managed Jupyter Notebooks and tools, such as Spark UI, to simplify debugging.

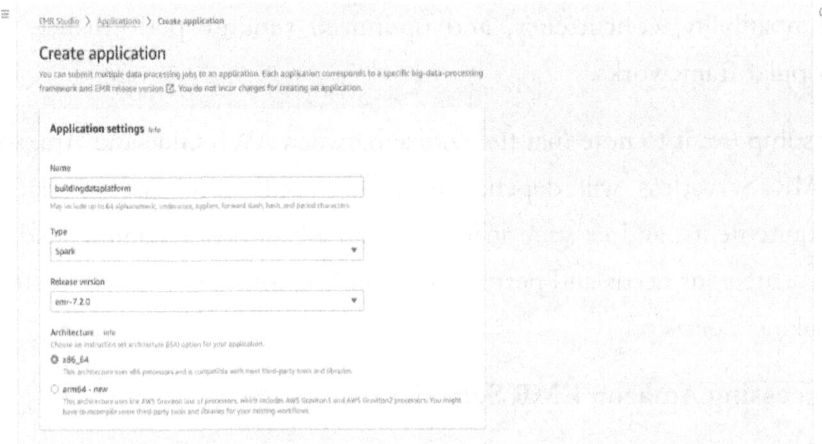

Figure 8.33: Create an application in Amazon EMR Studio

- After creating the application, you can access it and start submitting your data processing jobs or perform interactive analysis in Jupyter Notebooks.

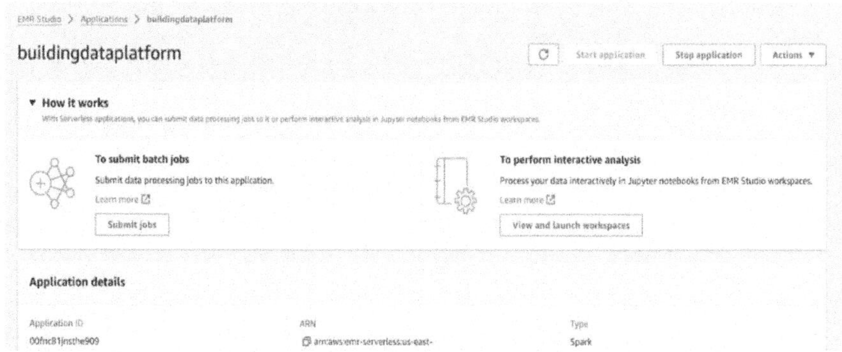

Figure 8.34: Application ready in Amazon EMR Studio

- From the application, we can submit a job run by simply accessing the script (JAR or Python) directly from Amazon S3. Furthermore, we can specify the location of the data store used to offload the data processed.

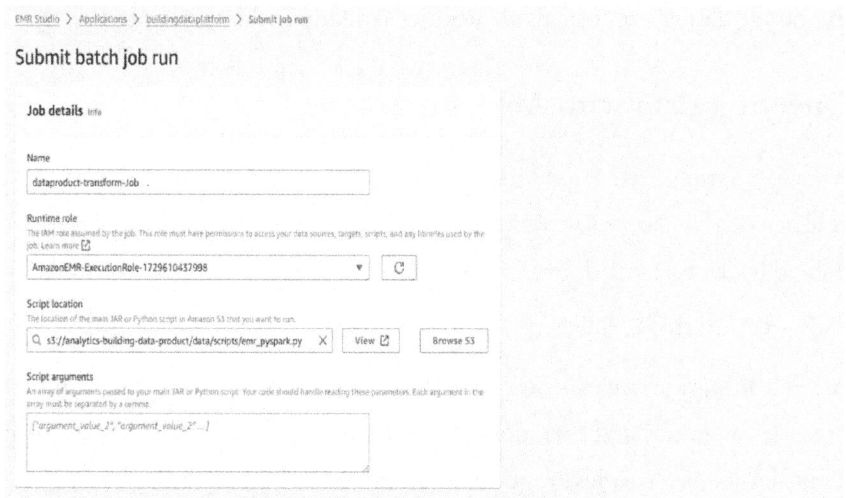

Figure 8.35: Submit a job run in EMR Studio

- Once the batch job run has been defined, it can be executed.

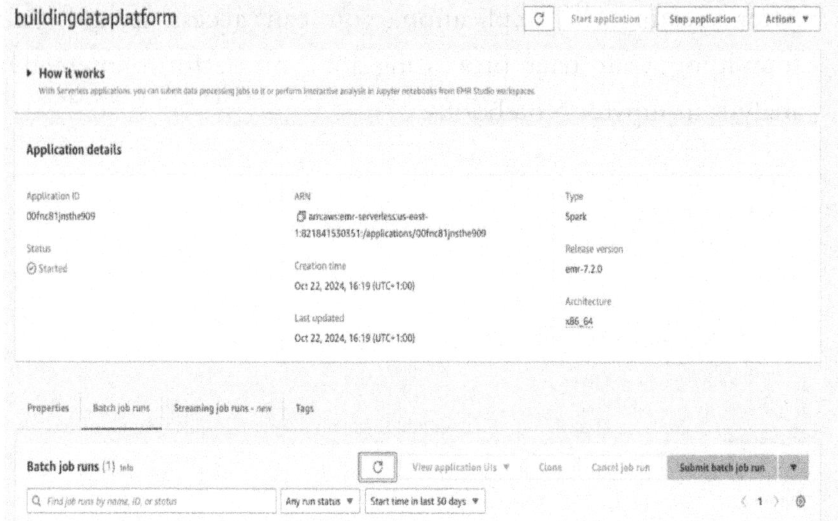

Figure 8.36: Execution of the job run in EMR Studio

Once the job has successfully been executed, you can view the process from the batch or streaming job run section. After processing the data, you can navigate to your data target to view the new, updated, processed data. Subsequent to validating that the right data has been loaded into the target data store, our data product is ready to be consumed.

Querying data with Amazon Athena

Amazon Athena is a serverless SQL query service that enables easy analysis of data stored in Amazon S3. Users start by pointing Athena to their data in S3 and defining the schema. Then, they can immediately begin querying the data using standard SQL.

Athena integrates seamlessly with the AWS Glue Data Catalog, which provides a centralized metadata store accessible across an AWS account. This allows users to leverage the schema and ETL capabilities of AWS Glue when querying their data with Athena. We will use Glue Data Catalog tables as the source to query your data in Athena. Once the data has been crawled and the schema is established in the AWS Glue Data

Catalog, you can seamlessly use Athena to query the data stored in AWS Glue. Athena is a serverless query service that allows you to run standard SQL queries against various data sources.

- We start by Opening the Athena Console.

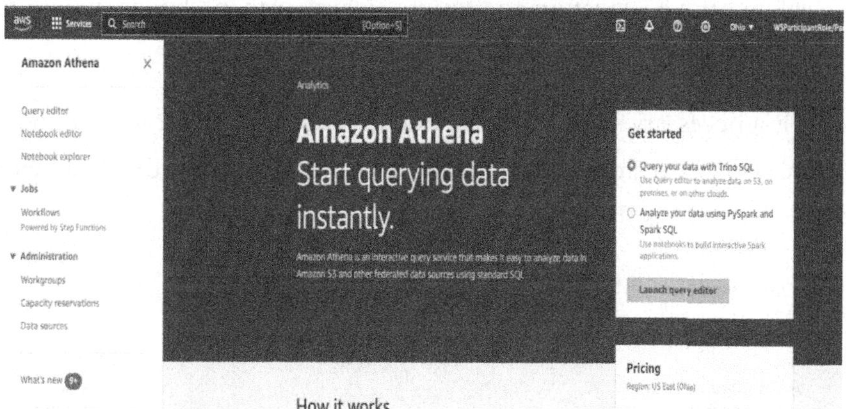

Figure 8.37: Amazon Athena console

- On the Amazon Athena page, click on Launch Query editor.

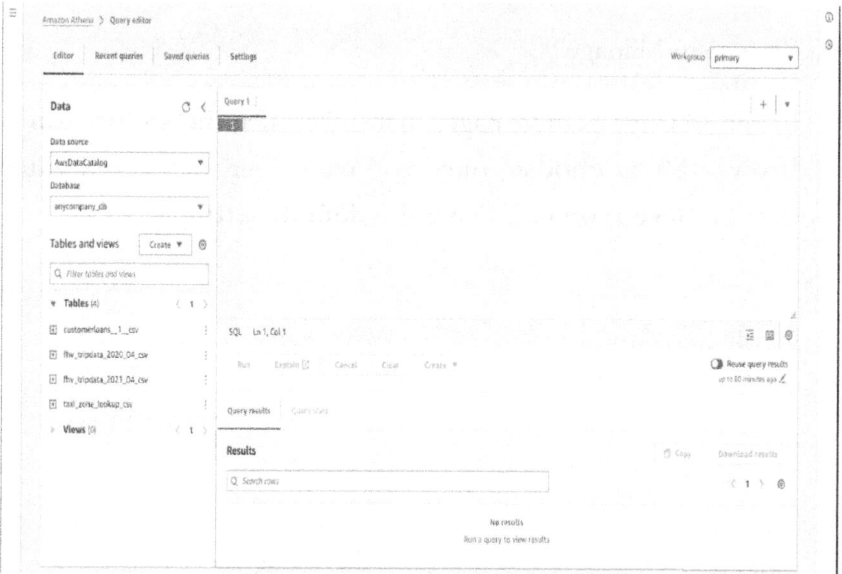

Figure 8.38: Amazon Athena query editor

- Next, Navigate to Settings to set up your query result location in S3

In order to use Athena, you need to specify an Amazon S3 location where Athena will store the results/ output of your SQL queries. Specifying the S3 location for results ensures Athena knows where to save the output of your SQL analyses.

This is a necessary setup step, as Athena is a serverless service and does not have its own storage. It relies on Amazon S3 to store the data being queried as well as the query results.

Figure 8.39: Amazon Athena settings

- Choose to Manage
- In the Manage setting page, manually enter the s3 location or **Browse S3 to choose**; once you have your location inputted, click on **Save (you can leave the default settings)**

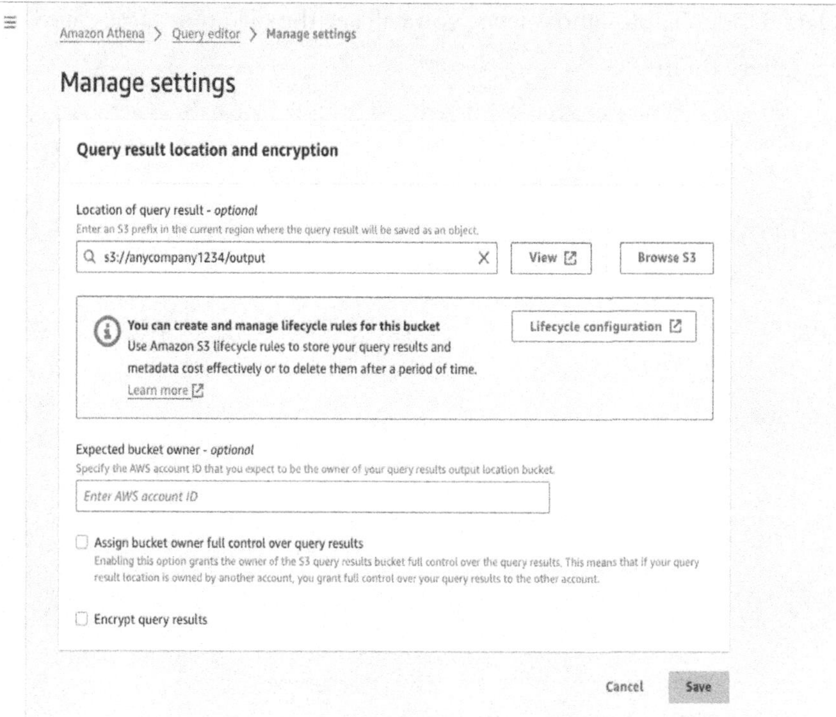

Figure 8.40: Manage the Amazon Athena settings

- Once saved, go ahead and click on **Editor** to navigate back to the Query Editor page.

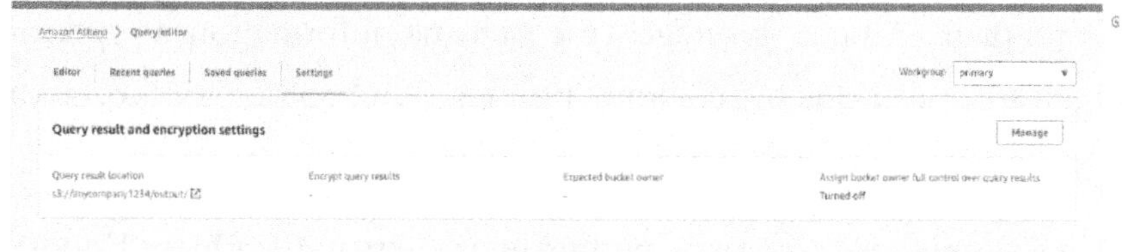

Figure 8.41: Manage the Amazon Athena settings

- On the **Query Editor** page

Note: The data source and a database are required, which, in our case, AWS Glue Data Catalog (data source), along with the database we created earlier, will be displayed in the Query Editor on the left under

Data. Under Tables and Views, you will see the different tables, and you can query them.

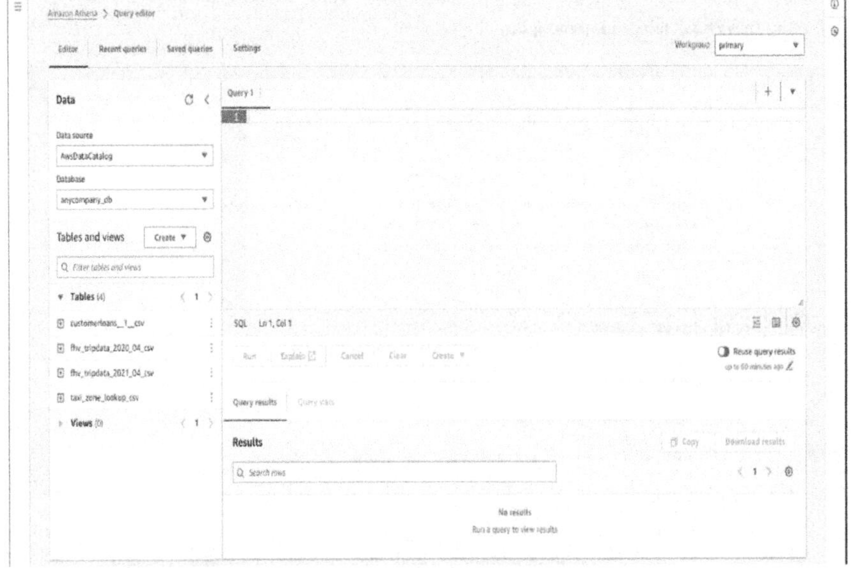

Figure 8.42: Amazon Athena query editor with settings defined

Executing queries in Amazon Athena

Executing a query in Athena utilizes the metadata stored in the Glue Data Catalog to understand the structure of the data and optimize the query plan. Athena leverages the schema information to perform predicate push-down, column pruning, and other optimizations, resulting in faster query execution.

Run a simple select query by putting your query in the Query Editor:

SELECT * FROM "anycompany_db"."taxi_zone_lookup_csv" limit 10;

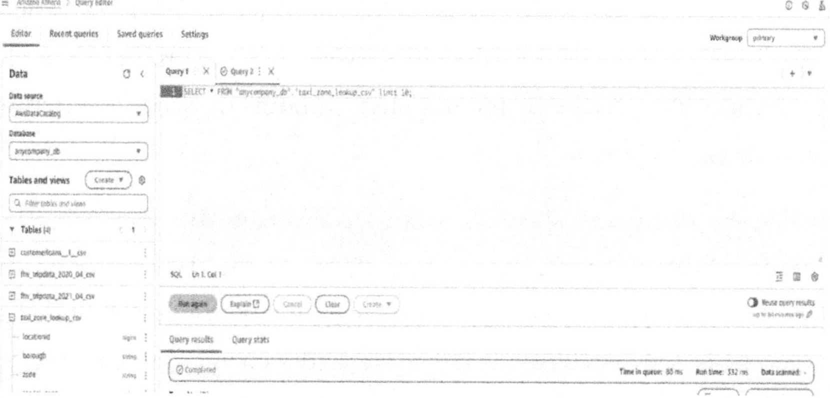

Figure 8.43: Execution of the query in the Amazon Athena query editor

Summary

This chapter presents a comprehensive guide to building a data product using AWS big data services. At the core, a data product leverages data to deliver valuable insights and capabilities to users. Key characteristics of effective data products include scalability, domain-centricity, modularity, discoverability, and continuous improvement.

To construct this data product, the chapter demonstrates how to load data into an Amazon S3 data lake, which serves as a scalable and durable foundation. It then shows the process of creating a centralized AWS Glue data catalog, where the Glue crawler automatically extracts metadata and generates tables to provide a structured view of the data assets.

With the data catalog in place, the chapter delves into two approaches for transforming and preparing the data. The first method utilizes the visual AWS Glue Studio interface, enabling users to intuitively design and execute ETL workflows through a drag-and-drop canvas. This includes applying data transformations, joining datasets, and loading the processed data back into S3.

As an alternative, the guide also covers using Amazon EMR Serverless, a managed big data processing service that simplifies running frameworks like Apache Spark and Hive without the need to provision and scale clusters manually.

Finally, the document showcases how to leverage Amazon Athena, a serverless SQL query service, to directly query the data stored in the Glue data catalog. Athena's seamless integration with Glue allows users to leverage the established metadata and schema information to optimize query execution.

By guiding the reader through this end-to-end process, the chapter demonstrates how organizations can leverage AWS big data services to build robust, scalable, and easily consumable data products that drive meaningful insights and support data-driven decision-making.

9. Build a Data Product on Data Warehouse

A data warehouse is a centralized, integrated repository of data that is specifically designed to support analytical and reporting workloads within an organization. Unlike operational databases that are optimized for transactional processing, a data warehouse is structured to enable efficient querying, aggregation, and analysis of large volumes of historical data from multiple sources.

The primary value of a data warehouse lies in its ability to provide a unified, consistent, and comprehensive view of an organization's data. By consolidating data from disparate systems and applications into a single repository, a data warehouse eliminates data silos and ensures that decision-makers have access to a "single source of truth." This enables more informed and data-driven decision-making, as users can analyze historical trends, identify patterns, and generate insights that inform strategic business initiatives.

Moreover, the dimensional model used in data warehouses, which organizes data into fact tables and dimension tables, allows for faster query performance and more intuitive data exploration. This structure aligns well with the analytical needs of business users, empowering them to explore data, generate reports, and perform ad-hoc analysis without the technical overhead of working with raw operational data. Additionally, data warehouses often incorporate advanced data processing and transformation capabilities, such as extraction, transformation, and loading (ETL) pipelines. These mechanisms ensure data quality, consistency, and integrity, ultimately increasing the trustworthiness and reliability of the information available to decision-makers.

By consolidating and structuring data in a centralized, purpose-built repository, data warehouses enable organizations to unlock the full value of their data assets. This, in turn, supports strategic decision-making, operational efficiency, and the development of data-driven products and services – all of which can contribute to an organization's competitive advantage in the market.

Create the Data Product in Amazon Redshift from Amazon S3

Amazon Redshift is a fully managed, petabyte-scale cloud data warehouse service offered by AWS. It enables users to analyze large volumes of structured and semi-structured data across various data sources, including data lakes, operational databases, and other data warehouses.

Loading data into S3

The first step to creating a data product in AmazonRedshift is to load data into Amazon S3.

We will be loading this data from our local machine into Amazon S3. It is relevant to point out that this is just one of the many various ways by which you can upload data into Amazon S3. In order to do so, you can follow these steps:

- Sign in to the AWS Management Console and open the Amazon S3 console
- In the left navigation pane, choose **Buckets**

Figure 9.1: Amazon S3 console

- Choose **Create bucket**

Once you get the **Create Bucket** page:

- Under **General configuration**, view the AWS Region where your bucket will be created
- For the **Bucket name**, enter a name for your bucket, e.g., "any company."
- Under **Object Ownership**, to disable or enable ACLs and control ownership of objects uploaded in your bucket, choose one of the following settings: **ACLs disabled or enabled** (you can leave at the recommended option)
- Under **Block Public Access settings for this bucket**, choose the Block Public Access settings that you want to apply to the bucket. By default, all four Block Public Access settings are enabled.

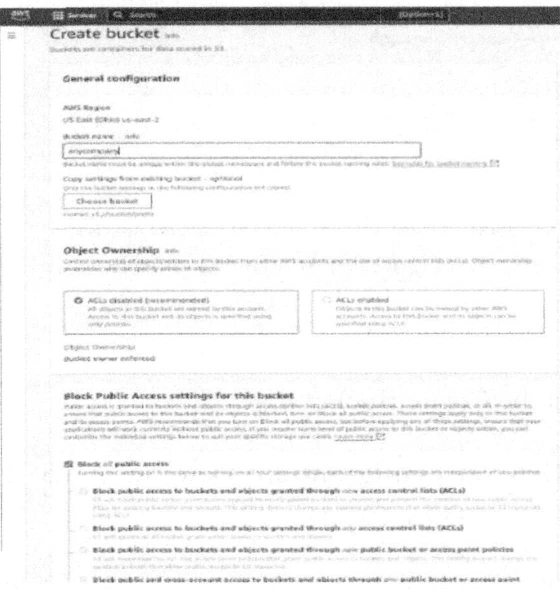

Figure 9.2: Parameters to create a bucket in Amazon S3

- (Optional) Under **Tags**, you can choose to add tags to your bucket. Tags are key-value pairs used to categorize storage. (To add a bucket tag, enter a Key and optionally a Value and choose Add Tag.)
- Under **Default encryption**, select an encryption type, or you can use the default selected.
- (Optional) Choose **Advanced Settings**. If you want to enable Object Lock, choose Enable, read the warning that appears, and acknowledge it
- Choose **Create bucket**.

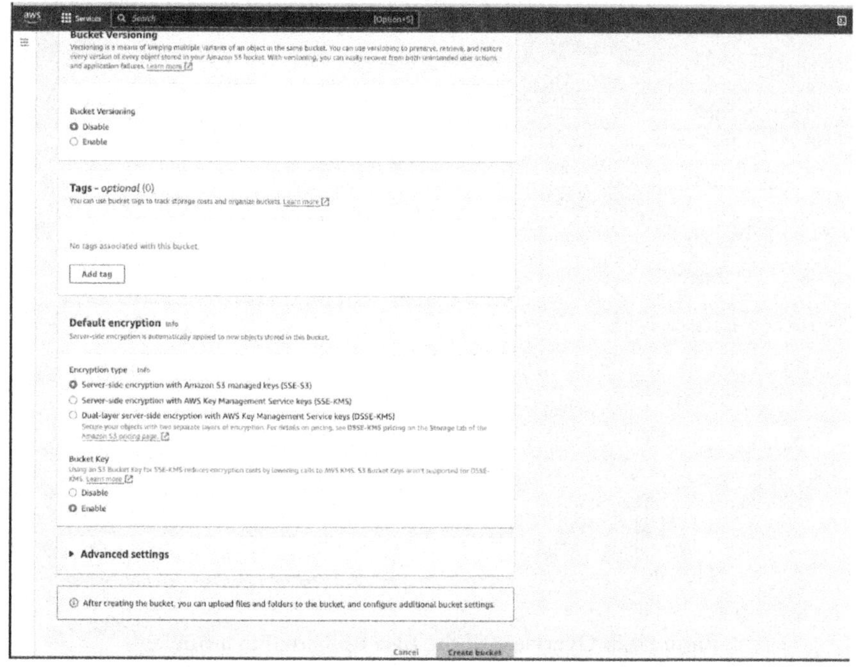

Figure 9.3: Parameters to create a bucket in Amazon S3

- After you have completed your bucket creation, go to the bucket (anycompanybucket1234)
- Navigate to the bucket and choose the "**Upload**" button.

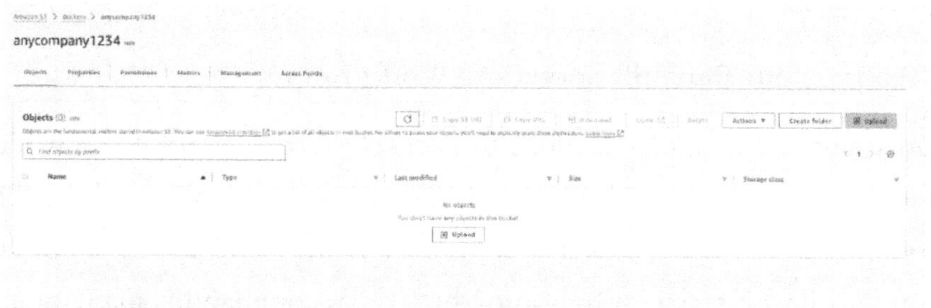

Figure 9.4: Upload a file into an Amazon S3 bucket

- Choose to add a file to add the file from your local drive
- Then **Upload**

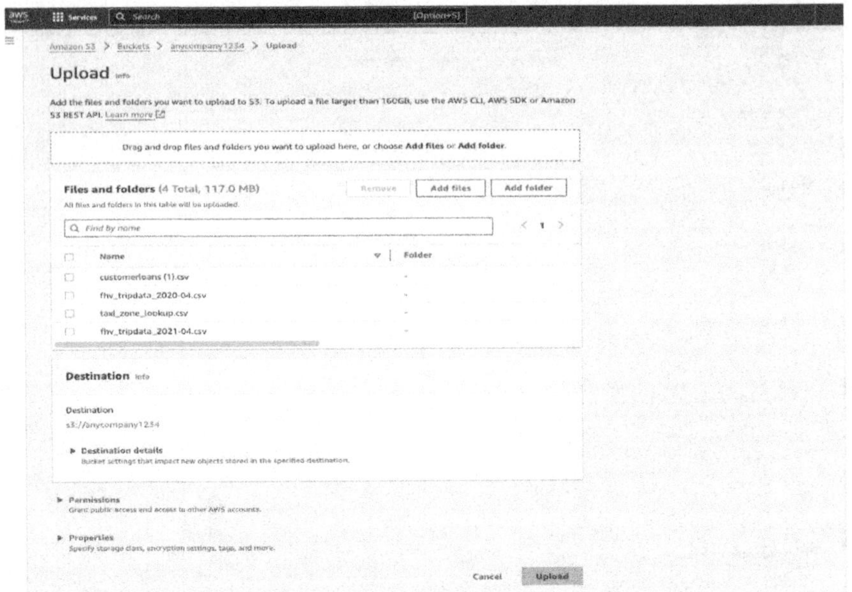

Figure 9.5: Overview of the files uploaded in a bucket

We uploaded our CSV files into an Amazon S3 bucket, which serves as the foundation for our data lake. Amazon S3 provides a scalable and durable object storage service that can handle large volumes of data, which is one of the characteristics of a data product. This S3 data lake will now act as the data source from which we will create an AWS Glue Data Catalog.

Creating your Redshift Serverless Workgroup

Once all the data has been added to buckets in Amazon S3, you can add data to your Amazon Redshift tables either by using an INSERT command or by using a COPY command. At the scale and speed of an Amazon Redshift data warehouse, the COPY command is many times faster and more efficient than INSERT commands.

The COPY command uses the Amazon Redshift massively parallel processing (MPP) architecture to read and load data in parallel from multiple data sources. You can load data files on Amazon S3, Amazon

EMR, or any remote host accessible through a Secure Shell (SSH) connection. You can also load directly from an Amazon DynamoDB table.

In this example, we would use the COPY command to load data from Amazon S3 into Redshift. Next, we need to create a workgroup to interact with Amazon Redshift. There are two different options for using Amazon Redshift: Amazon Redshift Serverless or Amazon Redshift provisioned clusters.

Amazon Redshift Serverless automatically provisions data warehouse capacity and intelligently scales the underlying resources. Amazon Redshift Serverless adjusts capacity in seconds to deliver consistently high performance and simplified operations for even the most demanding and volatile workloads. By using Amazon Redshift Serverless, you can access and analyze data without the need to set up, tune, and manage clusters. Furthermore, you can use the superior Amazon Redshift SQL capabilities, industry-leading performance, and data-lake integration to seamlessly query across a data warehouse, a data lake, and operational data sources, as well as deliver consistently high performance and simplified operations for the most demanding and volatile workloads with intelligent and automatic scaling. With Amazon Redshift Serverless, you use a console interface to reach a serverless data warehouse or APIs to build applications. Through the data warehouse, you can access your Amazon Redshift managed storage and your Amazon S3 data lake.

On the other hand, Amazon Redshift manages all of the work of setting up, operating, and scaling a data warehouse. These tasks include provisioning capacity, monitoring and backing up the cluster, and applying patches and upgrades to the Amazon Redshift engine. An Amazon Redshift cluster is a set of nodes that consists of a leader node and one or more compute nodes. The type and number of compute nodes that you need depend on the size of your data, the number of queries you will run, and the query runtime performance that you need.

When you launch a cluster, one option that you specify is the node type. The node type determines the CPU, RAM, storage capacity, and storage drive type for each node.

For this example, we will be using Amazon Redshift Serverless since it adapts better to our requirements. To access the service, sign in to the AWS Management Console and open the Amazon Redshift console.

- Click on the Amazon Redshift Serverless option.

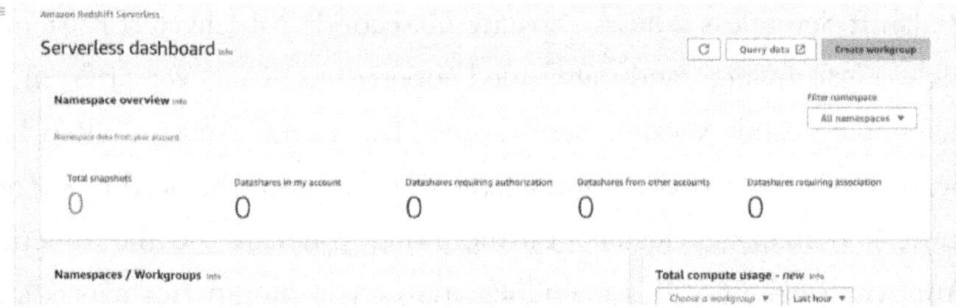

Figure 9.6: Amazon Redshift serverless dashboard

Next, we can create a workgroup. A workgroup is a collection of computing resources. The compute-related workgroup groups together compute resources like RPUs, VPC subnet groups, and security groups.

- Define the **workgroup name**.

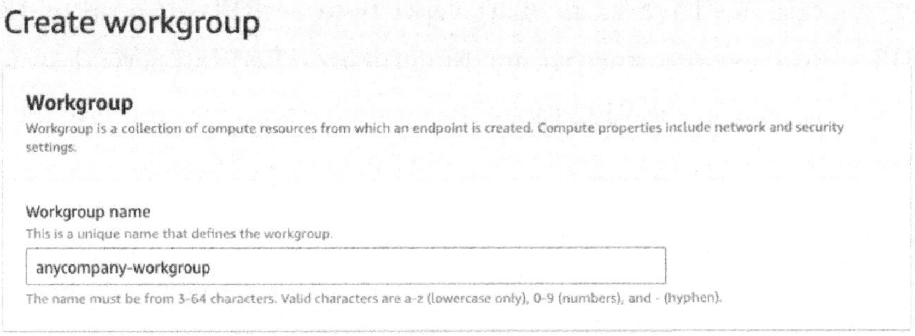

Create workgroup

Workgroup

Workgroup is a collection of compute resources from which an endpoint is created. Compute properties include network and security settings.

Workgroup name

This is a unique name that defines the workgroup.

anycompany-workgroup

The name must be from 3-64 characters. Valid characters are a-z (lowercase only), 0-9 (numbers), and - (hyphen).

Figure 9.7: Creation of Amazon Redshift serverless workgroup

Underperformance and control choose your base capacity ranging from 8- 1024 RPU (Redshift Processing Unit). A Redshift Processing Unit is a measure of compute capacity used in Amazon Redshift. This setting specifies the base data warehouse capacity Amazon Redshift uses to serve queries. One RPU provides 16 GB of memory. Setting higher base capacity improves query performance, especially for data processing jobs that consume a lot of resources. The default base capacity for Amazon Redshift Serverless is 128 RPUs. You can adjust the **Base capacity** setting from 8 RPUs to 512 RPUs in units of 8 (8,16,24...512) using the AWS console, the UpdateWorkgroup API operation, or the update-workgroup operation in the AWS CLI.

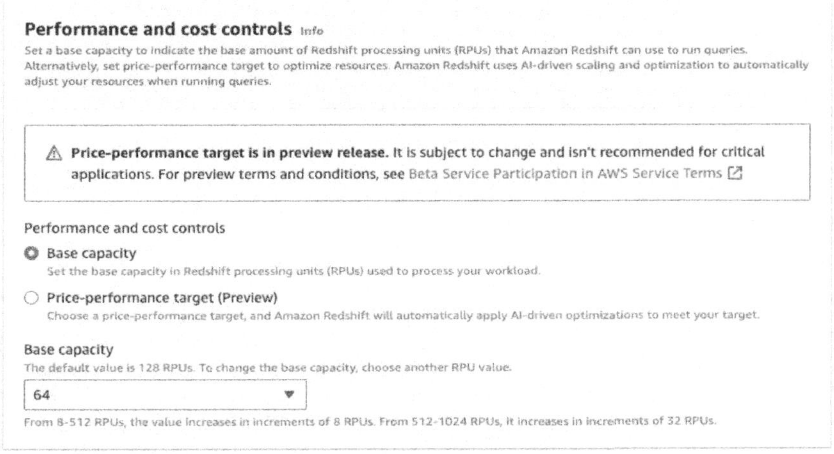

Performance and cost controls Info

Set a base capacity to indicate the base amount of Redshift processing units (RPUs) that Amazon Redshift can use to run queries. Alternatively, set price-performance target to optimize resources. Amazon Redshift uses AI-driven scaling and optimization to automatically adjust your resources when running queries.

Price-performance target is in preview release. It is subject to change and isn't recommended for critical applications. For preview terms and conditions, see Beta Service Participation in AWS Service Terms

Performance and cost controls

- Base capacity
  Set the base capacity in Redshift processing units (RPUs) used to process your workload.
- Price-performance target (Preview)
  Choose a price-performance target, and Amazon Redshift will automatically apply AI-driven optimizations to meet your target.

Base capacity

The default value is 128 RPUs. To change the base capacity, choose another RPU value.

64

From 8-512 RPUs, the value increases in increments of 8 RPUs. From 512-1024 RPUs, it increases in increments of 32 RPUs.

Figure 9.8: configuration of Amazon Redshift serverless

In this case, we have set the base capacity to 64 RPUs instead of 128 RPUs. Furthermore, since we are using Amazon Redshift Serverless, we can set a limit on the RPU capacity in order to set a maximum number of compute resources a workgroup uses at any point in time.

- We set the maximum capacity to **96 RPUs**

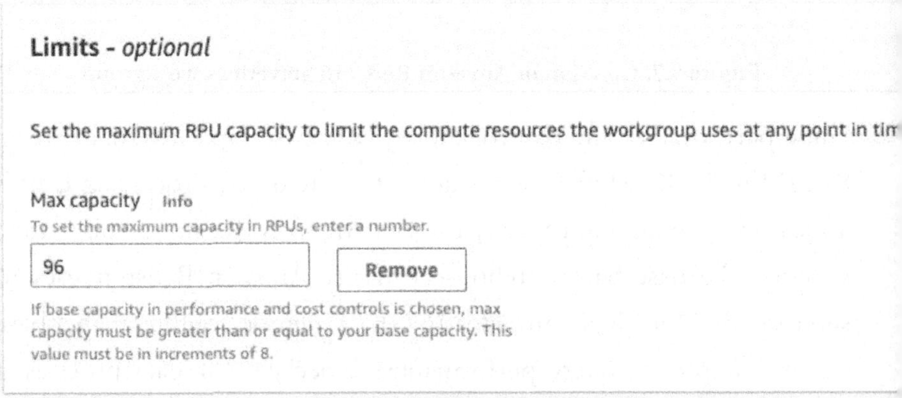

Limits - *optional*

Set the maximum RPU capacity to limit the compute resources the workgroup uses at any point in tim

Max capacity Info
To set the maximum capacity in RPUs, enter a number.

96 Remove

If base capacity in performance and cost controls is chosen, max capacity must be greater than or equal to your base capacity. This value must be in increments of 8.

Figure 9.9: Definition of the limits in Amazon Redshift serverless

- Under Network and Security, use the default created for you, or if you prefer, you can create your own VPC, subnets, and Security groups, then click on **Next:**

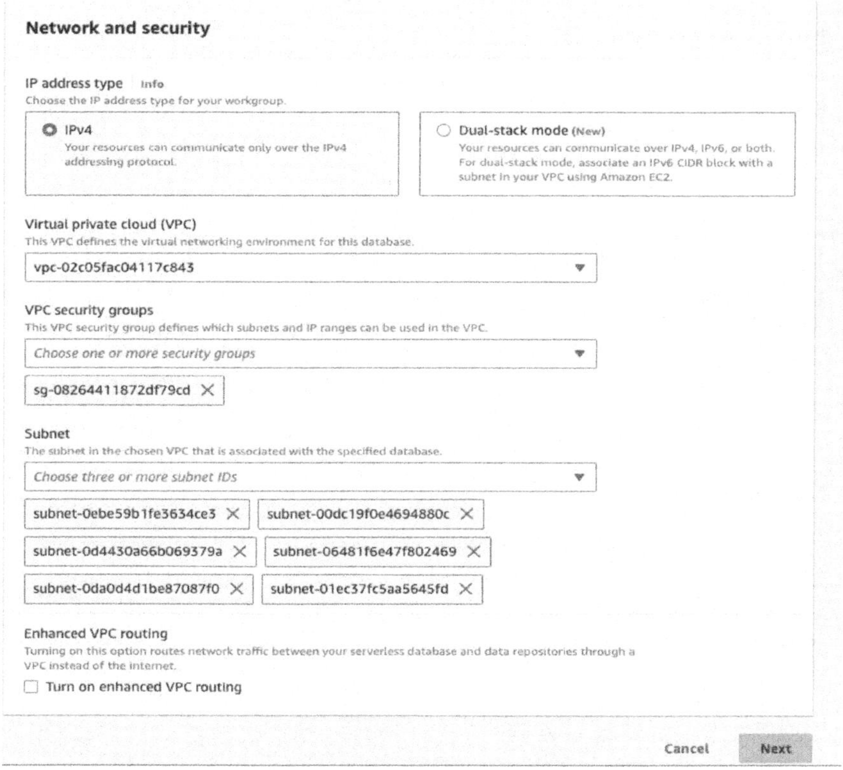

Network and security

IP address type Info

Choose the IP address type for your workgroup.

IPv4 — Your resources can communicate only over the IPv4 addressing protocol.

Dual-stack mode (New) — Your resources can communicate over IPv4, IPv6, or both. For dual-stack mode, associate an IPv6 CIDR block with a subnet in your VPC using Amazon EC2.

Virtual private cloud (VPC)

This VPC defines the virtual networking environment for this database.

vpc-02c05fac04117c843

VPC security groups

This VPC security group defines which subnets and IP ranges can be used in the VPC.

Choose one or more security groups

sg-08264411872df79cd

Subnet

The subnet in the chosen VPC that is associated with the specified database.

Choose three or more subnet IDs

subnet-0ebe59b1fe3634ce3

subnet-00dc19f0e4694880c

subnet-0d4430a66b069379a

subnet-06481f6e47f802469

subnet-0da0d4d1be87087f0

subnet-01ec37fc5aa5645fd

Enhanced VPC routing

Turning on this option routes network traffic between your serverless database and data repositories through a VPC instead of the internet.

Turn on enhanced VPC routing

Cancel Next

Figure 9.10: Configuration of network for Amazon Redshift serverless

- On the Choose Namespace page, create a new **Namespace**.

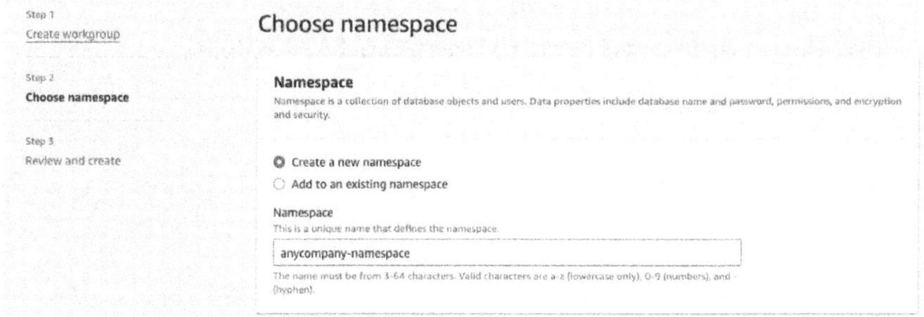

Figure 9.11: Creation of the namespace for Amazon Redshift serverless

- Next, enter your **Database name and password**. This information is crucial to later access your database.

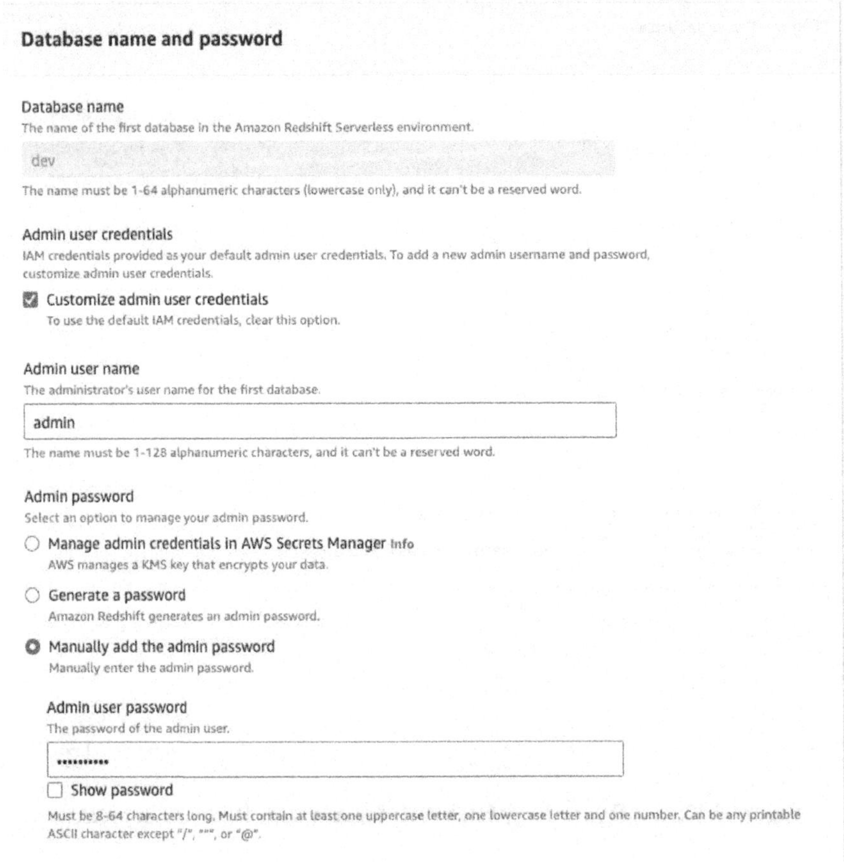

Database name and password

Database name

The name of the first database in the Amazon Redshift Serverless environment.

dev

The name must be 1-64 alphanumeric characters (lowercase only), and it can't be a reserved word.

Admin user credentials

IAM credentials provided as your default admin user credentials. To add a new admin username and password, customize admin user credentials.

☑ Customize admin user credentials

To use the default IAM credentials, clear this option.

Admin user name

The administrator's user name for the first database.

admin

The name must be 1-128 alphanumeric characters, and it can't be a reserved word.

Admin password

Select an option to manage your admin password.

○ Manage admin credentials in AWS Secrets Manager Info

AWS manages a KMS key that encrypts your data.

○ Generate a password

Amazon Redshift generates an admin password.

◉ Manually add the admin password

Manually enter the admin password.

Admin user password

The password of the admin user.

••••••••••

☐ Show password

Must be 8-64 characters long. Must contain at least one uppercase letter, one lowercase letter and one number. Can be any printable ASCII character except "/", """, or "@".

Figure 9.12: Configuration of database name and password

- For Permissions, we need to create an IAM role.

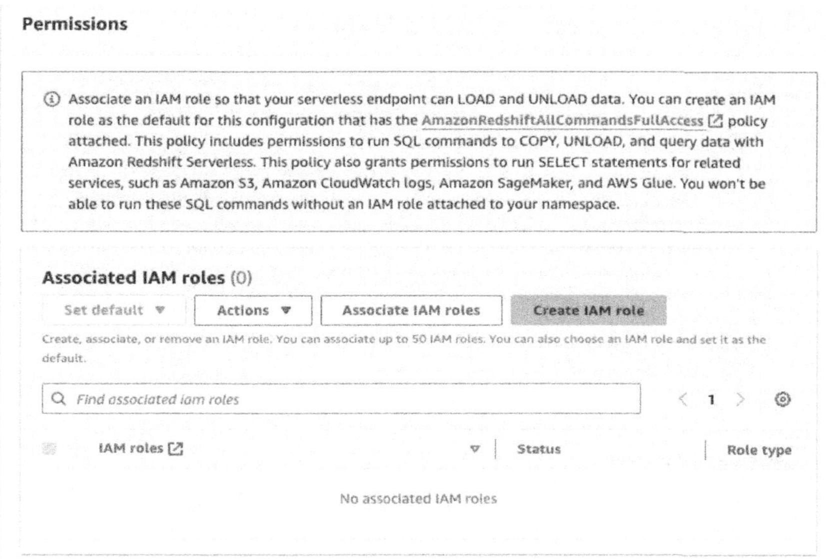

Permissions
Associate an IAM role so that your serverless endpoint can LOAD and UNLOAD data. You can create an IAM role as the default for this configuration that has the AmazonRedshiftAllCommandsFullAccess policy attached. This policy includes permissions to run SQL commands to COPY, UNLOAD, and query data with Amazon Redshift Serverless. This policy also grants permissions to run SELECT statements for related services, such as Amazon S3, Amazon CloudWatch logs, Amazon SageMaker, and AWS Glue. You won't be able to run these SQL commands without an IAM role attached to your namespace.
Associated IAM roles (0)
Set default
Actions
Associate IAM roles
Create IAM role
Create, associate, or remove an IAM role. You can associate up to 50 IAM roles. You can also choose an IAM role and set it as the default.
Find associated iam roles
1
IAM roles
Status
Role type
No associated IAM roles

Figure 9.13: Definition of the permission and IAM role

- A prompt will pop up to specify an Amazon S3 bucket for the IAM role to access and choose. One for this, we choose "Any S3 bucket" and click on "Create IAM role as default."

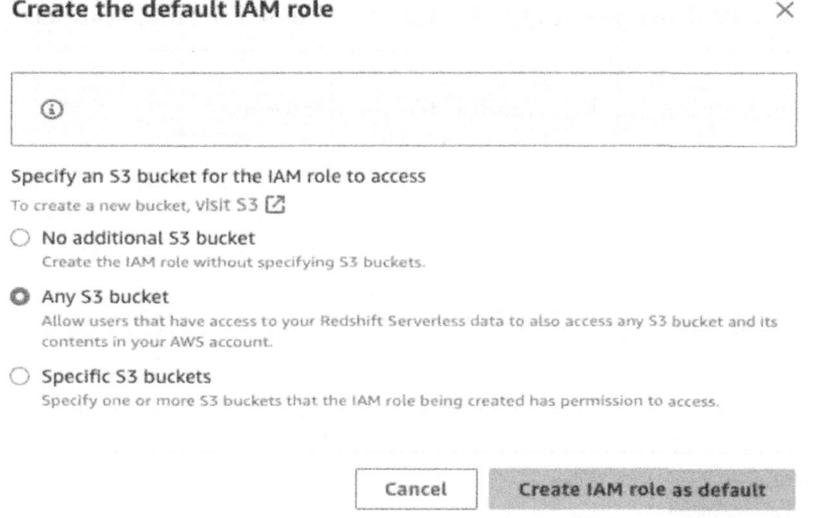

Create the default IAM role
Specify an S3 bucket for the IAM role to access
To create a new bucket, visit S3
No additional S3 bucket
Create the IAM role without specifying S3 buckets.
Any S3 bucket
Allow users that have access to your Redshift Serverless data to also access any S3 bucket and its contents in your AWS account.
Specific S3 buckets
Specify one or more S3 buckets that the IAM role being created has permission to access.
Cancel
Create IAM role as default

Figure 9.14: Figure 9.14 definition of the permission and IAM role

It will automatically create an IAM role for you.

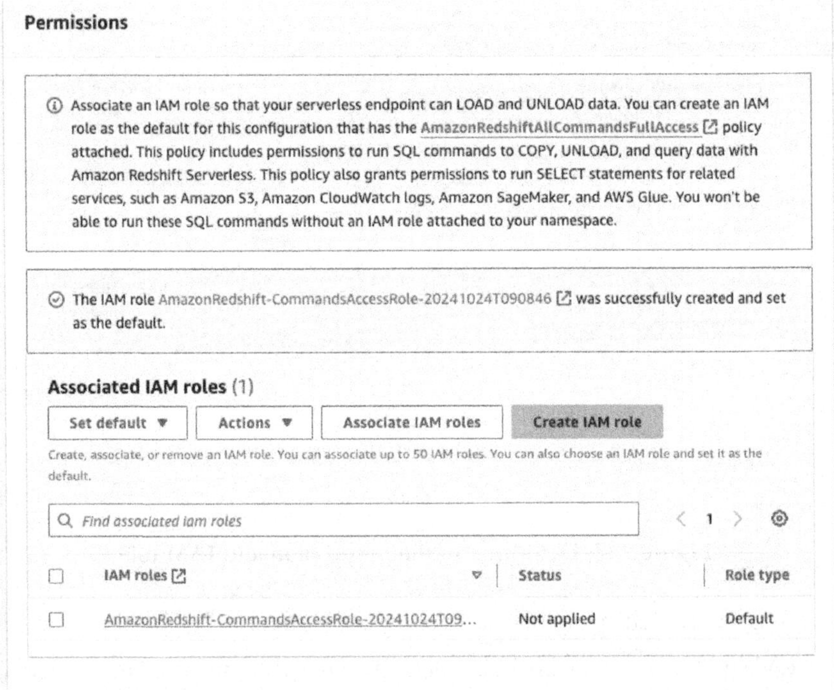

Figure 9.15: Definition of the permission and IAM role

- Under Encryption and Security for Audit Logging, you need to choose export to userlog, connection, and user activity logs to collect logging information for the database.

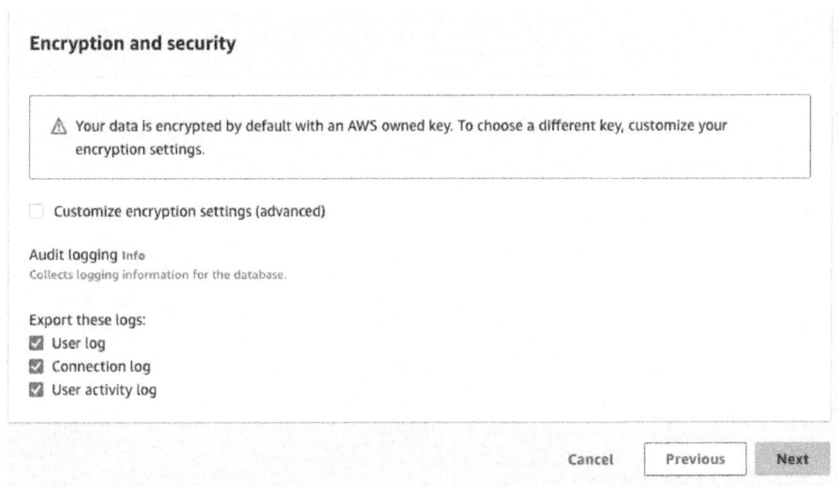

Figure 9.16: Configuration of encryption and security

- Click on Next, and you will be able to review all the steps created before finally creating the workgroup:

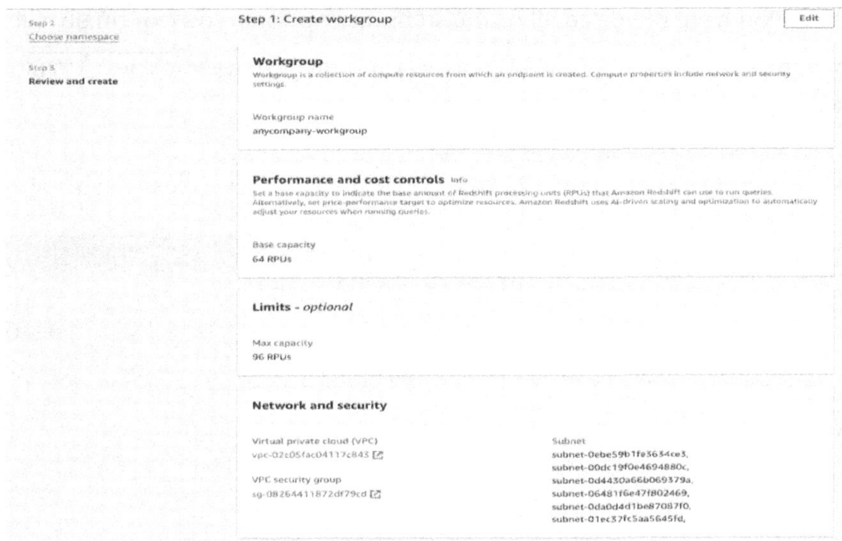

Figure 9.17: Configuration of encryption and security

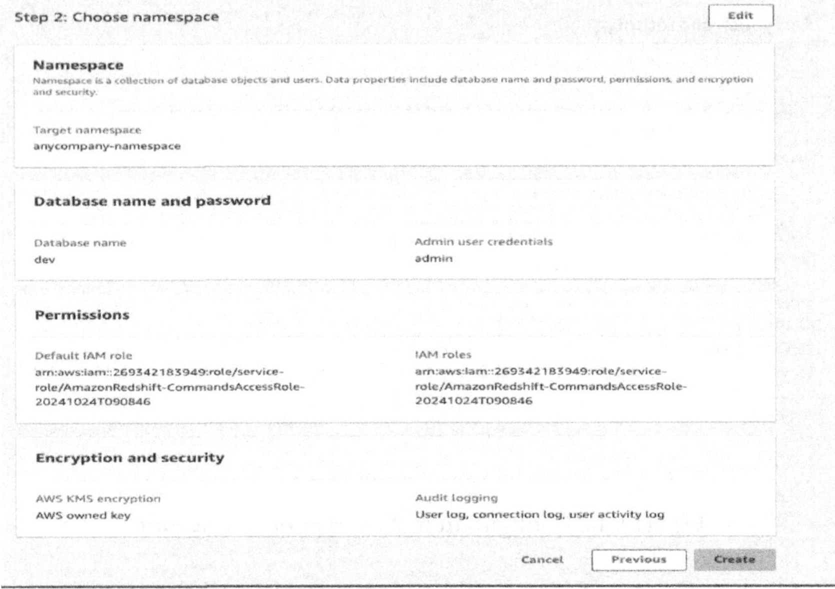

Figure 9.18: Configuration of encryption and security

After you have reviewed all of the steps and options, you can finally click on Create and see the new workgroup and namespace for your Amazon Redshift Serverless data warehouse.

- Once complete, you will be able to see your serverless dashboard:

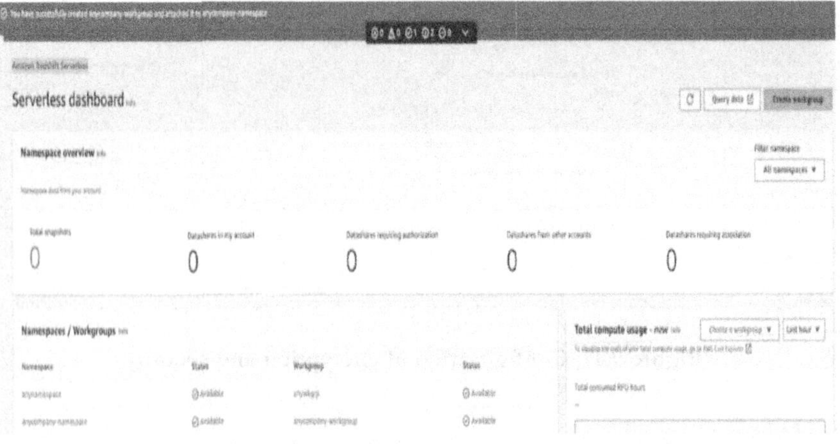

Figure 9.19: Amazon Redshift serverless dashboard

- From the namespace configuration, you can choose the namespace you created and then click on Query data:

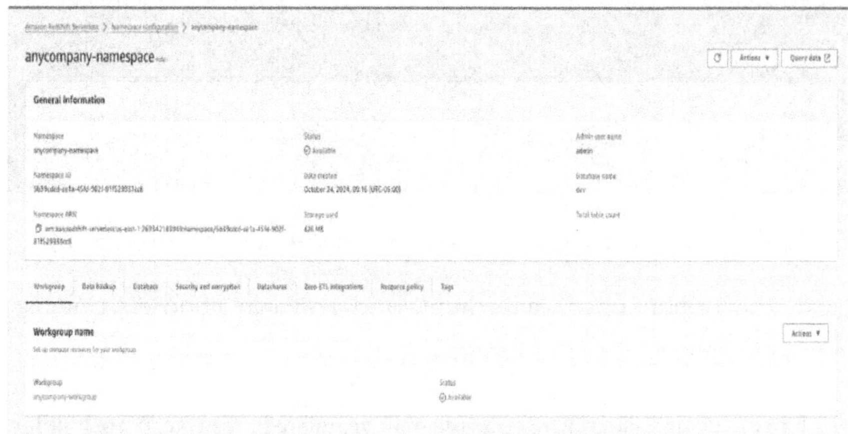

Figure 9.20: Selection of the namespace

After following those steps, your data warehouse solution has been created for your data product. Next, we will connect and load all of our data into Amazon Redshift.

Connecting and loading data into Amazon Redshift

Since our last step, clicking on Query data takes us to the Amazon Redshift Query Editor v2 page. Amazon Redshift Query Editor v2 is a web-based analyst workbench for you to securely explore, share, and collaborate on data with your teams using SQL within a common notebook interface. Amazon Redshift Query Editor v2 makes it easy to query your data using SQL and gain insights by visualizing your results using charts and graphs with a few clicks. In order to connect to your cluster, you can click on the three dots shown and create a connection.

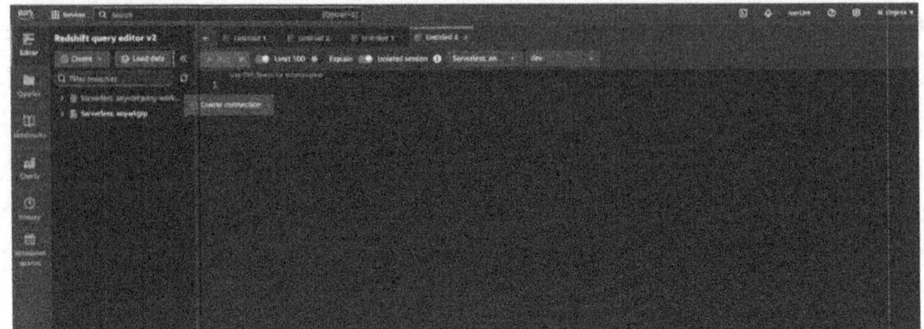

Figure 9.21: Connecting to the Amazon Redshift serverless workgroup

Next, the option opens a prompt, and you can choose "Database username and password" to connect.

- Enter your username password previously chosen and select Create Connection to connect:

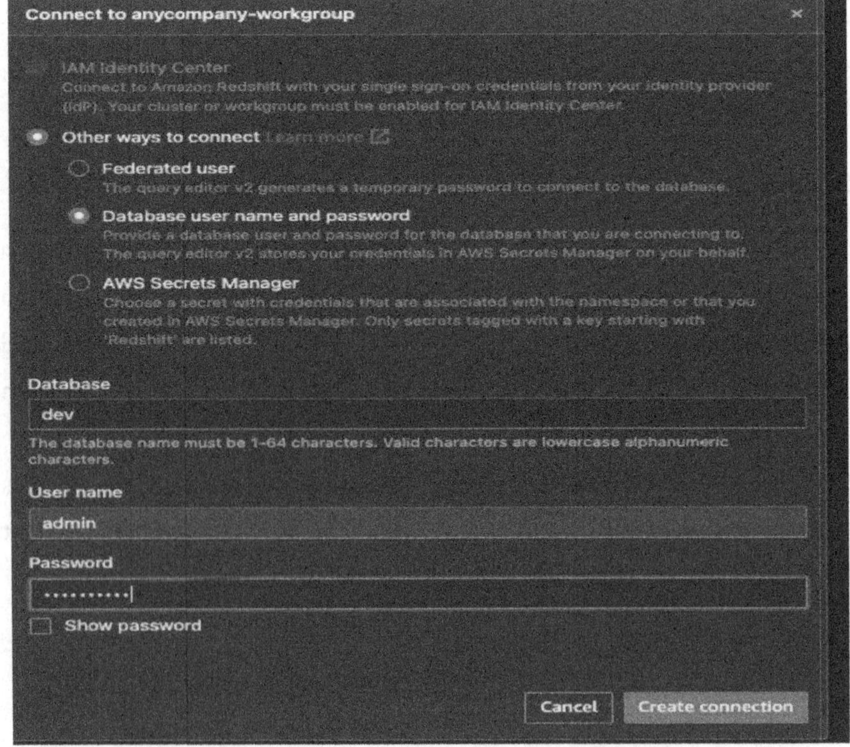

Figure 9.22: Connecting to the Amazon Redshift serverless workgroup

In order to import our data from Amazon S3 to Amazon Redshift, we are going to use the COPY command. To do so, we first create the table on the query editor by running the following command:

```
CREATE TABLE taxi_zone_lookup
( locationid bigint,
 borough varchar,
 zone varchar,
 service_zone varchar)
```

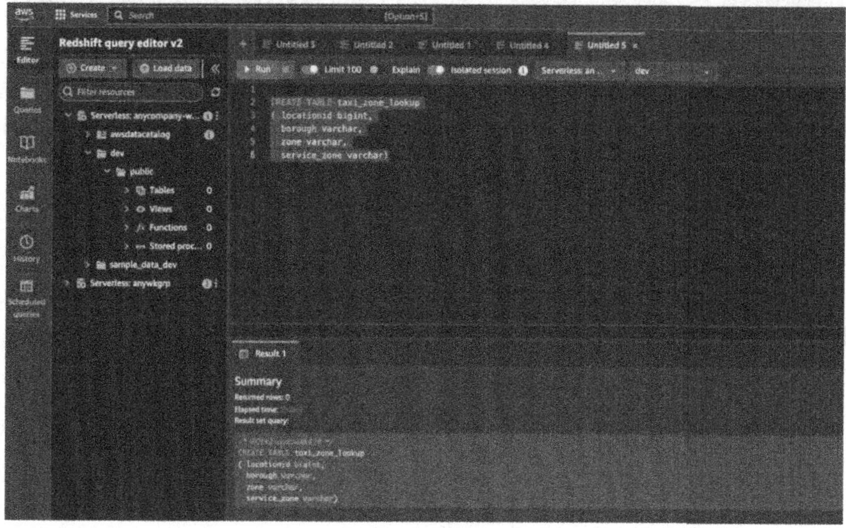

Figure 9.23: Creation of the table taxi_zone_lookup

Then, use the COPY COMMAND to copy data from Amazon S3 to Amazon Redshift. We will be copying the data we loaded in the Load table to Amazon S3:

```
COPY taxi_zone_lookup
FROM 's3://testbucketv3467/taxi_zone_lookup.csv'
IAM_ROLE DEFAULT
FORMAT AS CSV
IGNOREHEADER 1;
```

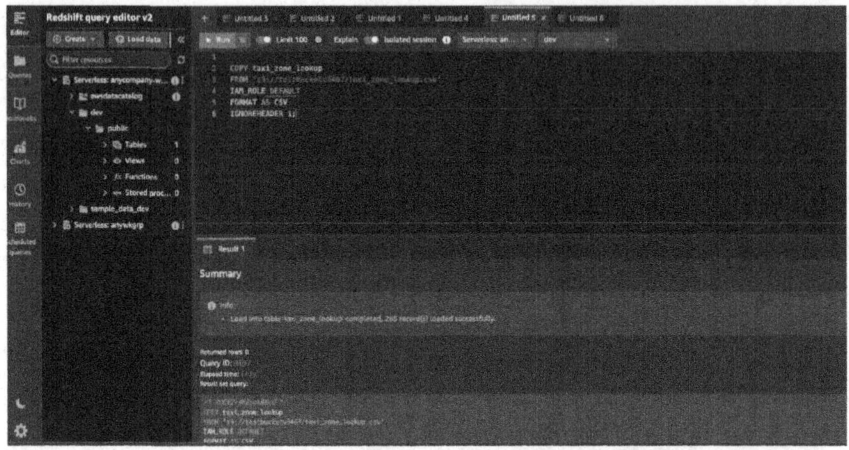

Figure 9.24: Data ingestion from Amazon S3 to Amazon Redshift

We have successfully created our table and, using the COPY command, loaded data from Amazon S3 to Amazon Redshift.

Transforming data with Amazon Redshift

In the next step, we need to perform some transformations to our data in order to process it. To transform data with Amazon Redshift, we can directly use the Query Editor v2. The transformations performed will be as follows:

1. Creating Views and using CTAS (CREATE TABLE AS SELECT) to create new tables
2. Perform CASE statements
3. Perform some aggregations and grouping

Note that the above is not limited to the type of transformations you can do in Amazon Redshift. You can also use UDF and Stored procedures to create different logic that fit your business logic.

Example1: Creating Views and using CTAS to create new tables

```
CREATE TABLE borough_summary AS
SELECT
  borough,
  COUNT(DISTINCT zone) AS num_zones,
  COUNT(DISTINCT service_zone) AS num_service_zones
FROM
  taxi_zone_lookup
GROUP BY
  borough;
```

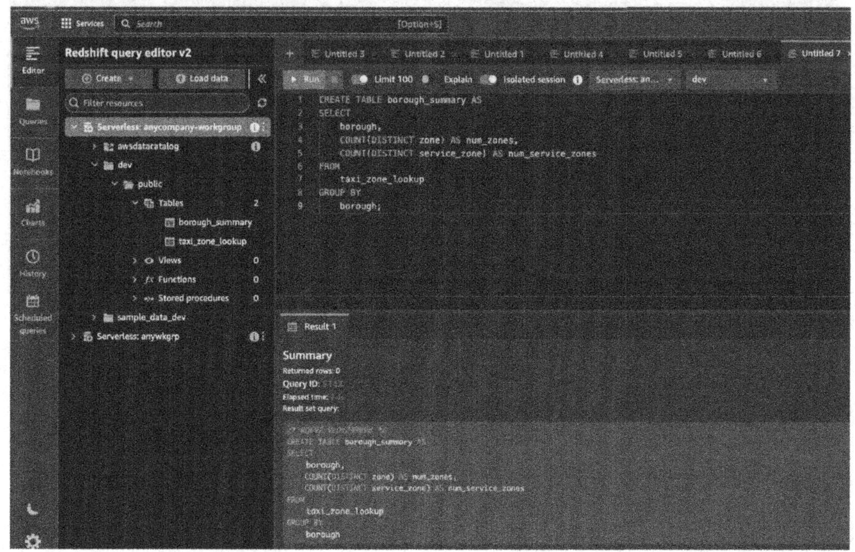

Figure 9.25: Creating a Table As Select (CTAS)

```
CREATE VIEW standardized_taxi_zones AS
SELECT
  locationid,
  CASE
    WHEN borough = 'Bronx' THEN 'The Bronx'
    WHEN borough = 'Staten Island' THEN 'Staten Island'
    ELSE INITCAP(borough)
  END AS standardized_borough,
```

```
    zone,
    service_zone
FROM
    taxi_zone_lookup;
```

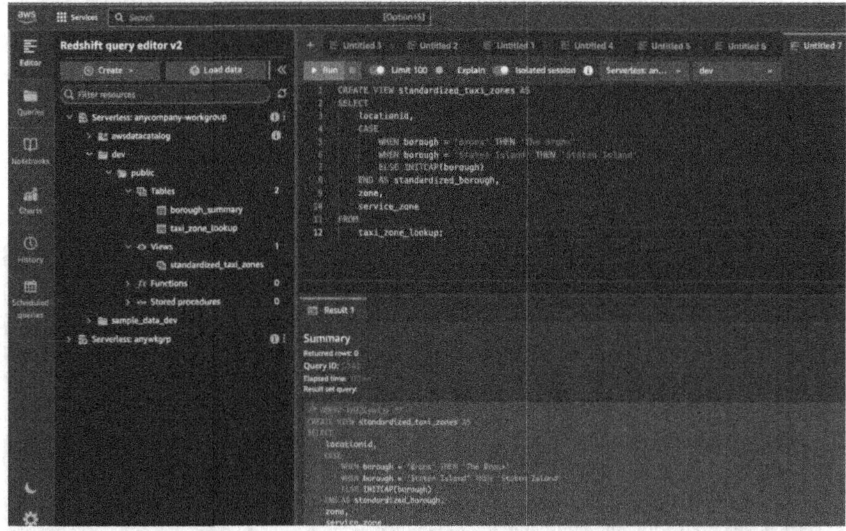

Figure 9.26: Creating a view in Amazon Redshift

Example 2: USING CASE WHEN

```
CREATE VIEW standardized_taxi AS
SELECT
    locationid,
    CASE
        WHEN borough = 'Bronx' THEN 'The Bronx'
        WHEN borough = 'Staten Island' THEN 'Staten Island'
        ELSE INITCAP(borough)
    END AS standardized_borough,
    zone,
    service_zone
FROM
    taxi_zone_lookup;
```

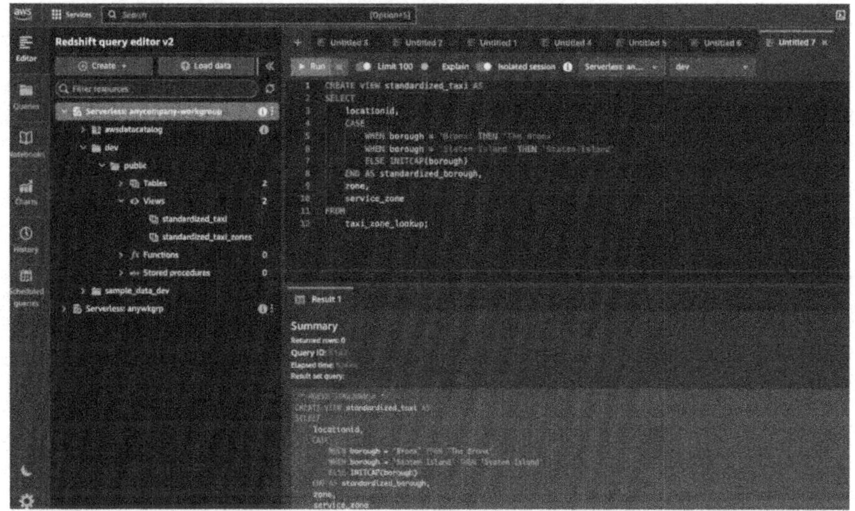

Figure 9.27: Creating a view in Amazon Redshift with Case When

Example 3: Perform some aggregations and grouping

```
REATE TABLE zone_distribution AS
SELECT
   zone,
   COUNT(DISTINCT borough) AS borough_count,
   COUNT(DISTINCT service_zone) AS service_zone_count
FROM
   taxi_zone_lookup
GROUP BY
   zone
HAVING
   COUNT(DISTINCT borough) > 1 OR COUNT(DISTINCT
service_zone) > 1;
```

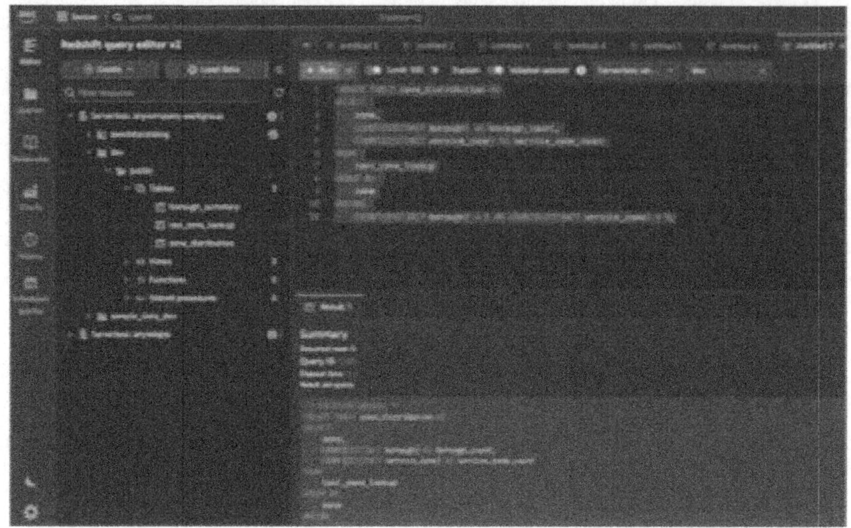

Figure 9.28: Creating a table in Amazon Redshift with aggregations and grouping

After the following transformations, we have processed our data by performing some aggregations and groupings as needed. The next step would be to query the data processed in our data warehouse to visualize the results.

Querying data with Amazon Redshift

In order to query the data, we can directly perform the action by using the Query Editor v2 and some simple SQL queries. Some examples could be:

Example 1: Retrieve all data from the table :

```
SELECT * FROM  taxi_zone_lookup;
```

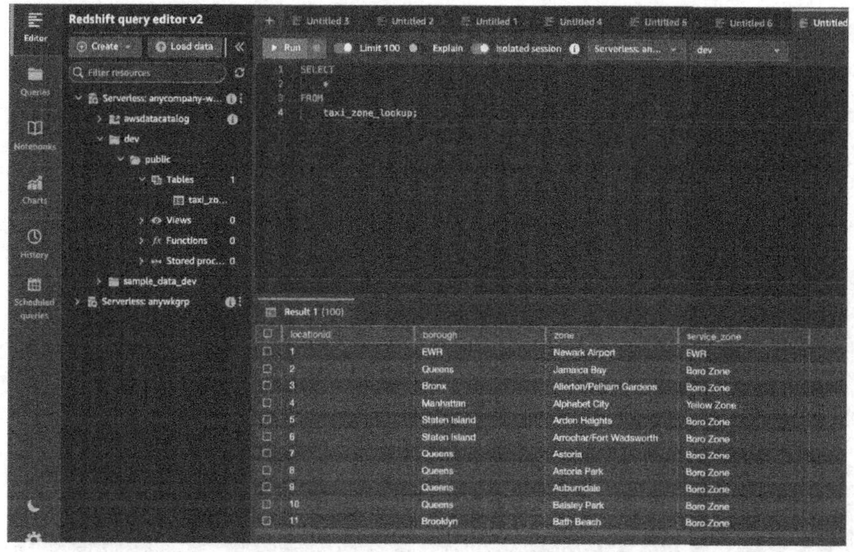

Figure 9.29: Query data in Amazon Redshit Query Editor V2

Example 2: Retrieve the location ID along with the borough and zone:

```
SELECT
    locationid,borough,zone
FROM
    taxi_zone_lookup
WHERE borough = 'Bronx';
```

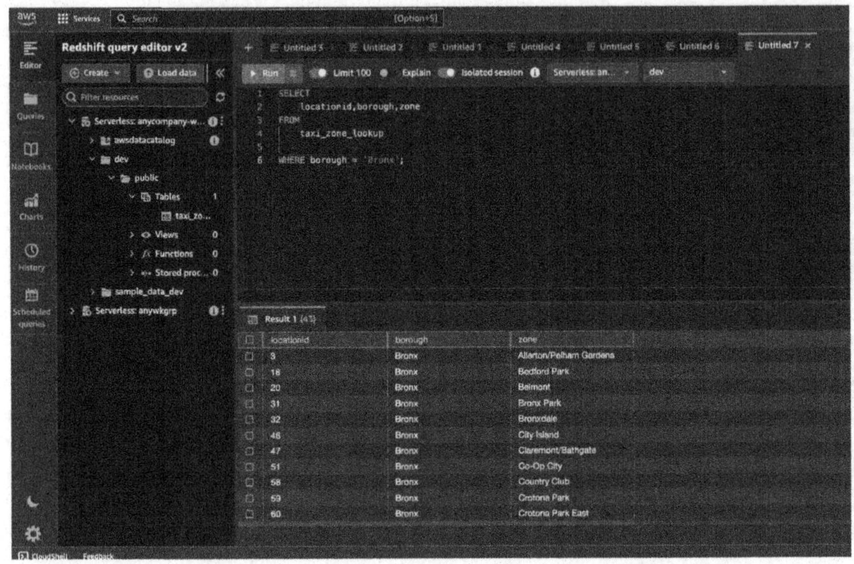

Figure 9.30: Query data in Amazon Redshit Query Editor V2

Example 3: Count the number of zones by borough

```
SELECT
  borough,
  COUNT(*) AS zone_count
FROM
  taxi_zone_lookup
GROUP BY
  borough
ORDER BY
  zone_count DESC;
```

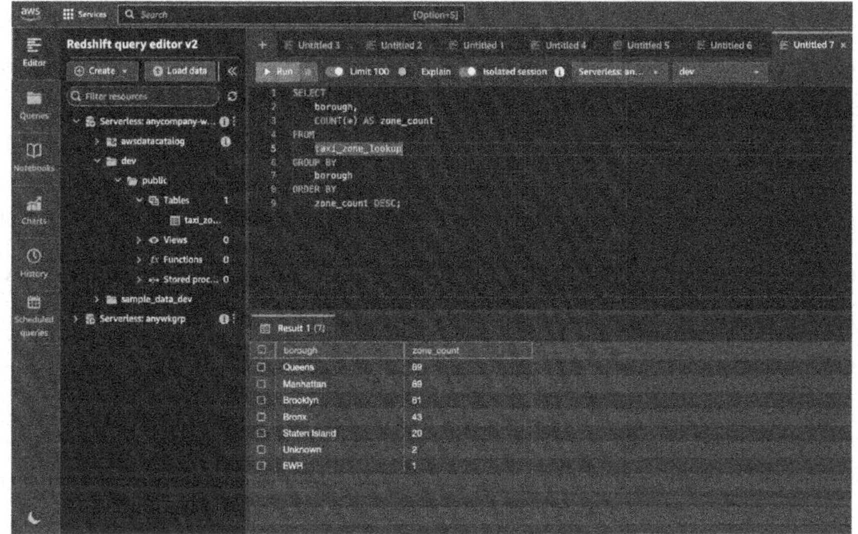

Figure 9.31: query data in Amazon Redshit Query Editor V2

As you can see from the result returned, the tables have changed from the previously loaded raw data. Our data warehouse would be finalized for our data product.

Summary

This chapter focuses on building a data product in a data warehouse and using SQL. It begins by explaining the purpose and value of a data warehouse - a centralized, integrated repository of data designed to support analytical and reporting workloads within an organization. Unlike operational databases optimized for transactional processing, a data warehouse provides a unified, consistent, and comprehensive view of an organization's data, enabling more informed and data-driven decision-making.

The chapter then outlines the steps to create a data product using Amazon Redshift, a fully managed, cloud-based data warehouse service. It starts by describing how to load data into an Amazon S3 bucket, which serves as the data lake foundation. Next, the process of creating an Amazon Redshift Serverless workgroup is detailed, including configuring the workgroup's performance, network, security, and permissions settings.

With the data warehouse infrastructure in place, the chapter covers connecting to Amazon Redshift and using the COPY command to load data from the S3 bucket into Redshift tables. It then demonstrates how to transform the data within Redshift, including creating views, using CTAS (Create Table As Select) to build new tables, applying CASE statements, and performing aggregations and grouping.

Finally, the chapter provides examples of querying the transformed data in the Redshift data warehouse using the Query Editor v2 tool. These queries showcase retrieving all data from a table, filtering and selecting specific columns, and aggregating data to count the number of zones by borough.

Throughout the chapter, we are guided through the end-to-end process of building a data product on a data warehouse, leveraging the capabilities of Amazon Redshift to ingest, store, transform, and query large volumes of data to support informed business decision-making.

10. Self-service Data Mesh: Democratize Analytics and AI using Amazon DataZone

By the end of this chapter, you'll have a comprehensive understanding of how different roles within your organization can effectively navigate and utilize the data mesh architecture to drive insights, innovation, and value. It mainly covers,

1. Data producers to list data products into a centralized technical catalog using Amazon Glue.
2. Data stewards to enrich the catalog and build a business glossary using Amazon DataZone.
3. Data consumer analysts subscribe to data products and build new data products using Amazon DataZone and its built-in Amazon Athena.
4. Data consumers and data scientists can consume data products and build ML models using Amazon Datazone and its built-in Amazon Sagemaker.

Technical skills needed

- Basic understanding of AWS cloud and how to navigate within AWS Console
- Basic understanding of Data Mesh design with roles and responsibilities

- A novice-level grasp of key AWS services, including Amazon DataZone for data management, Amazon Athena for SQL queries, Amazon Redshift for data warehousing, and Amazon SageMaker for machine learning, along with their primary functionalities.

In chapters 7 through 10, we explored various methods for creating data products within a data mesh architecture. Now that you've gained insight into data product development let's take a practical, step-by-step approach to understanding how different consumer personas in a Data Mesh architecture can discover, subscribe to, and query data for their specific use cases. This chapter will focus on four key consumer personas:

1. Data Stewards

2. Data Analysts

3. Data Scientists

Each of these roles plays an important part in leveraging the data mesh architecture to its fullest potential. We'll examine how they interact with the system to curate assets, locate assets in the catalog, request access, and utilize data for their individual needs.

The Data Steward's Crucial Role in Data Product Management Using Amazon DataZone

In the intricate world of data management, one role stands out as particularly vital: the Data Steward. Before we embark on our journey through the intricacies of querying a data product, it's crucial to understand the significance of this position.

Data Stewards are the bridge between the technical and business realms. They possess a deep understanding of both domains, allowing them to translate complex technical metadata into comprehensible business terms. Consider, for instance, a technical data asset named "cust_order_invoice." While this name hints at invoice data for customer orders, it leaves many questions unanswered. Is it specific to web orders? Does it pertain to business-to-business transactions? Or perhaps it relates to orders placed in physical stores?

In medium to large organizations, data product teams often operate in silos, focusing on their specific lines of business (LOBs) or even individual functions within a LOB. This is where the Data Steward's role becomes indispensable. They create a business glossary, effectively translating technical jargon into a language that resonates with business users across the organization.

But the Data Steward's responsibilities extend far beyond mere translation. They are tasked with defining and enforcing acceptable quality standards at the attribute level, working closely with data producers to ensure these standards are met. Additionally, they play a crucial role in establishing compliance standards for various business functions within the organization.

Perhaps one of their most critical duties is approving subscription access to data objects for consumers of data products. This gatekeeping function ensures that sensitive data is accessed only by authorized personnel, maintaining both security and regulatory compliance.

To better understand how these responsibilities are executed in practice, let's explore the steps a Data Steward would take using Amazon DataZone, a powerful tool designed to streamline data management processes.

In the following sections, we'll walk through each of these steps, providing you with a comprehensive understanding of how Data Stewards navigates their complex role in the modern data landscape.

Customer 360 Data Product

This data product would provide a comprehensive view of customers, including their demographics, addresses, and household information

Contributing tables in the TPC-DS data set for Customer 360 data product:

- customer
- customer_address
- customer_demographics
- household_demographics
- income_band

In our scenario, we have a data steward who is in the process of enhancing a comprehensive customer data product, often referred to as a "Customer 360" data product. The data producer ETL team, responsible for supplying the necessary information, has already contributed various data assets to this product. These assets, which we will interchangeably refer to as tables, have been published in the AWS Glue data catalog.

Tables (25)

View and manage all available tables.

Last updated (UTC) October 14, 2024 at 16:10:01

Delete

Filter tables

Name	Database	Location	Classification	De
call_center	tpcds3tb	s3:// /tpcds3t/call_center/	Parquet	-
catalog_page	tpcds3tb	s3:// /tpcds3t/catalog_page/	Parquet	-
catalog_returns	tpcds3tb	s3:// /tpcds3t/catalog_returns/	Parquet	-
catalog_sales	tpcds3tb	s3:// /tpcds3t/catalog_sales/	Parquet	-
customer	tpcds3tb	s3:// /tpcds3t/customer/	Parquet	-
customer_address	tpcds3tb	s3:// /tpcds3t/customer_address/	Parquet	-
customer_demographics	tpcds3tb	s3:// /tpcds3t/customer_demographics/	Parquet	-
date_dim	tpcds3tb	s3:// /tpcds3t/date_dim/	Parquet	-
household_demographics	tpcds3tb	s3:// /tpcds3t/household_demographics/	Parquet	-
income_band	tpcds3tb	s3:// /tpcds3t/income_band/	Parquet	-
inventory	tpcds3tb	s3:// /tpcds3t/inventory/	Parquet	-
item	tpcds3tb	s3:// /tpcds3t/item/	Parquet	-
promotion	tpcds3tb	s3:// /tpcds3t/promotion/	Parquet	-
reason	tpcds3tb	s3:// /tpcds3t/reason/	Parquet	-
ship_mode	tpcds3tb	s3:// /tpcds3t/ship_mode/	Parquet	-
store	tpcds3tb	s3:// /tpcds3t/store/	Parquet	-
store_returns	tpcds3tb	s3:// /tpcds3t/store_returns/	Parquet	-

Figure 10.1: Tables contributing to customer 360 data product

The AWS Glue data catalog serves as a centralized metadata repository, housing the schema and location information for these tables. Figure 11.1 illustrates the tables within the TPC-DS public dataset in the AWS Glue catalog that represents a typical retail company's decision support system. The tables highlighted in the image collectively form the foundation of our Customer 360 data product.

By leveraging these tables, the data steward can now begin the process of enriching and refining the Customer 360 view, ultimately creating a more robust and valuable data product for the organization.

Data Steward practical execution steps

This section will showcase the execution steps performed by the data steward in order to build a customer 360 data product from the TPCDS sales dataset.

At this point, we assume that the Datazone Domain is pre-created with the domain name *Retail-Demo,* and the data steward name *book-steward* is provided access to the domain to create a Datazone project. Now, let's get you into the role of the data steward as we walk you through the steps.

1. Create a datazone project with the name customer, which becomes a workspace to curate and enrich the customer 360 data product. Figure 10.2 illustrates the creation of a datazone project.

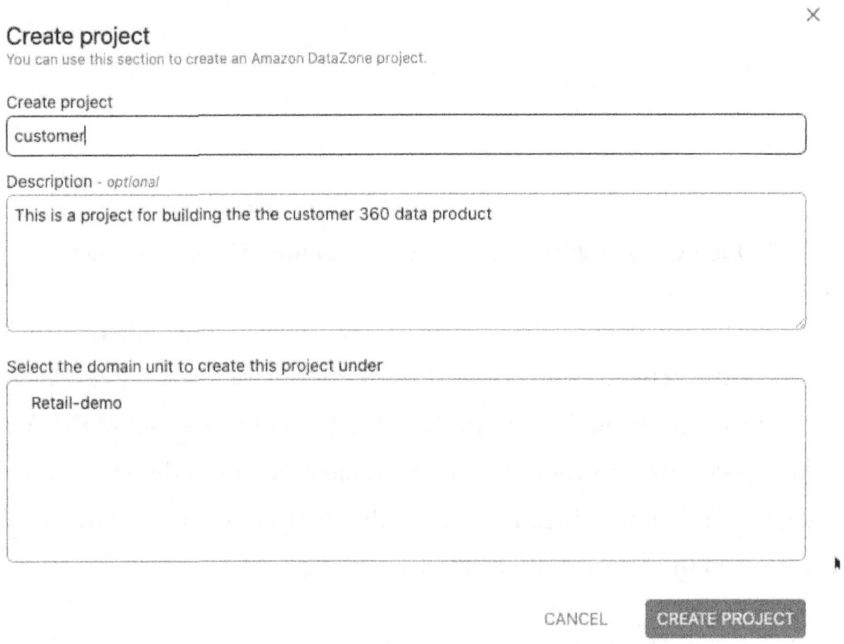

Figure 10.2: DataZone project creation

2. An Amazon DataZone environment profile is a template used to create environments within the Amazon DataZone service. It serves as a blueprint that simplifies the process of environment creation by embedding key configuration details and parameters.

Create a datazone env profile named customer360ENVProfile, as shown in Figure 10.3. Notice the environment profile is under the customer created in Step 1.

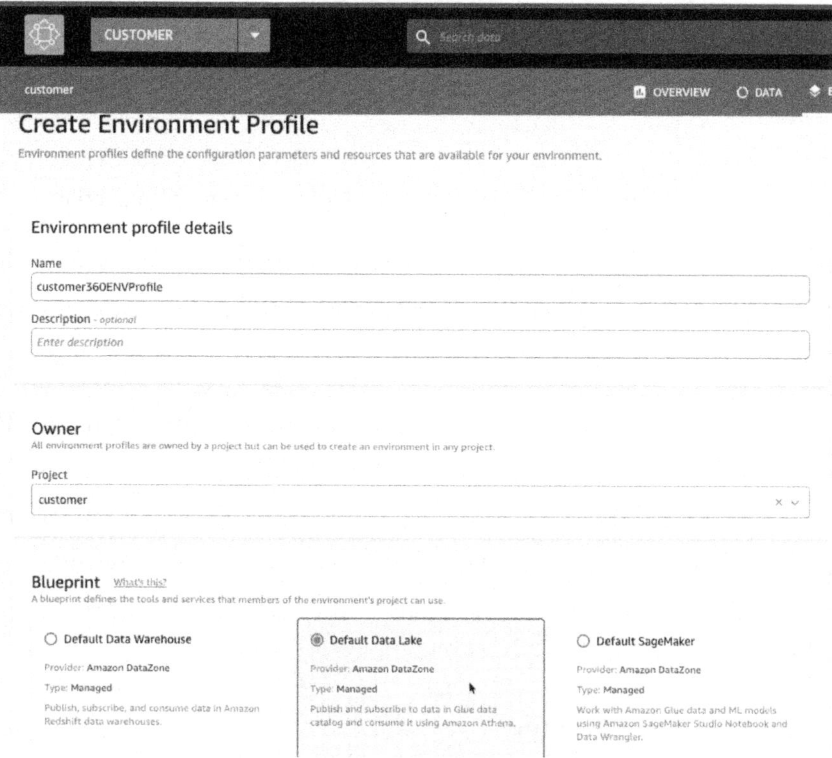

Figure 10.3: Creating Datazone Environment Profile

3. An Amazon DataZone environment is a collection of configured resources and authorized users within a project that enables data collaboration and analysis.

Amazon DataZone environments and environment profiles are closely related components within the DataZone ecosystem. Their relationship can be described as follows:

Environment profiles serve as templates or blueprints for creating DataZone environments. This relationship is fundamental to the efficient and governed creation of workspaces within DataZone.

Create a DataZone environment as shown in Figure 10.4

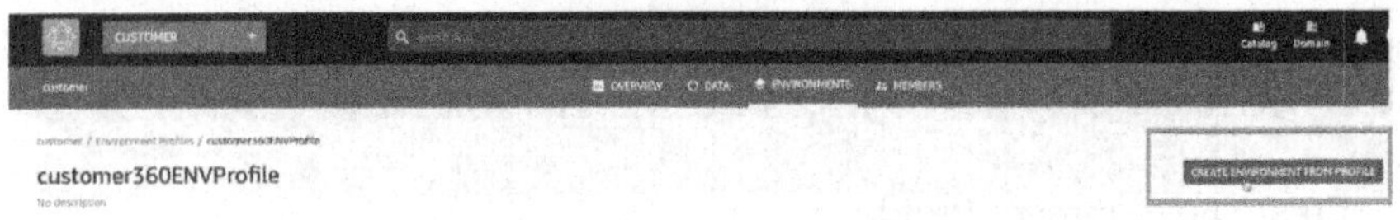

Figure 10.4: Creating datazone environment from profile

During the creation process, there is an important consideration. Parameters allow a level of customization to meet your enterprise nomenclature.

During the creation of an Amazon DataZone environment, the parameters section includes fields for Producer Glue DB name, Consumer Glue DB name, and Workgroup name. These parameters are applicable when using the Data Lake blueprint and are essential for setting up the environment's data infrastructure. Here's a brief explanation of each:

Producer Glue DB Name

This parameter specifies the name of the AWS Glue database that will be used for data production activities within the environment. It's applicable when:

- Data producers need to create and manage tables for data publishing
- The environment is used for data ingestion, transformation, or preparation tasks

Consumer Glue DB Name

This parameter defines the name of the AWS Glue database that will be used for data consumption activities. It's relevant when:

- Data consumers need to access and query data within the environment

- The environment is used for data analysis or reporting purposes

Workgroup Name

This parameter sets the name of the Amazon Athena workgroup associated with the environment. It's applicable when:

- Users need to query data using Amazon Athena within the environment
- The environment requires a dedicated space for running Athena queries

The Athena workgroup is created as part of the Data Lake blueprint and allows users to create and query Lake Formation tables.

These parameters are particularly relevant when using the Data Lake blueprint, which provides users with the ability to create and query Lake Formation tables using Amazon Athena, as well as access to AWS Glue databases with appropriate permissions for both production and consumption activities.

Update the parameters section as shown in Figure 10.5.

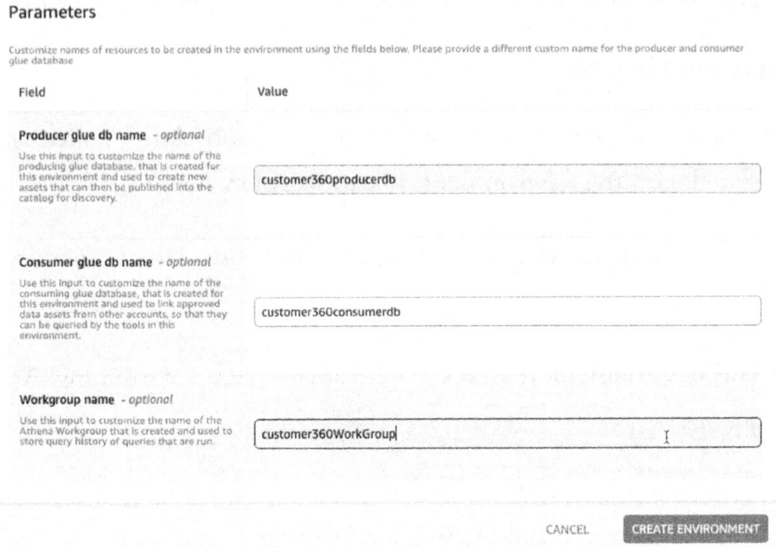

Figure 10.5: Illustrates the Configuration for Parameters

4. At this point, you have all the tooling and computing required to perform your role as a data steward. Create a source connection to the Glue catalog and fetch the 5 tables that you need to curate the customer 360 data product. Figure 10.6 shows the connection configuration.

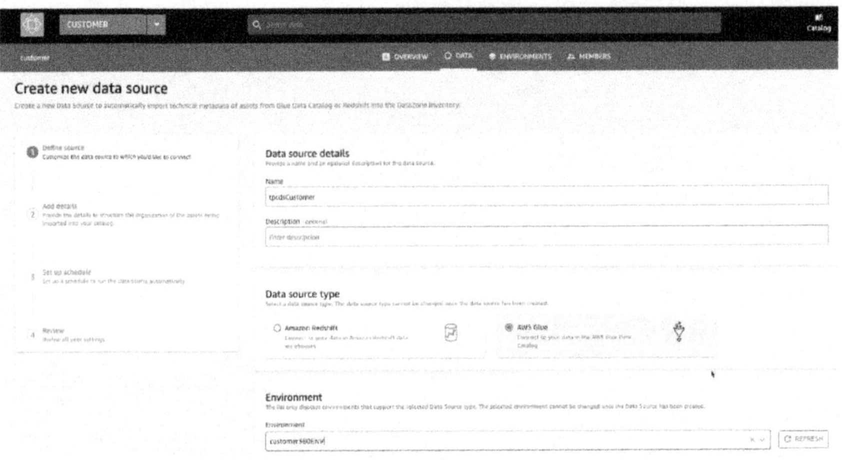

Figure 10.6: Create a data source connection configuration-1

Select the source tables relevant to the customer 360 data product. These are the 5 tables of interest from the Glue catalog shown in Figure 10.1

Figure 10.7: Data source connection configuration-2

Run the data source to fetch the tables in the Glue catalog. Upon completion, the tables and their associated metadata are now fetched inside the Datazone's own internal catalog, and each table will now appear as a data asset in Datazone. Figure 10.8 illustrates this.

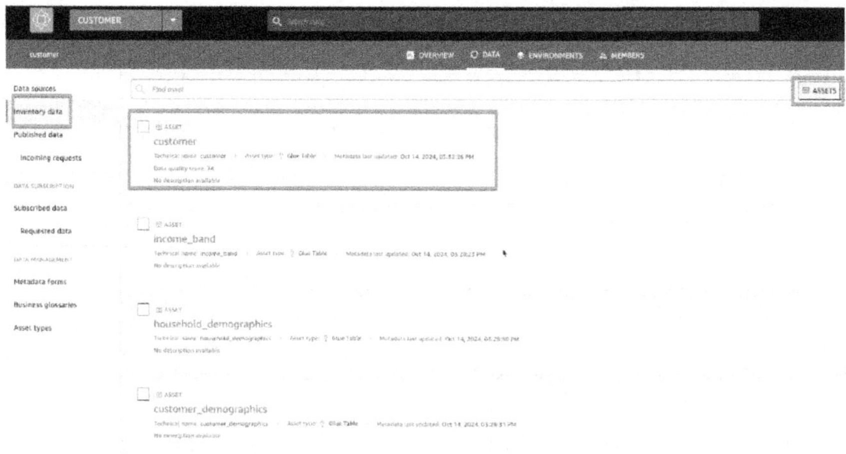

Figure 10.8: Datazone assets in inventory view

There is a subtle difference between inventory data and published data, which is highlighted in Figure 10.8.

Inventory data refers to assets that have been brought into a specific project within Amazon DataZone. These assets are only discoverable and accessible to members of that particular project. It serves as a staging area where data producers can organize, curate, and prepare assets before making them widely available. Project owners and contributors can enrich inventory assets with business metadata, descriptions, and other relevant information.

Published data refers to assets that have been made available in the Amazon DataZone catalog. All domain users who have access to DataZone can discover these assets. It represents data that has been approved for wider use and consumption across the organization. Users can search, discover, and request subscriptions to published data assets.

5. Poor data leads to poor insights. This is a universal truth. Before a data asset can be published, there are certain established guidelines, typically defined by data stewards within the organization, to certify a data asset as consumable. We covered a good deal of depth on what guidelines are available in this book under chapters 3 and 5.

For the purposes of this section, let's use the following guidelines that each data asset must meet before a data steward can certify and publish it for consumption.

- Establish Data quality standards.
- Business-friendly names for Table and Column objects
- Business-friendly descriptions of the Table and Column objects
- Manage metadata relevant to data consumers

- Manage Glossary definitions for data assets

Establish Data Quality Standards

Amazon DataZone acquires data quality information for data assets through two primary methods:

- Integration with AWS Glue Data Quality:
    - DataZone directly integrates with AWS Glue to import data quality scores for AWS Glue Data Catalog assets.
    - When creating or editing an AWS Glue data source in DataZone, users can enable data quality by selecting "Enable data quality for this data source."
    - Once enabled, DataZone automatically fetches data quality scores from AWS Glue during each data source run.
    - For existing assets, users can enable data quality in the DataZone project's "Inventory Data" pane.
- APIs for external data quality solutions:
    - DataZone offers APIs that allow data quality scores to be imported from third-party or external data quality systems.
    - Organizations can use these APIs to push data quality metrics from their existing quality assessment tools into DataZone.

6. Review data quality of the data assets as shown in Figure 10.9

Figure 10.9: Illustrates the data quality for Customer data asset

Notice the overall data quality score, which reflects all the columns in the customer table in the Glue catalog on which data quality rules were defined. Notice the rules failed, which allows you to reach out to the data producer team to investigate and fix data quality before promoting this data asset for publishing.

Now, let's assume the data producer fixed the data quality, and the score meets your data quality standards for publishing. So, you move forward with your curation.

Business-friendly name descriptions for Table and Column objects

Amazon DataZone provides a powerful capability to generate business-friendly descriptions for table and column data assets using generative AI. Here's a brief overview of this feature:

- Automated Generation: DataZone can automatically generate high-quality descriptions for data assets, including tables and columns, using AI models powered by Amazon Bedrock with its fully managed foundation models.

- Contextual Understanding: The system uses available metadata such as table names, column names, and optional metadata provided by data producers to generate relevant descriptions.
- Domain-Specific Insights: The AI-first infers the domain (e.g., automotive, finance, healthcare) of the data asset, then tailors the descriptions and use cases to that specific industry context.
- Comprehensive Coverage: Generated descriptions include:

  a. Overall meaning of the table in the context of the identified industry

  b. Narrative descriptions of the most important columns

  c. How columns relate to each other

  d. Potential use cases for the data
- Enhanced Discoverability: These AI-generated descriptions improve data discovery by providing a richer context for search functionality and helping users quickly understand the relevance of data assets.
- Time-Saving: Data producers can generate contextual descriptions with a single click, saving time on manual catalog curation and encouraging more data to be made available.
- User-Friendly Interface: Users can easily generate these descriptions through the DataZone data portal by clicking "Generate summary" on an asset's page.
- Customization Options: Data producers can provide additional context as metadata in the readme section or metadata form content for more tailored descriptions.

This feature significantly enhances the ability of data consumers to find, understand, and trust data quickly and easily while also streamlining the process for data producers to provide meaningful context for their data assets.

7. Click on the Generate Descriptions button found under the Business Metadata tab for each of the data assets. Upon completion, you will see the descriptions for Customer data assets, as shown in Figure 10.10

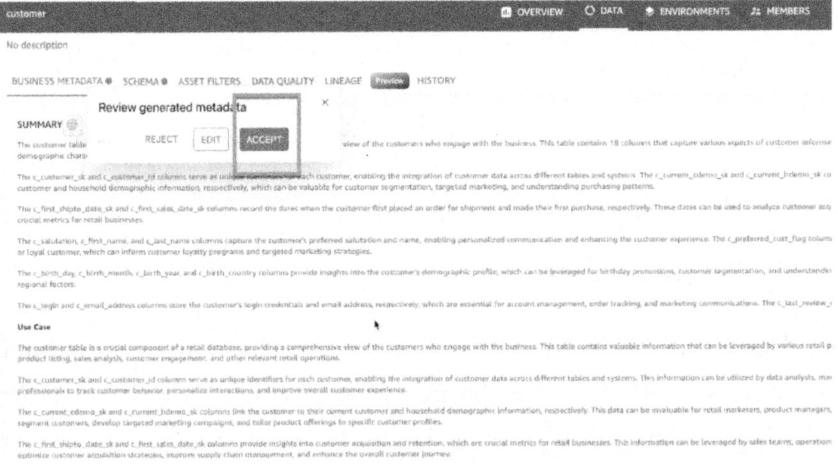

Figure 10.10: Generative AI produced table description

Review the description and choose to either reject and regenerate descriptions edit or accept the generated description.

Similarly, Figure 10.11 depicts the schema descriptions for the customer table.

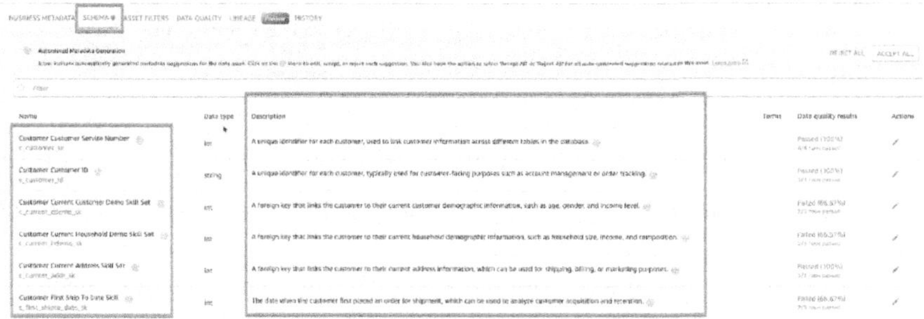

Figure 10.11: Column names and descriptions generated by generative AI

You must take note of the level of effort this capability alleviates off of the data stewards. In a typical organization with thousands of tables with 10s to 100's of columns, manually creating and keeping up-to-date with the descriptions is very complex and is a leading indicator of why organizations cannot maintain an enriched business glossary for their data objects. It simply becomes a non-starter in most organizations.

Metadata forms: Manage metadata relevant to data consumers

A metadata form in Amazon DataZone is a powerful tool used to augment and enrich asset metadata in the catalog. Metadata forms serve several important purposes:

- Enriching Asset Information: They allow data owners to add additional business context to asset metadata, making it easier for data users to search for and understand the data.
- Enforcing Consistency: Metadata forms help maintain consistency across assets published to the Amazon DataZone catalog.
- Extending Metadata Models: They enable you to extend a data asset's metadata model by adding custom-defined attributes, such as sales region, sales year, or sales quarter.

A metadata form consists of the following elements:

- Field Definitions: Each form is composed of one or more field definitions
- Data Types: Fields can support various data types, including boolean, date, decimal, integer, string, and business glossary terms

8. To create and manage metadata forms, Navigate to the Amazon DataZone data portal and log in. Access the Catalog menu, select Metadata forms, and choose Create form to start a new form, as shown in Figure 10. 12 below

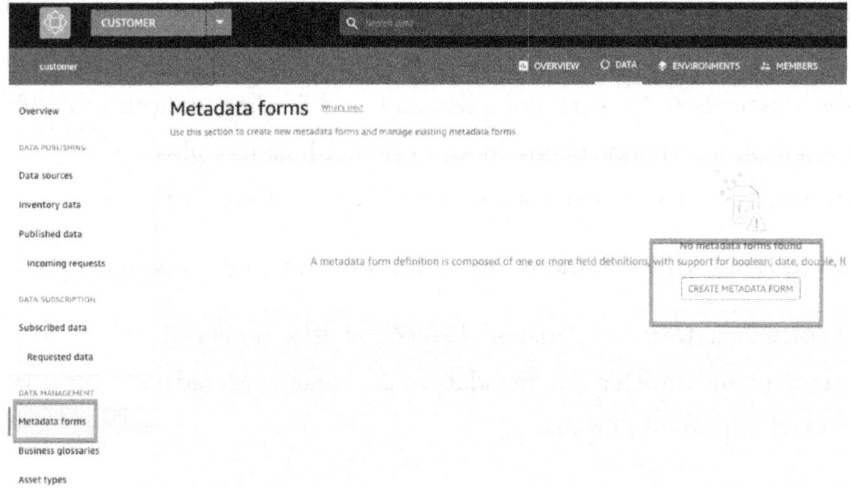

Figure 10.12: Creating metadata forms

Specify the form name, description, and owner as seen in Figure 10.13

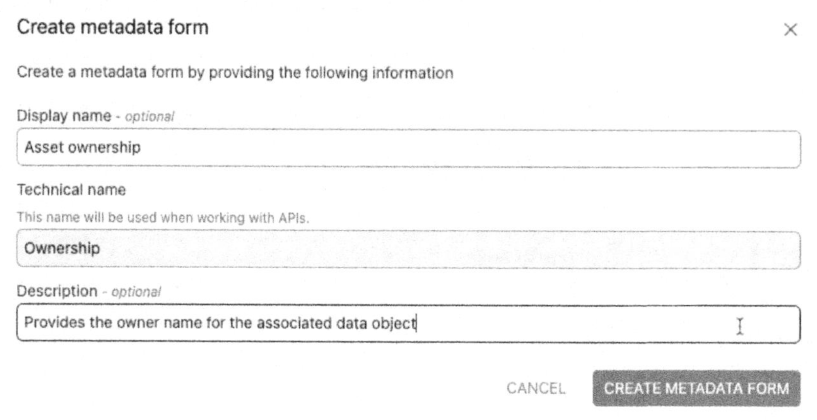

Figure 10.13: Metadata form creation

Add fields to the form by choosing Create field and specifying the field name, description, type, and whether it's required. Figure 10.14 shows the configuration for creating a business SME field.

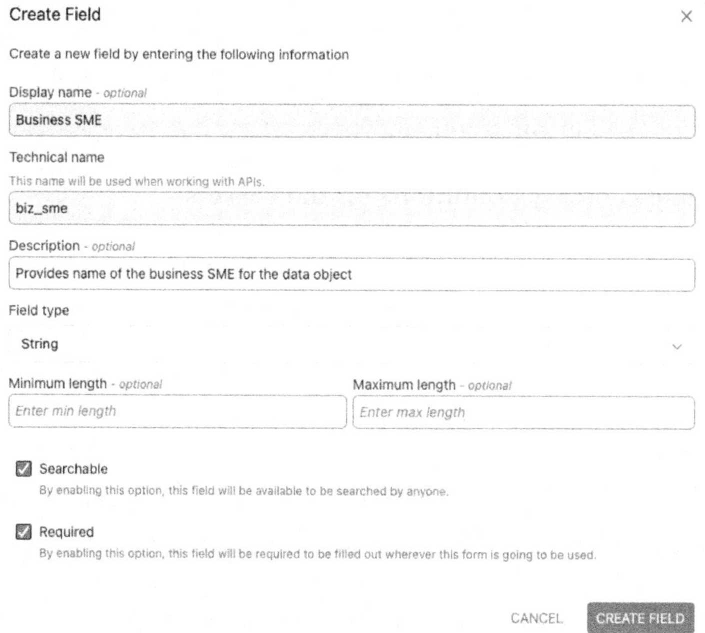

Figure 10.14: Metadata form field configuration

Follow the steps in the figure above and create another field for technical SME.

At this point, you will have two fields, as shown in Figure 10.15.

Figure 10.15: Metadata fields and enabling them for use

Amazon DataZone provides APIs for programmatic interaction with metadata forms. The GetFormType API allows you to retrieve metadata form type information, including its model, imports, and status.

By utilizing metadata forms effectively, organizations can significantly improve the quality and completeness of their data asset metadata, making it easier for users to discover, understand, and utilize data resources within Amazon DataZone.

Manage Glossary definitions for data assets

A business glossary in Amazon DataZone is a powerful tool for organizing and standardizing business terminology across an organization.

Business glossaries serve several important purposes:

- Standardization: They provide a collection of business terms with their definitions to ensure consistent usage across the organization.
- Context: Glossaries help set the context for data assets by associating relevant business terms with them.

- Clarity: They improve understanding of data assets by providing clear, agreed-upon definitions for business terms.
- Collaboration: Glossaries facilitate better communication between different teams and departments by establishing a common language.

A business glossary in Amazon DataZone consists of:

- Terms: Individual business words or phrases with their definitions.
- Relationships: Connections between terms that provide additional context.
- Metadata: Additional information about terms, such as ownership and status.

9. To create and manage a business glossary for confidentiality, Access the Catalog menu and select Glossaries. Choose Create Glossary to start a new glossary. Enter the field values shown in Figure 10.16

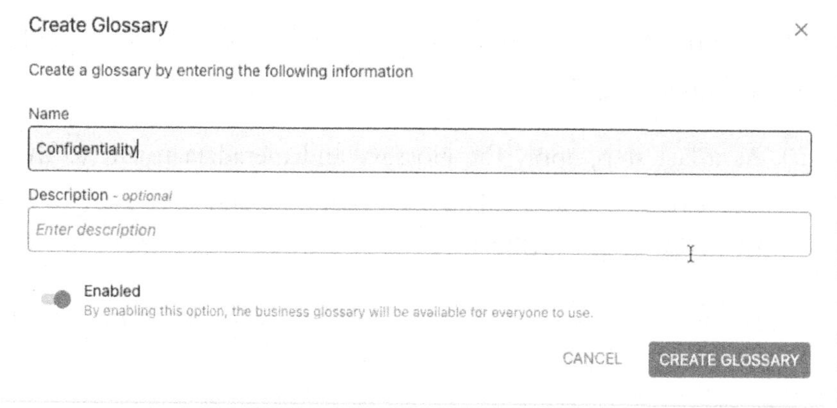

Figure 10.16: Creating a business glossary

Glossary terms are the lifeblood of a glossary definition. Create terms that represent the Confidentiality of data. Figure 10.17 illustrates 4 terms that are applicable to Confidentiality.

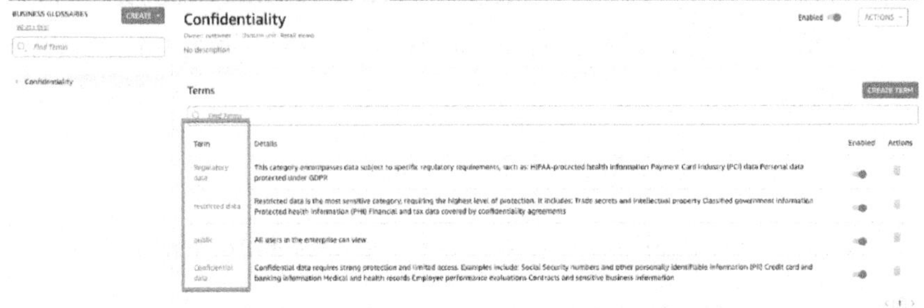

Figure 10.17: Glossary Terms for Confidentiality

Business glossary terms can be associated with:

- Entire data assets
- Specific columns within data assets

This association helps users understand the business context of the data they're working with.

This completes the definition and configuration of the guidelines defined under step 5.

10. As a last step, apply the glossary and metadata forms to the data assets by selecting the data asset customer and navigating to the tab BUSINESS METADATA.

Scroll down to the section named Glossary Terms and apply the term as seen in Figure 10.18

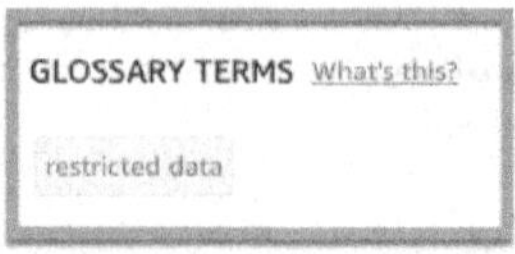

Figure 10.18: Mapping Confidentiality glossary term to table object

Similarly, you can apply at individual column level for the customer data asset by visiting the SCHEMA tab.

Scroll down to the section named METADATA FORMS and attach the Asset ownership metadata form defined in step 8.

Figure 10.19: Attaching metadata form

Provide the names of the owners, as shown in Figure 10.19.

11. At this point, the role of the data steward is complete, and the data assets are ready to be published. Figure 10.20 illustrates how to publish a data asset.

Figure 10.20: Publishing a data asset

12. Once all the data assets are published, you can see them from the published view, as shown in Figure 10.21 below.

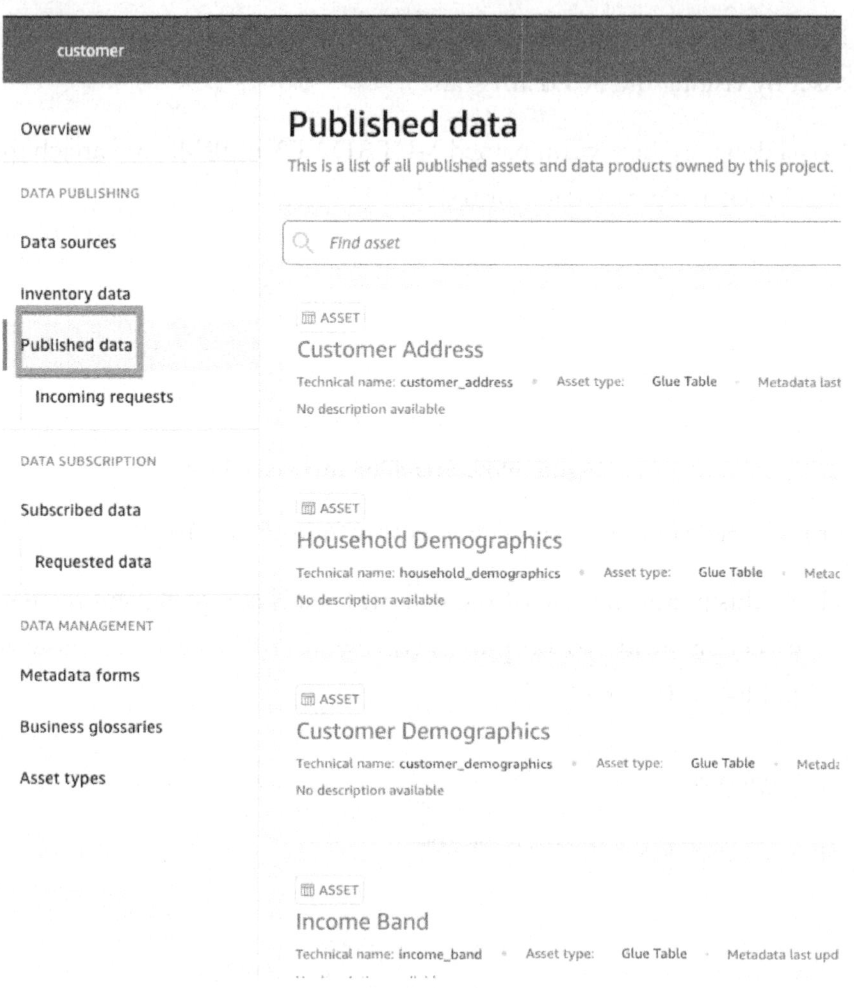

Figure 10.21: Published data assets

Create a data product using data assets in Amazon DataZone

At this point, the data assets are enriched for business use and can be discoverable by all consumers of the data. There is one task left before you want to open up the consumers to use these assets. It will be hard for your consumers to understand what data assets will make up a data product. That's why the final authoring task of a data steward is to bundle up all data assets that represent a data product. Since the objective is to create a customer 360 data product, let's bundle the assets that represent it.

13. Create a new data product from the Inventory data section of the left-hand pane in the portal. Add all the data assets, as illustrated in Figure 10.22, that make up the customer 360 data product.

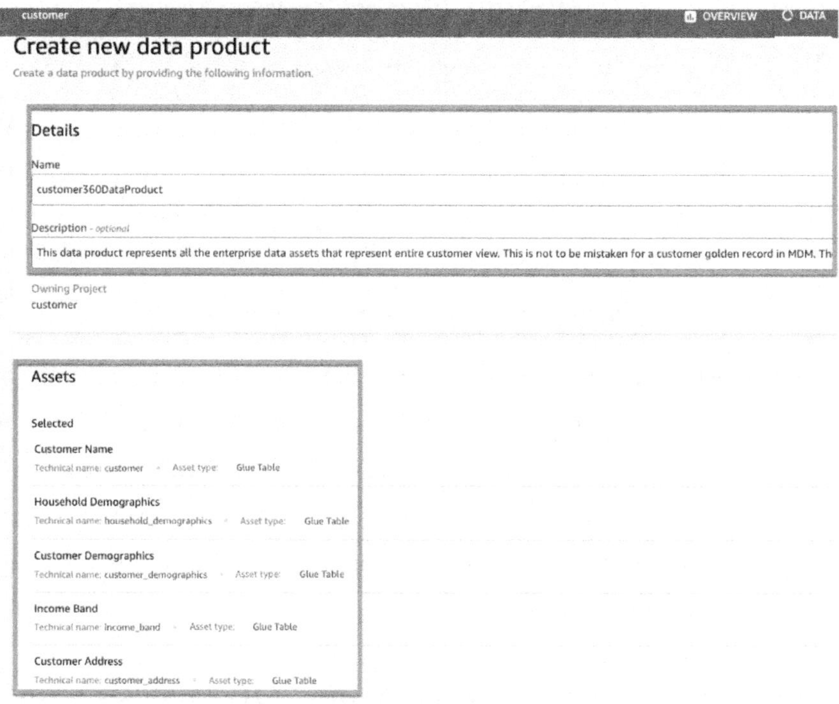

Figure 10.22: Creating data product using data assets in DataZone

Customer360 data product is now created, as seen in Figure 10.23.

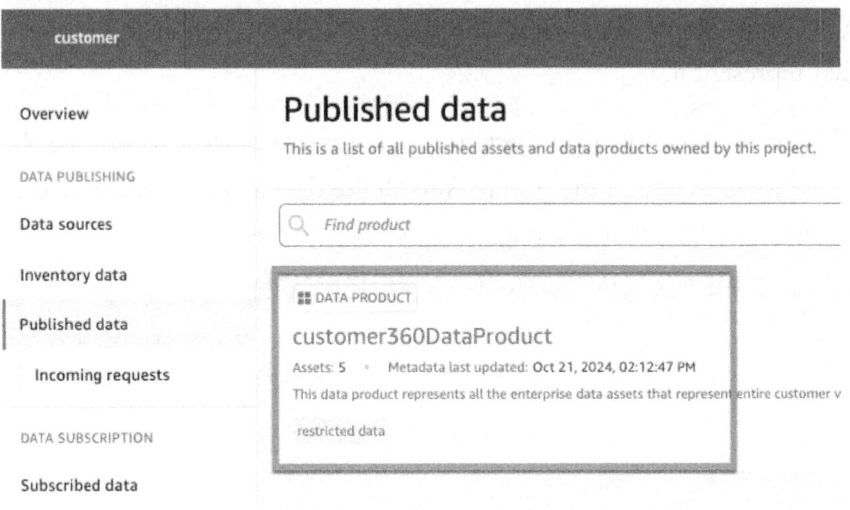

Figure 10.23: Customer 360 data product

To summarize, in this section, you have seen the role of a data steward with step-by-step instructions on how to enrich a data asset from the technical catalog using auto-generated AI descriptions, assess data quality, create and apply metadata and business glossary terms to assets and finally publishing a customer 360 data product. Let's now move on to the analyst role.

Role of Data Analysts: Maximizing SQL Analysis with Amazon DataZone

A modern data analyst primarily relies on SQL analysis to derive insights from large datasets to support data-driven decision-making within an organization. Here's an overview of their role and responsibilities:

- Working with Stakeholders
    - Understanding business requirements and translating them into SQL queries
    - Presenting findings and insights to non-technical stakeholders

- Cross-functional Collaboration
    - Supporting data scientists with exploratory data analysis
- Data Querying
    - Writing complex SQL queries to retrieve relevant data from relational databases
    - Using SELECT statements with various clauses (WHERE, GROUP BY, HAVING, ORDER BY) to filter and organize data
    - Joining multiple tables to combine data from different sources

By mastering these SQL-centric skills and responsibilities, a modern data analyst can effectively turn raw data into valuable insights, driving informed decision-making across their organization.

Now, let's look at how a data analyst can leverage Amazon DataZone to discover the data product, request access to the data product, and perform SQL analysis on the data.

Let us use an example scenario to illustrate the role of the analyst. Imagine the analyst is a marketing analyst who is creating a product market campaign analysis for a recent product launch. The analyst needs access to Customer360 data products, and web returns data assets and will use SQL to prepare data.

Data analyst practical execution steps

1. The marketing analyst, username book-analyst, first logs on to the Amazon Datazone and creates a new project named marketing campaign. Then, he will choose a data lake environment backed by Amazon Athena for SQL analysis. This is very similar to the steps the data steward had to perform in the previous section, and

therefore, we skip directly to the data discovery task. Figure 1-.24 below depicts the marketing campaign project showing the data assets available to query, which at this point is 0, and the env to query the data as Athena.

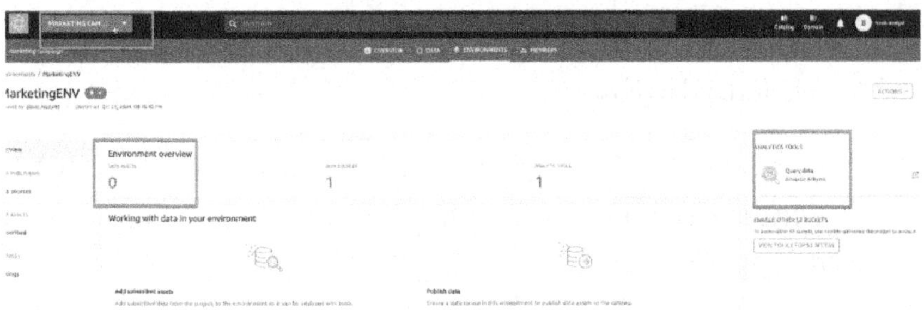

Figure 10.24: Marketing campaign project with Analytics tool

2. The analyst uses the search bar to discover the data assets required for marketing analysis. The analyst starts by finding the customer360 data product. Figure 10.25 below depicts the intuitive search that makes it easy for the analyst to locate and inspect all the customer data assets and data products and request access to the desired data.

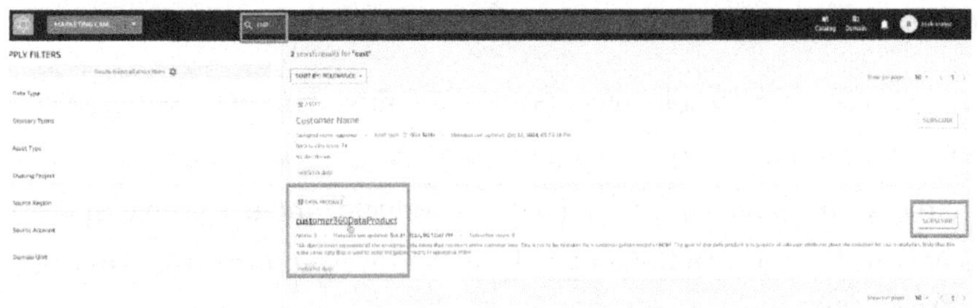

Figure 10.25: Search term Customer shows related data assets and data products

The analyst inspects the data product and confirms it has all the data assets needed for marketing campaign analysis for customers. The analyst then requests a subscription, as shown in Figure 10.25.

Similarly, an analyst searches for web returns data assets and requests access to them.

The data steward gets notified and can see all subscription requests under the notification screen shown in Figure 10.26.

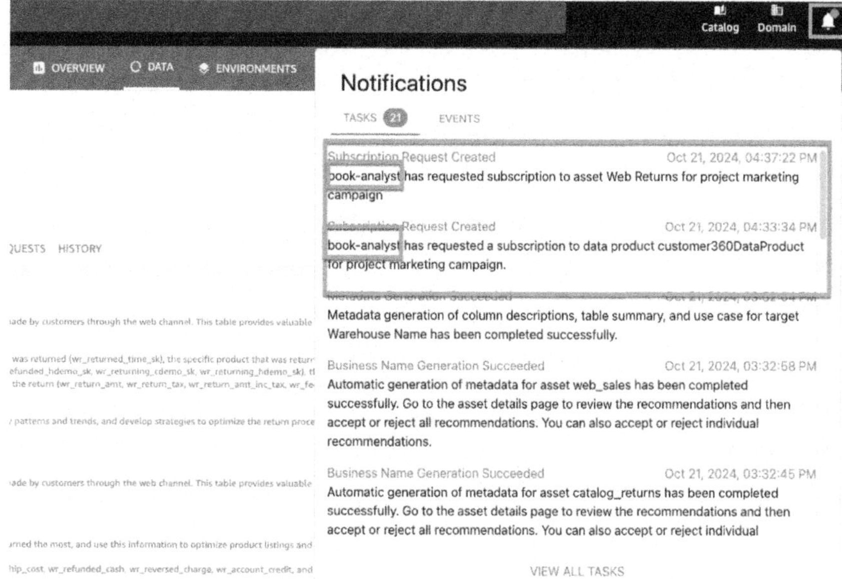

Figure 10.26: Data Steward finds subscription notifications in DataZone

3. The steward reviews the request and provides access, or the steward can choose to deny it. In this case, the request is approved, as shown in figure 10.27.

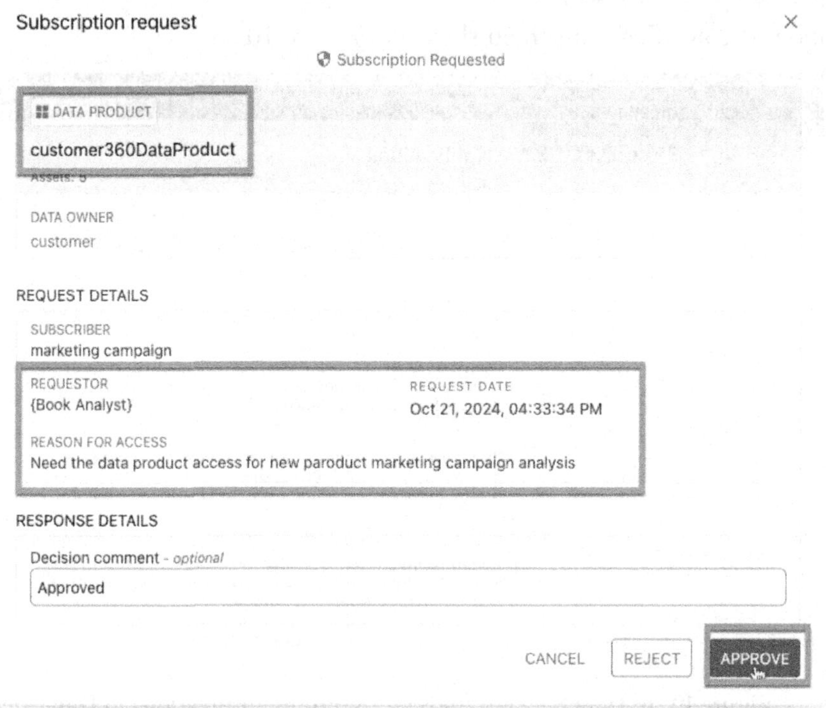

Figure 10.27: Data Steward approves subscription request for data product

For data assets, the data steward can also provide fine-grained access, including specific columns and rows, as shown in Figure 10.28.

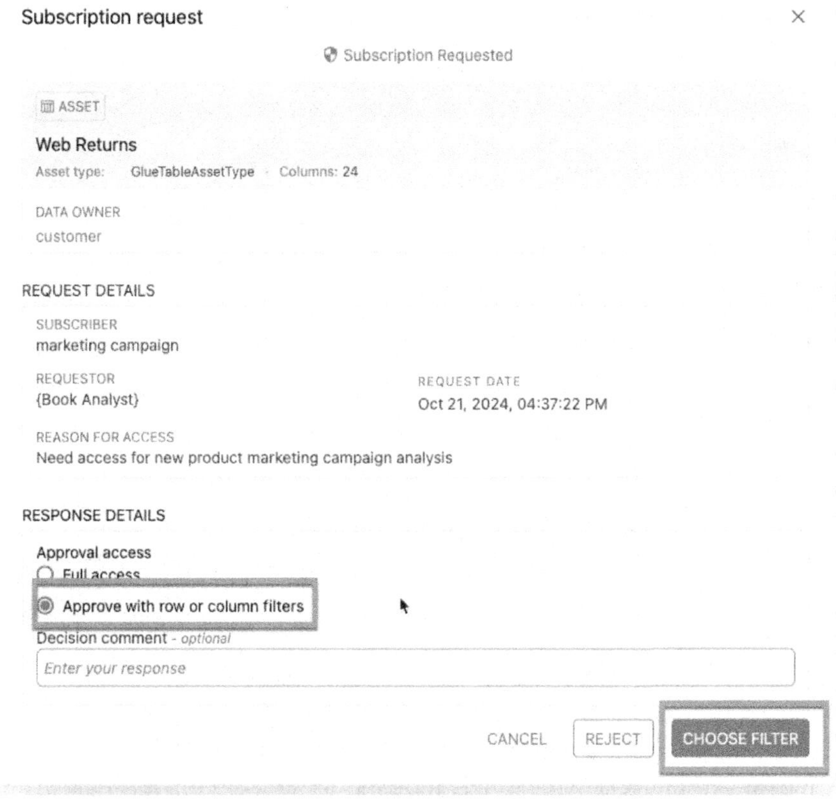

Figure 10.28: DataZone asset filters

Fine-grained access control (FGAC) can be achieved by creating a filter. A filter with specific columns has been created by the data steward for marketing analyst use, and the steward simply selects the filter and provides approval, as shown in Figure 10.29.

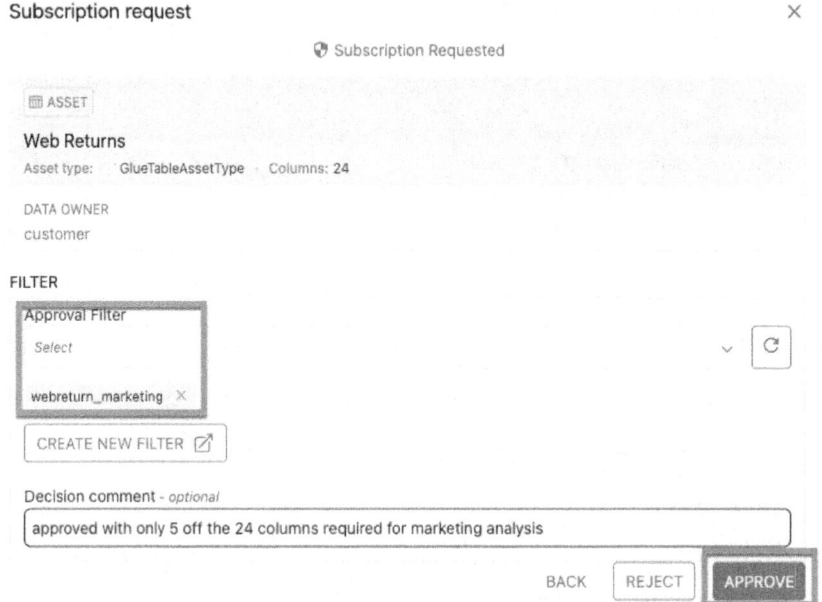

Figure 10.29: Data steward approves access with FGAC

Now, the marketing analyst has access to all required data and will use Amazon Athena via Amazon DataZone to work with the data using SQL.

4. The analyst can validate the approved subscription request under the data subscriptions section on the portal's left pane.

Now, the analyst is ready to use the analytics tool, Amazon Athena, from the DataZone portal, as shown in Figure 10.30 for SQL analysis.

Figure 10.30: Analytics tool to query data from Amazon DataZone

5. Notice the Athena workgroup shown in Figure 10.31 as the *Datazone Environment* name, created using the project creation step. The workgroup and the access are fully managed by datazone. Permissions are only limited within this environment and won't be accessible directly through Amazon Athena outside of the DataZone portal.

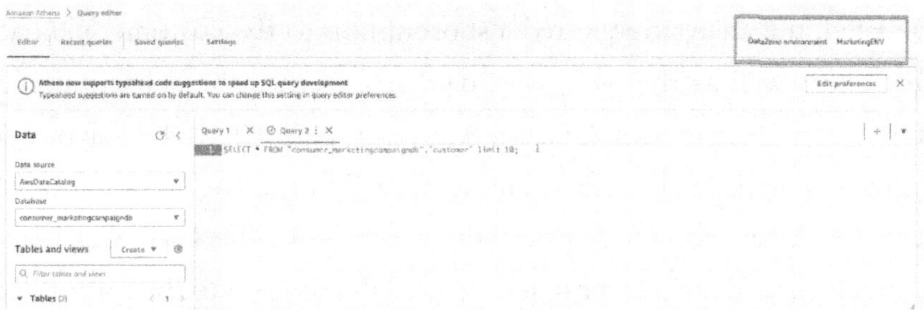

Figure 10.31: Athena SQL query editor and the workgroup name

6. The analyst can also use SQL DML operations using this functionality. In this case, the analyst creates new tables in the producer database, producer_marketingcampaigndb, as shown in Figure 10.32. The new tables will be available in the Glue data catalog immediately and can also be used to query outside DataZone.

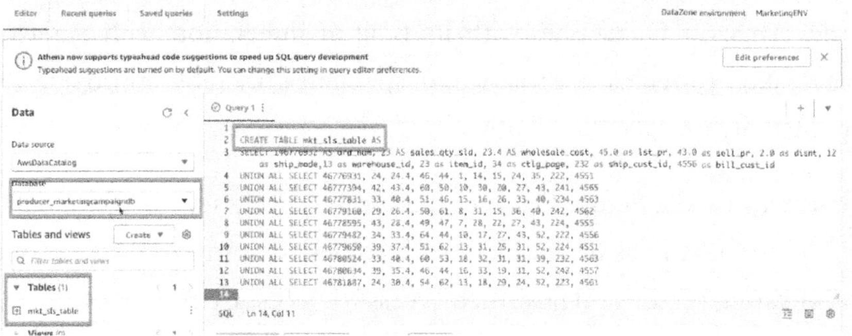

Figure 10.32: CTAS creating a new table in the producer database

Note that the data files from the table created using the CTAS statement will reside in your AWS bucket created for Amazon DataZone. It usually has the naming format, amazon-datazone-<YOURAWSACCTNUMBER>-us-east-1-xxx

In Summary, the analyst started off by performing data discovery using Amazon Datazone's powerful search capability. Once data quality was validated, the analyst requested a subscription to the customer360 data product as well as the web_sales data asset. Once the subscription is granted, the analyst uses Amazon Athena to perform SQL analytics on the data. You have also learned how the analyst can use CTAS to create new data assets, which can be written back into the Glue Catalog, a central technical metadata catalog. Now, let's move on to the role of data scientist.

Empowering Data Scientists for Large-Scale ML and Generative AI using Amazon DataZone

Data Scientists are required to do several tasks in their role, and they need the right capabilities to discover and get access to data, setup an environment for data preparation, and use the right tooling for model development with the ability to collaborate and govern ML artifacts at scale. Amazon DataZone, with its built-in integration with Amazon SageMaker, provides the following capabilities, thereby improving the productivity of the data scientists.

- Environment Setup: Data scientists can quickly set up a SageMaker environment using predefined profiles in Amazon DataZone, ensuring secure and governed access to necessary resources.
- Data Access and Discovery: They can search, discover, and subscribe to data and machine learning (ML) assets from the DataZone business catalog directly within SageMaker Studio.

- ML Development: Within SageMaker Studio, data scientists perform tasks such as data preparation, model training, and feature engineering using tools like JupyterLab and SageMaker Canvas.
- Collaboration: They collaborate on ML projects by sharing insights and assets with other team members through the integrated platform.
- Publishing Assets: After completing ML tasks, data scientists can publish models, datasets, and feature groups back to the DataZone catalog for governance and discoverability by other users.

This integration streamlines the workflow for data scientists by providing a unified platform for accessing data, developing models, and managing ML assets with robust governance controls. Figure 10.33 illustrates the supported capability, which is fairly new at the time of writing this book.

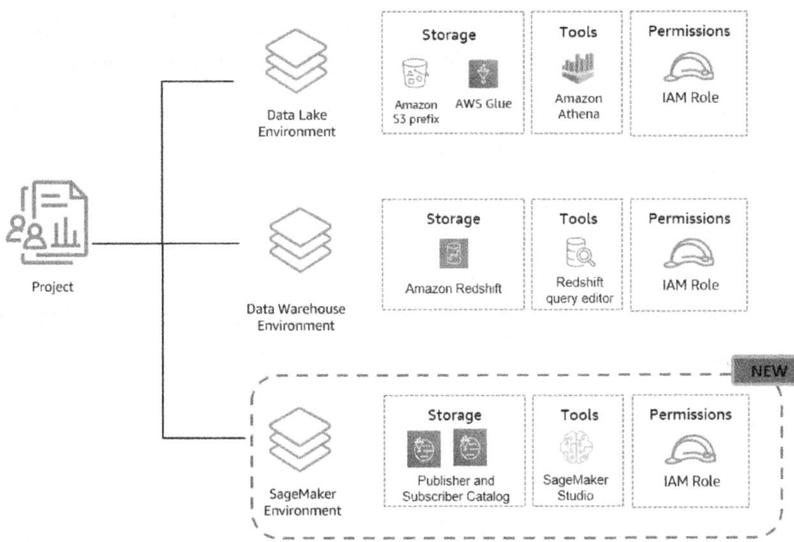

Figure 10.33: DataZone blueprints with supported tool capability

Assets in Amazon DataZone are publishable, discoverable, and shareable data or machine learning resources. Originally, these assets included Amazon Redshift and AWS Glue tables. Now, the platform expands its capabilities with two new asset types: SageMaker Feature Groups and Model Package Groups.

SageMaker Feature Groups serve as centralized stores for machine learning features, promoting consistency and reusability across projects. Model Package Groups, on the other hand, facilitate the organization and management of machine learning models throughout their lifecycle.

This integration enhances Amazon DataZone's ecosystem, bridging traditional data management with advanced machine learning practices. By incorporating these new asset types, organizations can streamline their data and ML workflows, fostering improved collaboration and innovation.

Data Scientist practical execution steps

Once the data scientist logs on to the Amazon DataZone portal, a datazone project is created to perform data science functions. This project's purpose and the steps to create it are no different than what you have already seen with Data Steward and Data Analyst roles earlier in the section. So, we will not cover all the steps in detail in this section, but we will list the key ones so you understand the execution overall.

1. The data scientist created a new project named campaign prediction, as shown in Figure 10.34, to perform data science functions.

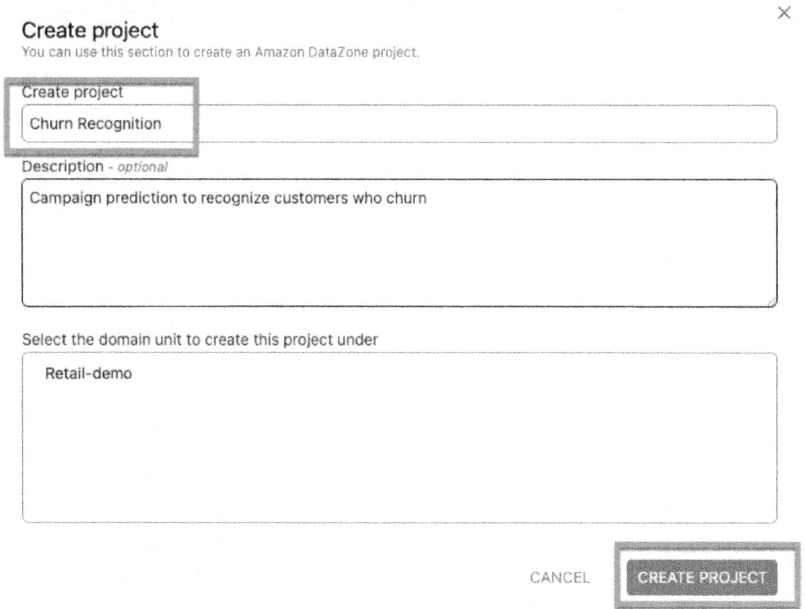

Figure 10.34: Data scientist project for churn recognition

2. The data scientist then continues to create a new environment profile with Amazon Sagemaker as the tool of choice and creates the environment. This is very similar to how Data Steward created a Data Lake environment with Amazon Athena as the tooling choice in the previous section.

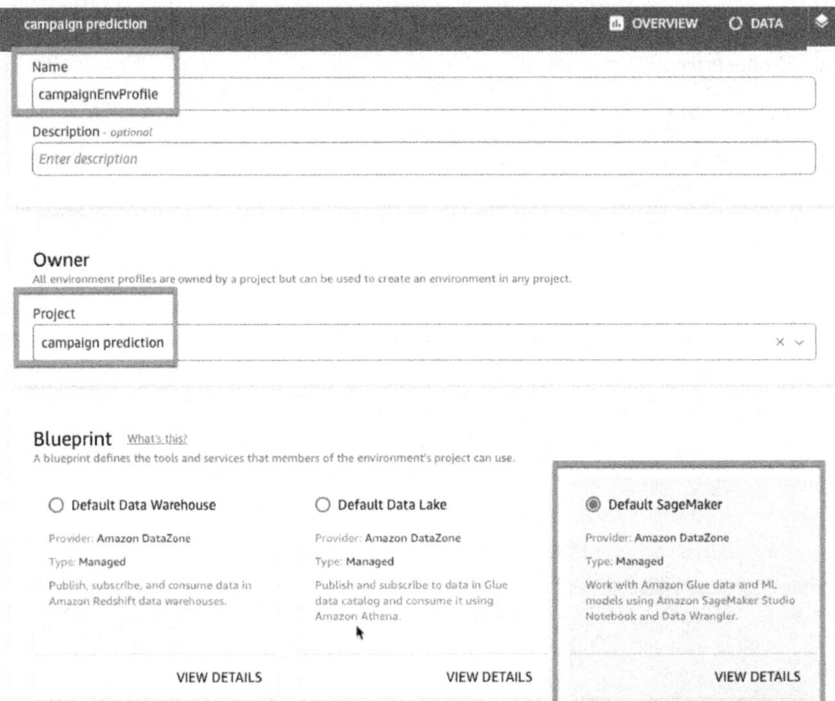

Figure 10.35: Project environment with SageMaker blueprint

Figure 10.35 outlines the creation of an environment profile with Sagemaker as the blueprint.

Once the env is created and attached to the project, the data scientist will use the search bar as shown in figure 10.36 to find the data product customer360DataProduct as well as web_returns asset using the same approach the analyst took in the previous section and request subscription. The data steward then approves the request.

Figure 10.36: Search bar to discover and subscribe to data assets with SageMaker Studio as the tool to perform data science development

Asset Management using Amazon Sagemaker Studio

SageMaker Studio empowers ML builders with a robust asset management system. Here, they can effortlessly search, discover, and utilize data and ML assets from their business catalog.

Asset Discovery and Utilization

ML builders can access a wealth of resources through the Assets option in the navigation pane. This feature allows them to:

- Search and discover data and ML assets without administrative overhead
- Consume assets for various ML workflows, including data preparation, model training, and feature engineering
- Utilize these assets in both SageMaker Studio and SageMaker Canvas

Streamlined Search Process

The Assets page offers an intuitive search experience:

- Results display asset names and descriptions
- Filters enable narrowing down results by asset type
- Search criteria can be customized to find specific assets

Contribution to the Ecosystem

Upon completing ML tasks, builders can publish their work back to the business catalog, enhancing:

- Governance
- Discoverability
- Collaborative potential

This cyclical process of discovery, utilization, and contribution fosters a rich ecosystem of ML resources within the organization.

3. Discover from the asset catalog to find available assets, and use the search bar to filter if necessary. Data scientists can also see the type of the asset, whether it's a data table, a view, or even an ML model, as shown in Figure 10.37.

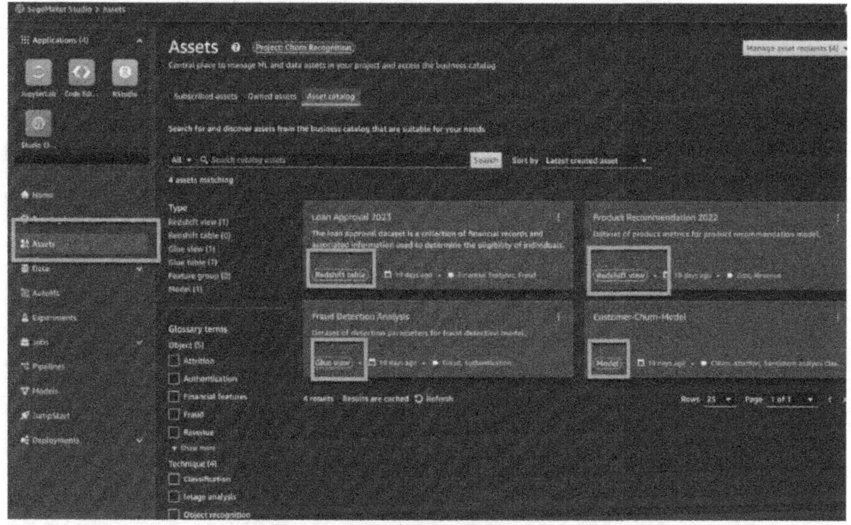

Figure 10.37: Discover data and ML assets

Asset subscription

SageMaker Studio offers ML builders a structured process for accessing valuable assets. This system ensures both ease of use and proper data governance.

To gain access to an asset:

- ML builders initiate a request by selecting "Subscribe"
- This action triggers an access request to the asset owner
- Asset owners review requests in the "Incoming subscription requests" section
- Owners can approve or reject requests, providing justifications for their decisions
- ML builders can track their requests in the "Outgoing subscription requests" section

The Assets page features a "Subscribed Assets" tab, allowing users to manage their accessed resources efficiently, as shown in Figure 10.38.

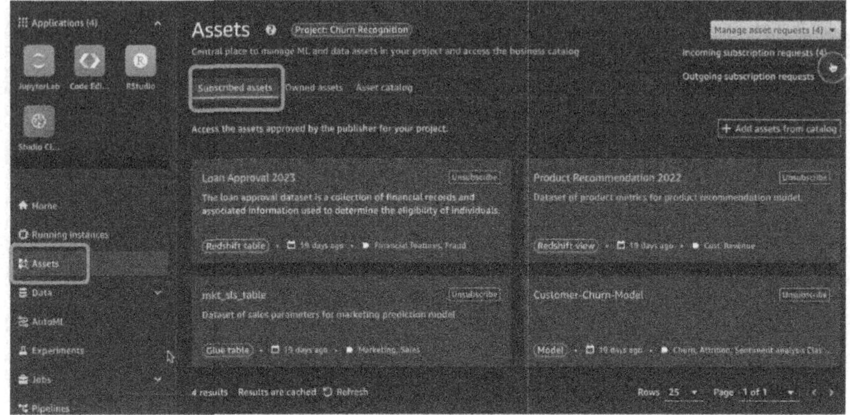

Figure 10.38: Subscribed assets view after subscription approval

4. Once subscribed, assets like "mkt_sls_table" (data asset) and "Customer-Churn-Model" (ML asset) shown in Figure 10.37 become available for use within SageMaker, enabling ML builders to integrate these resources into their workflows.

This process balances accessibility with proper data governance, ensuring that organizational assets are used responsibly and effectively.

Utilizing Subscribed Assets in SageMaker Studio

Once ML builders gain approval to access subscribed assets, they can leverage these resources within SageMaker Studio's ecosystem. This process offers flexibility and powerful tools for asset utilization.

Accessing Model Package Groups

To view and use subscribed Model Package Groups:

5. Navigate to the asset details page and select "Open in Model Registry," as shown in Figure 10.39.

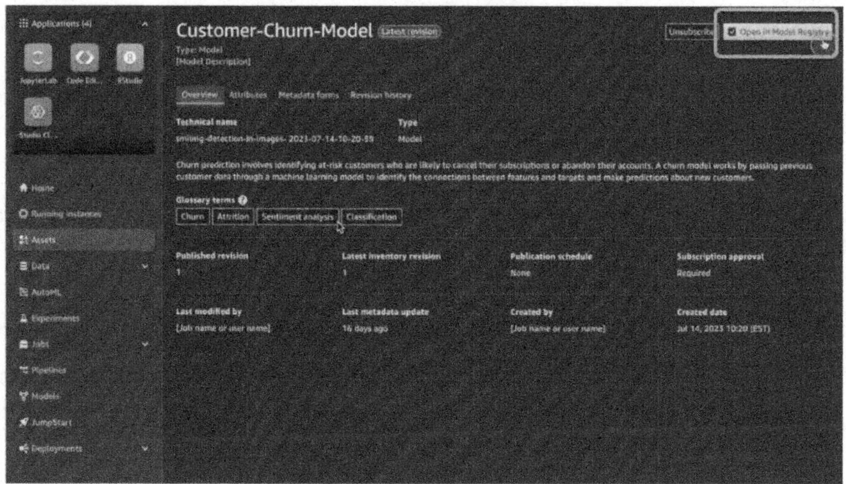

Figure 10.39: Accessing model registry

Asset utilization Options

ML builders can choose between two primary platforms:

- Amazon SageMaker Canvas
- JupyterLab within SageMaker Studio

Utilizing Subscribed Data Assets in SageMaker Canvas

SageMaker Canvas provides ML builders with a user-friendly interface to utilize subscribed data assets for experimentation and model building.

When ML builders launch SageMaker Canvas from SageMaker Studio, they can:

- Use Amazon SageMaker Data Wrangler for data preparation
- Access their subscribed datasets

When organizing data, subscribed assets are conveniently organized:

- Visible under the "sub_db" section

- New assets can be published via "pub_db"

This allows ML builders to seamlessly perform data preparation tasks, generate features, and build models using the prepared features.

Finally, they can register created models in the Amazon SageMaker Model Registry directly from SageMaker Canvas.

This integration streamlines the process from data access to model creation and registration, enhancing productivity and ensuring proper asset management within the

Utilizing Subscribed Data Assets in SageMaker Jupyter Lab

In SageMaker Studio, ML builders can harness the power of subscribed data assets within JupyterLab notebooks for advanced experimentation and model development. By navigating to JupyterLab from the SageMaker Studio interface, builders can launch notebooks that provide direct access to their subscribed data resources.

6. This seamless integration allows ML practitioners to effortlessly query and manipulate subscribed assets, such as the mkt_sls_table, directly within their notebook environment, as seen in Figure 10.40.

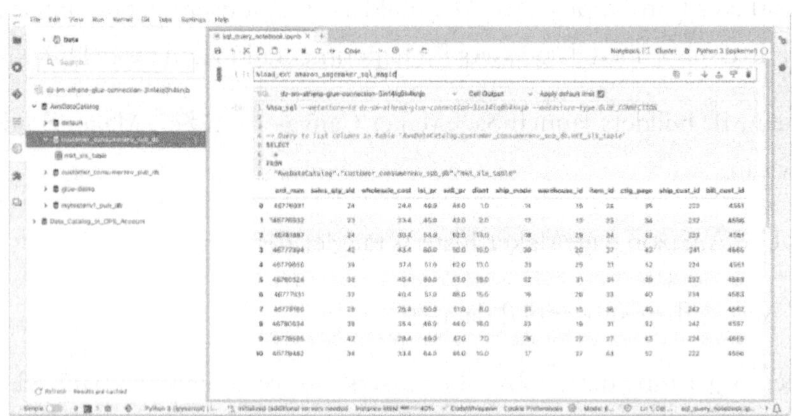

Figure 10.40: Accessing subscribed data from Sagemaker Studio jupyter notebook

The ability to instantly access and work with these data assets streamlines the data preparation process, enabling ML builders to focus on experimentation and model construction without the need for complex data retrieval procedures. This efficient workflow exemplifies how SageMaker Studio facilitates a smooth transition from data access to hands-on machine learning tasks, enhancing productivity and enabling more rapid iteration in the model development cycle.

Model Deployment

ML builders can operationalize subscribed models by:

Deploying the model to an endpoint for prediction purposes. This streamlined process allows ML builders to seamlessly integrate subscribed assets into their workflows, enhancing productivity and leveraging pre-existing resources within the organization. The ability to quickly access and deploy models from the Model Registry facilitates efficient machine-learning operations and collaboration among teams.

Publish assets to Amazon Datazone

SageMaker Studio empowers ML builders to share their work efficiently after completing experimentation and analysis. The platform offers flexible publishing options to cater to different collaboration needs. ML builders can choose to make their assets widely available by publishing them to the Amazon DataZone business catalog, ensuring organization-wide access. Alternatively, for more targeted sharing, they can publish assets exclusively to the project inventory, restricting access to project members only. These publishing tasks can be accomplished either programmatically using the SageMaker SDK or directly through the SageMaker Studio interface. The process is straightforward: users navigate to the specific asset tab and select either "Publish to asset catalog" or "Publish to inventory," depending on their sharing requirements. This streamlined publishing workflow exemplifies

SageMaker Studio's commitment to fostering collaboration and knowledge sharing within organizations while also providing granular control over asset visibility and access.

7. The data scientist can finally publish the feature group that was created during feature engineering in the catalog, as seen in Figure 10.41.

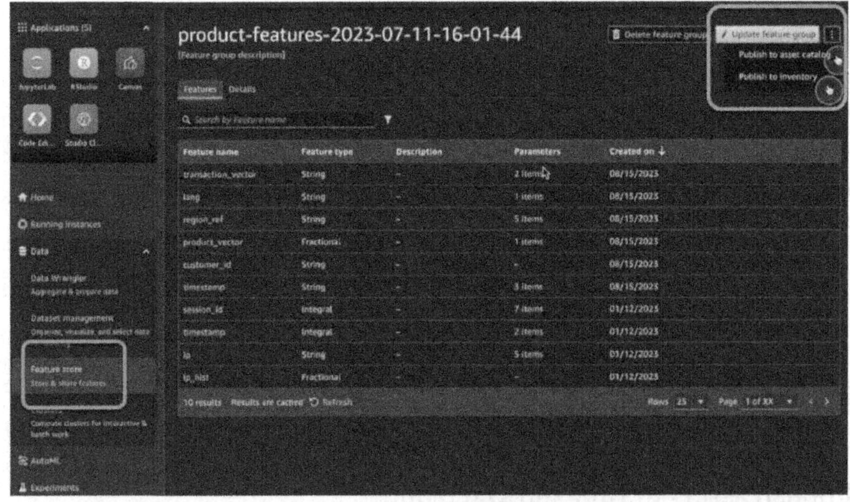

Figure 10.41: Publishing feature assets to Glue catalog

The integration of Amazon SageMaker and Amazon DataZone marks a significant advancement in ML governance, addressing the multifaceted challenges organizations face when scaling their machine-learning operations. This powerful combination streamlines infrastructure controls, permissions management, and governance of both data and ML assets within ML projects. Providing a secure, scalable, and reliable environment enables teams to access resources and develop models with confidence while simultaneously mitigating technical and operational risks.

This new capability represents a crucial step forward in helping organizations implement comprehensive ML governance strategies. It encompasses essential aspects such as infrastructure management, data stewardship, model oversight, access control, and policy enforcement. As organizations expand their ML initiatives across diverse use cases, the importance of robust governance frameworks becomes increasingly apparent. The SageMaker and DataZone integration offers a solution that not only facilitates this expansion but also ensures that it occurs within a well-governed ecosystem.

As this integration continues to evolve, feedback from users will play a vital role in shaping its future development. Organizations are encouraged to explore this new ML governance capability and share their experiences. By leveraging these tools, businesses can enhance their ML workflows, ensure compliance, and drive innovation while maintaining control over their valuable data and ML assets. The ongoing dialogue between users and developers will be crucial in refining and expanding these governance features to meet the ever-changing needs of the ML community.

Summary

This chapter provides a comprehensive overview of how different roles within an organization can effectively utilize the data mesh architecture using Amazon DataZone and related AWS services. Here's a summary of the key points:

Data Stewards:

- Use Amazon DataZone to enrich and manage data assets.
- Create and manage business glossaries and metadata forms.
- Establish data quality standards and review data quality scores.

- Use generative AI to create business-friendly descriptions for data assets.
- Publish data products and manage access requests.

Data Analysts:

- Discover and request access to data products and assets using Amazon DataZone.
- Use Amazon Athena within DataZone for SQL analysis.
- Create new tables and perform data manipulations.

Data Scientists:

- Set up SageMaker environments within Amazon DataZone.
- Discover, access, and subscribe to data and ML assets.
- Use SageMaker Studio for ML development, including data preparation and model training.
- Publish models, datasets, and feature groups back to the DataZone catalog.
- Utilize subscribed assets in SageMaker Canvas and JupyterLab notebooks.
- Deploy models and publish assets to the DataZone business catalog or project inventory.

The chapter emphasizes how Amazon DataZone integrates various AWS services to create a seamless workflow for data management, analysis, and machine learning. It highlights the importance of data governance, collaboration, and the democratization of data access within an organization. The step-by-step instructions provided for each role demonstrate how to practically implement these concepts using AWS tools.

References:

SageMaker integration with Amazon DataZone blog: https://aws.amazon.com/blogs/machine-learning/amazon-sagemaker-now-integrates-with-amazon-datazone-to-streamline-machine-learning-governance/

Index

A

U

V

Made in United States
North Haven, CT
24 November 2024

60319317R00196